Edward Hewitt is a barrister at 5 Stone Buildings in Lincoln's Inn. He has a private client practice with a particular emphasis on inheritance and trust disputes. He is frequently asked to advise on the correct construction of wills and trust instruments. He has also acted in some of the leading recent cases involving the construction and rectification of wills and trust instruments, some of which have included ancillary professional negligence proceedings against the relevant draftsman.

A Practical Guide to the Construction and Rectification of Wills and Trust Instruments

A Practical Guide to the Construction and Rectification of Wills and Trust Instruments

Edward Hewitt, LL.B., B.C.L.
Barrister of Lincoln's Inn

Law Brief Publishing

Published 2020 by Law Brief Publishing, an imprint of Law Brief Publishing Ltd
30 The Parks
Minehead
Somerset
TA24 8BT

www.lawbriefpublishing.com

Paperback: 978-1-912687-20-6

For my wonderful parents, without whom nothing would have been possible.

CONTENTS

CHAPTER ONE
INTRODUCTION

1.1 The problem

Construction and rectification problems in wills and other trust instruments[1] come in many different shapes and sizes. When considering a provision in a will or other trust instrument which is unclear and/or can be interpreted in different ways, the PRs or trustees, beneficiaries and other interested parties may ask themselves: what did the testator or settlor mean? Alternatively, a provision may be clear on its face, but the particular surrounding circumstances may lead interested parties to ask themselves: is that really what the testator or settlor meant? These sorts of questions are often a good indication that the provision in question may give rise to a construction or a rectification problem.

1.2 Structure of this book: distinction between wills and other trust instruments

Many trusts are created by will. These are usually – and unsurprisingly – referred to as 'will trusts'. A will can therefore itself be a trust instrument. However, there are some important differences between the rules governing the construction and rectification of wills on the one hand, and those governing the construction and rectification of other trust instruments (typically trust deeds by which a settlor settles property on trust during his lifetime) on the other. As a result, this book distinguishes between wills (whether or not they create any will trusts), which are considered in chapters 2 and 3, and other trust instruments (i.e. any instrument which creates a trust except a will), which are considered in chapters 4 and 5.

---

1 Other fertile ground for these problems are contracts and patents. In particular, contractual construction and rectification are huge subjects in their own right, which are beyond the scope of this book.

In order to avoid a large amount of unwieldy cross-referencing, each of those four chapters has been written as self-standing. Because there is some similarity and overlap between the topics, this has resulted in some inevitable repetition across the chapters. However, that seemed to be a price worth paying to achieve what it is hoped are four chapters which are clearer and more straightforward to consult.

1.3 A bit of history

As this is intended to be a practical guide, and this particular section is not at all practical, it has been kept short. However, it has been included because, as with most legal doctrines, some knowledge of history is likely to help better understand how we have got the current position, and why.

Wills and certain other trust instruments have a long history of being documents which are required by law to be in writing. Section 9 of the Wills Act 1837 has required wills to be "*in writing*" (save for some limited exceptions) for nearly 200 years, but the requirement can be traced back a further 300 years to the Statute of Wills of 1540. Similarly, sections 52 and 53 of the Law of Property Act 1925 impose some familiar writing requirements, the origin of which dates back to the Statute of Frauds of 1677. As a result, the courts have had to grapple with problematic drafting in wills and trust instruments for centuries. Unsurprisingly, the case law on the subject is enormous.

For the practitioner, one of the important points to emerge from history is a shift in the courts' approach to construction from what can be described as a strict literalist approach to a more purposive approach. A large amount of judicial and academic ink has been devoted to this topic,[2] which continues to be controversial. It will only be considered briefly – and thus no doubt overly-simplistically – here.

2 For more in-depth treatment of this interesting and difficult topic, see e.g. *Theobald on Wills*, 18th ed., chapter 13; *Williams on Wills*, 10th ed., chapter 50; *Lewin on Trusts*, 19th ed., chapter 6; Kessler, *Drafting Trusts and Will Trusts*, 13th ed., chapter 4; Kerridge, *Parry and Kerridge: The Law of Succession*, 13th ed., chapter 10.

The shift can be illustrated by contrasting the following two quotes, the first from 1833, the second from 2014:

> *In expounding a will, the Court is to ascertain, not what the testator actually intended, as contradistinguished from what his words express, but what is the meaning of the words he has used. I consider it doubtful what the testator actually meant should be done. But I have no doubt as to the meaning of the words used by him.*[3]

> *19. When interpreting a contract, the court is concerned to find the intention of the party or parties, and it does this by identifying the meaning of the relevant words, (a) in the light of (i) the natural and ordinary meaning of those words, (ii) the overall purpose of the document, (iii) any other provisions of the document, (iv) the facts known or assumed by the parties at the time that the document was executed, and (v) common sense, but (b) ignoring subjective evidence of any party's intentions.*

> *20. When it comes to interpreting wills, it seems to me that the approach should be the same. Whether the document in question is a commercial contract or a will, the aim is to identify the intention of the party or parties to the document by interpreting the words used in their documentary, factual and commercial context.*[4]

The more strict literalist approach had generated several rules of construction which compelled judges to interpret particular words in a particular way, irrespective of context and no matter how absurd the result.

A landmark moment in the shift away from this approach was the House of Lords decision in *Perrin v Morgan*[5] in January 1943. Emily Morgan died in 1939 leaving a home-made will by which she gifted some cottages, and then included the following provision: "*all moneys of*

---

3 *Doe v Gwillim* (1833) 5 B & Ad 122 *per* Parke J.

4 *Marley v Rawlings* [2015] AC 129 *per* Lord Neuberger.

5 [1943] AC 399.

which I die possessed of shall be shared by my nephews and nieces now living". The issue was whether the word "*moneys*" included the testatrix's investments, which represented the bulk of her estate.

At first instance, Farwell J followed a well-established rule of construction dating back to 1725[6] that, unless the context allowed a wider construction, "*money*" included only cash or currency in a testator's possession or due to him (such as sums on current or deposit account at a bank). As the context did not allow a wider construction on the facts, a partial intestacy arose in relation to the investments.

The Court of Appeal felt it had no option but to uphold Farwell J's decision because of previous binding authority.[7] It did so reluctantly, describing the rule as "*a blot on our jurisprudence*" and commenting that it had been "*said more than once by judges, members of the profession and laymen, that it defeats the intention of the testatrix*".

The House of Lords unanimously allowed the appeal. Although the result was unanimous, the different members of the Committee reached it in different ways. Perhaps the most colourful speech was that of Lord Atkin, who in his inimitable style held:

> "*The result of your Lordships' decision will be to relieve judges in the future from the thraldom, often I think self-imposed, of judgments in other cases believed to constrain them to give a meaning to wills which they know to be contrary to the testator's intention. [...] I anticipate with satisfaction that henceforth the group of ghosts of dissatisfied testators who, according to a late Chancery judge, wait on the other bank of the Styx to receive the judicial personages who have misconstrued their wills, may be considerably diminished. It will be a relief to the whole legal profession that at last what the Master of the Rolls rightly called a blot on our jurisprudence has been removed.*"[8]

---

6 *In re Shelmer* (1725) Gilb 200.

7 [1942] Ch 345.

8 [1943] AC 399 at 415.

Although this shift has not been linear,[9] in general terms it can be said that the courts have tried to free themselves somewhat from the shackles of the 'strict literalist' approach and nowadays can adopt a fairly liberal and flexible approach to construction (where the circumstances allow it). This more liberal approach has also had an impact on the development of the doctrine of rectification, as discussed in the next section.

Another important historical point in relation to the rectification of wills is that prior to the enactment of the Administration of Justice Act 1982, it seems the courts had no power to rectify a will. Therefore this jurisdiction, and the case law which explores its limits, is still relatively young.

1.4 Relationship between construction and rectification

It is now tolerably clear that the courts will generally approach a drafting problem by deciding its correct construction first, and only then moving on to consider whether the document should be rectified (if that issue arises at all).[10]

In relation to wills, this follows from the 3-stage approach to rectification identified in *Re Segelman*:[11]

> *The subsection [viz. section 20(1) of the Administration of Justice Act 1982] requires the court to examine three questions. First, what were the testator's intentions with regard to the dispositions in respect*

9 For a notable example of literalism prevailing in the Court of Appeal nearly 20 years after *Perrin v Morgan*, see *Re Rowland* [1963] Ch 1. The decision led to a large amount of correspondence, most of it critical, in *The Times*: see Albery, *Coincidence and the Construction of Wills*, (1963) 26 MLR 353.

10 See for example *Parkinson v Fawson* [2009] EWHC 1953 (Ch) at [5], *Burnard v Burnard* [2014] EWHC 340 (Ch) at [61]-[66], *Slattery v Jagger* [2015] EWHC 3976 (Ch) at [56], *Reading v Reading* [2015] EWHC 946 (Ch) at [40]. See also *Jump v Lister* [2016] EWHC 2160 (Ch), where only a will construction claim was advanced.

11 [1996] Ch 171. This is considered in more detail in chapter 3.

> *of which rectification is sought. Secondly, whether the will is so expressed that it fails to carry out those intentions. Thirdly, whether the will is expressed as it is in consequence of either (a) a clerical error or (b) a failure on the part of someone to whom the testator has given instructions in connection with his will to understand those instructions.*

The second question requires the court to construe the will. Only then will the court be able to determine whether there is a mismatch between the testator's intentions (i.e. the answer to the first question) and the effect of the will when properly construed (i.e. the answer to the second question).

There is authority for the proposition that the same approach applies in relation to other trust instruments.[12] In *Kevern v Ayers*[13] the court refused to rectify a deed of variation where the parties had asked it not to determine its construction first because that issue was to be determined by the tax tribunal. The court described the approach as "*unreal*"[14] and indicated that the separation between construction and rectification as "*essentially artificial*".[15]

On the other hand, in cases involving instruments other than wills, the court may be asked to decide whether to rectify the instrument without deciding its construction first.[16] This tends to happen where the rectification claim is considered to be very strong on the merits. If the circumstances justify it, this approach has the advantage of avoiding the "*mental gymnastics that are required to ensure the evidence of subjective*

---

12 See e.g. *Millar v Millar* [2018] EWHC 1926 (Ch) at [16].

13 [2014] EWHC 165 (Ch).

14 [2014] EWHC 165 (Ch) at [12].

15 [2014] EWHC 165 (Ch) at [11].

16 See e.g. *Re Hampel Discretionary Trust* [2012] EWHC 2395 (Ch), *Merchant Navy Officers Pension Fund Trustees v Watkins* [2013] EWHC 4741 (Ch) and *Re Chas A Blatchford & Sons Ltd Group Pension Scheme* [2019] EWHC 2743 (Ch).

intent [which is admissible in relation to a rectification claim] is disregarded when dealing with the issue of construction".[17]

Although the approach of (usually) determining construction first and then rectification appears well settled as a matter of authority, it is right to point out that its correctness has been questioned by some academics.[18]

1.5 Miscellaneous

References to the male singular are used for ease and to avoid a repetitive overuse of "he or she" and "his or her". Personal representatives are referred to as "PRs". In chapters 2 and 3, references to PRs should be read as references to "PRs or trustees, as the case may be" (unless the context requires otherwise).

Unless otherwise stated, all references to the Chancery Guide are to the February 2016 edition as updated in August 2019. I have attempted to state the law as at 31 October 2019.

In the conventional way, the responsibility for any error or omission – as well as for any offence my examples might cause to opera purists – is solely mine.

17 *A v D* [2017] EWHC 2222 (Ch) at [30]. In *Re Chas A Blatchford & Sons Ltd Group Pension Scheme* [2019] EWHC 2743 (Ch) Chief Master Marsh described construction and rectification as "*two separate and conflicting exercises*" (at [18]).

18 See Kerridge, *Parry and Kerridge: The Law of Succession*, 13th ed., at 10-02.

CHAPTER TWO
CONSTRUCTION OF WILLS

2.1 The law

Entire books have been written on the construction of wills,[1] and a large part of both *Theobald on Wills*[2] and *Williams on Wills*[3] is devoted to the construction of particular clauses in wills. It is beyond the scope of this short guide to attempt to consider this large subject in a similar level of detail. Instead, what follows is a summary of the key principles which apply to the construction of wills generally. For a more in-depth analysis of these principles and for guidance on how particular words and expressions have been construed in previous cases, reference should be made to the works mentioned above.

In *Marley v Rawlings*[4] the Supreme Court explained the modern approach to the construction of wills in a passage which is worth citing in full:

> *19. When interpreting a contract, the court is concerned to find the intention of the party or parties, and it does this by identifying the meaning of the relevant words, (a) in the light of (i) the natural and ordinary meaning of those words, (ii) the overall purpose of the document, (iii) any other provisions of the document, (iv) the facts known or assumed by the parties at the time that the document was executed, and (v) common sense, but (b) ignoring subjective evidence of any party's intentions. [...]*
>
> *20. When it comes to interpreting wills, it seems to me that the approach should be the same. Whether the document in question is a commercial contract or a will, the aim is to identify the intention of*

1 See e.g. Kerridge, *Hawkins on the Construction of Wills*, 5th ed.

2 *Theobald on Wills*, 18th ed., Section C, chapters 12 to 30.

3 *Williams on Wills*, 10th ed., volume 1, Parts J to M.

4 [2014] UKSC 2.

the party or parties to the document by interpreting the words used in their documentary, factual and commercial context. [...]

23. [...] the well known suggestion of James LJ in Boyes v Cook (1880) 14 Ch D 53, 56, that, when interpreting a will, the court should "place [itself] in [the testator's] arm-chair", is consistent with the approach of interpretation by reference to the factual context.

24. However, there is now a highly relevant statutory provision relating to the interpretation of wills, namely section 21 of the 1982 Act ("section 21"). Section 21 is headed "Interpretation of wills—general rules as to evidence", and is in the following terms:

> *"(1) This section applies to a will— (a) in so far as any part of it is meaningless; (b) in so far as the language used in any part of it is ambiguous on the face of it; (c) in so far as evidence, other than evidence of the testator's intention, shows that the language used in any part of it is ambiguous in the light of surrounding circumstances.*
>
> *"(2) In so far as this section applies to a will extrinsic evidence, including evidence of the testator's intention, may be admitted to assist in its interpretation."*

25. In my view, section 21(1) confirms that a will should be interpreted in the same way as a contract, a notice or a patent, namely as summarised in para 19 above. In particular, section 21(1)(c) shows that "evidence" is admissible when construing a will, and that that includes the "surrounding circumstances". However, section 21(2) goes rather further. It indicates that, if one or more of the three requirements set out in section 21(1) is satisfied, then direct evidence of the testator's intention is admissible, in order to interpret the will in question.

26. Accordingly, as I see it, save where section 21(1) applies, a will is to be interpreted in the same way as any other document, but, in addition, in relation to a will, or a provision in a will, to which section 21(1) applies, it is possible to assist its interpretation by ref-

> *erence to evidence of the testator's actual intention (eg by reference to what he told the drafter of the will, or another person, or by what was in any notes he made or earlier drafts of the will which he may have approved or caused to be prepared).*

This authoritative statement has been followed in several subsequent first instance decisions.[5]

Although in many authorities these are not expressly spelt out, it is suggested that the court's approach can be broken down into three stages:[6]

(a) At the first stage, the court will identify the meaning of the relevant words in the light of: (i) the natural and ordinary meaning of those words, (ii) the overall purpose of the will, (iii) any other provisions of the will, (iv) the facts known or assumed by the testator at the time the will was executed, and (v) common sense.[7] In doing so, at this first stage the court cannot take into account any extrinsic evidence of the testator's intention, the most common type of which (in the case of a professionally prepared will) will be the draftsman's attendance note of the meeting(s) at which the testator gave instructions. As the judge pointed out in *Re Freud*,[8] "*To lay people involved in a single piece of litigation, this may seem surprising. Suppose a testator gives clear and unequivocal instructions in writing as to what he wants to achieve by his will, his solicitor sends him a draft will with a covering letter explaining how*

---

5 See for example *Burnard v Burnard* [2014] EWHC 340 (Ch), *Re Huntley* [2014] EWHC 547 (Ch), *Re Freud* [2014] EWHC 2577 (Ch), *Reading v Reading* [2015] EWHC 946 (Ch), *Re Harte* [2015] EWHC 2351 (Ch), *Guthrie v Morel* [2015] EWHC 3172 (Ch), *Slattery v Jagger* [2015] EWHC 3976 (Ch), *Royal Society v Robinson* [2015] EWHC 3442 (Ch), *Jump v Lister* [2016] EWHC 2160 (Ch), *Re Aspinall* [2017] EWHC 454 (Ch), *Hives v Machin* [2017] EWHC 1414 (Ch), *Re Bathurst* [2018] EWHC 21 (Ch), *Re Wippell* [2018] EWHC 730 (Ch), *Tish v Olley* [2018] EWHC 1069 (Ch) and *MacIntyre v Oliver* [2018] EWHC 3094 (Ch).

6 See e.g. *Reading v Reading* [2015] EWHC 946 (Ch) at [40]-[49].

7 *Marley v Rawlings* [2014] UKSC 2 at [19] (cited in the text above).

8 [2014] EWHC 2577 (Ch) at [15].

the solicitor has sought to reflect those intentions in the draft will, and the testator signs the will and returns it to the solicitor with a letter saying that he is happy that his intentions have been achieved? Some might think all that a good aid to interpretation".

(b) At the second stage, the court will consider whether any of the three gateways in section 21 of the Administration of Justice Act 1982 ("AJA") is engaged. Those three gateways are:

 (i) any part of the will is meaningless (section 21(1)(a) AJA);

 (ii) the language used in any part of the will is ambiguous on the face of it (section 21(1)(b) AJA);

 (iii) evidence, other than evidence of the testator's intention, shows that the language used in any part of the will is ambiguous in the light of surrounding circumstances (section 21(1)(c) AJA).

 It is important to note that section 21(1)(c) AJA in particular makes it clear that at this second stage the court is still not permitted to take into account any extrinsic evidence of the testator's intention; only if the court decides that one of the gateways is open will such evidence become admissible.

(c) If at the second stage the court concludes that one of the section 21 gateways is engaged, then at this third stage the court may take into account "*extrinsic evidence, including evidence as to the testator's intention*" to "*assist in [the] interpretation*" of the will. As indicated above, in the case of a professionally prepared will, this will typically be in the form of the attendance note of the draftsman which records the testator's instructions, and perhaps any other contemporaneous document which records the testator's intentions.[9] Taking that evidence into account may

9 In *Marley v Rawlings* [2014] UKSC 2 at [26] (cited in the text above) Lord Neuberger indicated that evidence of the testator's intentions could for example be evidence of "*what he told the drafter of the will, or another person, or [...] what was in any notes he made or earlier drafts of the will which he may have approved or*

reinforce the construction the court had already reached at the first stage,[10] or may lead to a different one. On the other hand, if none of the section 21 gateways is engaged, then there will be no third stage and instead the court will construe the will in the accordance with the conclusion it had reached at the first stage.

Although each case inevitably turns on its own particular facts, some of the decisions which have followed *Marley v Rawlings* illustrate the flexibility of the court's approach to construction (where the circumstances allow it). For example:

(a) In *Reading v Reading*[11] a reference to "*issue of my mine*" was construed as including the testator's step-children,[12] even though the court observed that "*the ordinary and natural meaning of the word "issue" does not in its ordinary and natural meaning include stepchildren*".[13]

(b) In *Slattery v Jagger*[14] the court read the words "*to my Wife*" into a specific devise of a property from which they had accidentally been omitted by a process of construction.[15]

(c) In *Royal Society v Robinson*[16] a reference to "*the United Kingdom*" was construed as including the Channel Islands and the Isle of

---

caused to be prepared".

10 As happened e.g. in *Reading v Reading* [2015] EWHC 946 (Ch) (see [49]) and *Royal Society v Robinson* [2015] EWHC 3442 (Ch), in which the judge commented that if extrinsic evidence had not been admissible under section 21 AJA he "*would then have found it much more difficult to conclude with the same confidence that I have that the proper construction of the Will would be that which I have adopted*" (at [35]).

11 [2015] EWHC 946 (Ch).

12 [2015] EWHC 946 (Ch) at [47].

13 [2015] EWHC 946 (Ch) at [41].

14 [2015] EWHC 3976 (Ch).

15 [2015] EWHC 3976 (Ch) at [93].

16 [2015] EWHC 3442 (Ch).

> Man,[17] even though the court observed that "*There is no doubt that the technical meaning of "United Kingdom" would not include Jersey in the Channel Islands or the Isle of Man*".[18]

In *Re Hand*[19] the court accepted that human rights considerations can be relevant to the construction of a will. The reference in a 1946 will to "*children*" *prima facie* had to be construed as excluding adopted children as a result of the Adoption of Children Act 1926, which treated adopted children as children of their natural, rather than their adoptive, parents for succession purposes. Although that position had been reversed in 1950, it had been preserved in relation to existing dispositions. However, the court concluded that it was required by the Human Rights Act 1998 to read down the relevant preserving legislation,[20] and to construe "*children*" as including two adopted children so as not to breach their human rights.[21] The full impact of this decision is yet to be explored.[22]

It is also worth bearing in mind that several provisions of the Wills Act 1837 contain important statutory rules of construction. Those which are engaged most frequently are:

(a) section 18A, which provides that where after a will his made the testator's marriage is terminated by dissolution or annulment, the will is to be construed as if the testator's former spouse had died on the date of the dissolution or annulment, unless a contrary intention appears;

---

17 [2015] EWHC 3442 (Ch) at [34].

18 [2015] EWHC 3442 (Ch) at [26].

19 [2017] EWHC 533 (Ch).

20 Paragraph 6(1) of Schedule 2 to the Adoption Act 1976.

21 The relevant human rights were the right to respect for private and family life, protected by article 8 of the European Convention on Human Rights, and the right not to be discriminated against on the on the ground of "*birth or other status*", protected by article 14.

22 See e.g. *PQ v RS* [2019] EWHC 1643 (Ch), in which Chief Master Marsh expressed no view as to whether *Re Hand* had been correctly decided (at [24]).

(b) section 18C, which contains equivalent provisions in relation to the dissolution or annulment of a civil partnership;

(c) section 24, which provides that a will must be construed to "*speak and take effect as if it had been executed immediately before the death of the testator*", unless a contrary intention appears;

(d) section 33, which may prevent a gift to a child or children of the testator from lapsing where such child or children have predeceased the testator leaving issue, unless a contrary intention appears.[23]

2.2 Practice and procedure

2.2.1 Who is affected?

The first question PRs should ask themselves when faced with a construction problem is: who is affected by it?

The reason for this is that construction problems have a right answer – and one, or possibly several, wrong ones. Therefore PRs should not try to decide themselves what they think the answer is and then act on that basis. If they do and if they proceed on the basis of an answer which later turns out to be the wrong one, they can be personally liable for *devastavit* (i.e. for having administered or distributed the estate incorrectly).

It follows that the main concern for PRs faced with a construction problem is to ensure that before they take any step based on a particular construction they protect themselves from potential personal liability for *devastavit*, which they can do by obtaining either the binding consent of all affected beneficiaries or authorisation from the court. To get to that position, the PRs will first have to establish who the affected beneficiaries are.

23 Section 33 and the existence of a contrary intention were considered in *Hives v Machin* [2017] EWHC 1414 (Ch).

Needless to say, the answer to this will depend on the particular circumstances, and can vary widely. In simple terms, the way to go about ascertaining the affected beneficiaries is to consider the different possible constructions (which may be two or more) and then consider who would benefit under each possible construction, as illustrated by the following examples.

Example 1

Violetta's will gives her country estate to "*my husband Alfredo*", and the residue of her estate to the British Thoracic Society. At her death Violetta has been in a cohabiting relationship with Alfredo for 15 years, but the couple never married.

There are two possible constructions: either the gift to Alfredo takes effect or it does not. The affected beneficiaries are therefore Alfredo and the British Thoracic Society.

Example 2

Siegmund dies leaving a will which includes the following specific gift: "*I give my prized sword Nothung to my son absolutely free of tax*". The residuary estate is left to Siegmund's wife Sieglinde. Siegmund was survived by two sons: Siegfried, who was the child of Siegmund's marriage to Sieglinde; and Trevor, who was born from an extra-marital affair Siegmund had with a babysitter.

There are four possible constructions:

(a) the gift takes effect and passes Nothung to Siegfried;

(b) the gift takes effect and passes Nothung to Trevor;

(c) the gift takes effect and passes Nothung to both Siegfried and Trevor; or

(d) the gift fails and Nothung falls into residue and passes to Sieglinde.

The affected beneficiaries are therefore:

(a) Siegfried;

(b) Trevor; and

(c) Sieglinde.

Example 3

By his will, Buoso left his entire estate to "*those inhabitants of Fucecchio who were kind to me during my lifetime, if more than one in equal shares absolutely*".

There are two possible constructions:

(a) the gift takes effect and passes the estate to the inhabitants of Fucecchio who were kind to Buoso during his lifetime; or

(b) the gift fails and an intestacy arises.

The affected beneficiaries are therefore:

(a) the inhabitants of Fucecchio who were kind to Buoso during his lifetime; and

(b) Buoso's intestacy beneficiaries.

If the construction problem affects the amount of tax payable, some thought should be given to whether it is also necessary to involve HMRC.

The corollary to the above is that PRs should bear in mind that they have no personal interest in how the construction problem is resolved between the affected beneficiaries. It is not for the PRs to try to second guess what the testator might have intended, nor to form a view as to which of the affected beneficiaries is more 'worthy' or 'deserving'. The PRs should remain neutral and impartial, and simply do what they are told, either by a unanimous binding agreement reached by all of the affected beneficiaries, or by the court.

2.2.2 Can the problem be resolved by agreement?

In principle, a construction problem can be resolved by the unanimous agreement of all of the beneficiaries affected by it. Therefore, once the PRs have identified all of the affected beneficiaries, the next question they should ask themselves is: can the problem be resolved by agreement?

Suppose that in Example 1 above the British Thoracic Society agrees that Violetta's country estate should pass to Alfredo. They are the only two parties affected by the uncertainty.[24] If they are able to agree what should happen to the property, then provided Alfredo is a capacitous adult, they can resolve the construction problem between themselves without having to go to court. The PRs' only concern will be to ensure that the agreement is properly documented so that they cannot later be criticised by the British Thoracic Society or Alfredo for acting in accordance with it.

Resolving the problem by agreement is usually significantly cheaper and quicker than asking the court to do so. Moreover, if an agreement is reached within two years of the deceased's death, it may be possible for the agreement to be 'read back' for IHT and/or CGT purposes if doing so is advantageous.[25]

As indicated above, if the construction problem affects the amount of tax payable, some thought should be given to whether it is also necessary to obtain the agreement of HMRC. Typical examples are cases in which the problem concerns whether property passes to an IHT-exempt beneficiary (such as a surviving spouse or charity). HMRC's involvement will generally not be required if an agreement is reached and implemented by an instrument which is executed within

24 This assumes the estate is sufficiently solvent for there to be residue.

25 See section 142 of the Inheritance Tax Act 1984 and section 62 of the Taxation of Chargeable Gains Act 1992.

two years of the testator's death, because in such cases it should be possible for the affected beneficiaries to determine the tax consequences.[26] However, if an agreement is only reached or implemented more than two years after the testator's death and affects (or purports to affect) the amount of tax payable, HMRC's agreement is likely to be required.

Suppose that in Example 2 above, Siegmund, Trevor and Sieglinde agree that Nothung should pass as part of residue to Sieglinde. As Sieglinde is the surviving spouse and thus an IHT-exempt beneficiary, whereas Siegmund and Trevor are sons and are not, this could affect the amount of IHT payable. It may therefore be necessary to involve HMRC.

In practice, construction problems are generally only resolved by agreement in the most straightforward cases. Two reasons can be identified for this. First, beneficiaries often have different views about what the testator did or did not intend, and are therefore simply unable to reach an agreement. Secondly, to avoid exposing themselves to potential personal liability to disappointed beneficiaries, PRs must obtain the binding consent of all of the beneficiaries who are affected by the construction problem. This will not be possible if the construction problem affects beneficiaries who are minors, unborn, lack capacity and/or cannot be found. As those types of beneficiaries are unable to give the PRs their binding consent, in cases in which they are affected, the court's intervention is likely to be necessary.

A useful way to explore whether the construction problem can be resolved by agreement is for the PRs, who are often the first to spot the problem, to obtain advice from counsel on the construction problem and then share that advice with all affected beneficiaries and canvass their views. If the will incorporates clause 12.3 of the STEP Standard Provisions (2nd edition), the PRs should consider obtaining the advice of counsel of "*at least five years' standing*" if they want to rely on the protection from liability afforded by that clause.[27]

---

26 By availing themselves of the 'reading back' mechanisms in section 142 of the Inheritance Tax Act 1984 and/or section 62 of the Taxation of Chargeable Gains Act 1992.

27 Clause 12.3 and the following two clauses provide:

This process should help both the PRs and all the affected beneficiaries to understand their respective positions, which in turn should inform all involved whether there is any hope of the construction problem being resolved by agreement and, if so, how this might be achieved. Depending on the circumstances, the affected beneficiaries may wish to try to reach an agreement by, for example, negotiating in correspondence, at a round-table meeting or at a mediation.

As indicated above, PRs should bear in mind that they have no personal interest in how the construction problem is resolved between the affected beneficiaries. Their focus should be to ensure:

(a) that they obtain the binding consent of all affected beneficiaries so they are protected from potential personal liability for *devastavit* (i.e. for having distributed to the wrong person); and

(b) that the agreement is one which the PRs can in fact implement. For example, the PRs should consider whether the agreement has tax consequences and, if so, how these should be addressed.

However, if all affected beneficiaries manage to reach a binding agreement which the PRs can implement, it is not for the PRs to 'approve' or 'disapprove' of it in any moral or ethical sense, e.g. on the

---

12.3 A Trustee shall not be liable for acting in accordance with the advice of counsel, of at least five years' standing, with respect to the Trust. The Trustees may in particular conduct legal proceedings in accordance with such advice without obtaining a court order. A Trustee may recover from the Trust Fund any expenses where he has acted in accordance with such advice.

12.4 Clause 12.3 does not apply:

12.4.1 in relation to a Trustee who knows or has reasonable cause to suspect that the advice was given in ignorance of material facts;

12.4.2 if proceedings are pending to obtain the decision of the court on the matter;

12.4.3 in relation to a Trustee who has a personal interest in the subject matter of the advice; or

12.4.4 in relation to a Trustee who has committed a breach of trust relating to the subject matter of the advice.

12.5 Clause 12.3 does not prejudice any right of any Person to follow property or income into the hands of any Person, other than a purchaser, who may have received it.

basis that they think the testator would or would not have liked it. It also follows from this that PRs are generally not required to actively participate in any negotiations between the affected beneficiaries; indeed, PRs should ensure they do not incur unnecessary costs by doing so.

In cases in which professional negligence proceedings against the draftsman have also been threatened or are on foot, it may be sensible to try to compromise those proceedings at the same time.

There are two further tools which can help achieve a pragmatic solution without the court's intervention in a suitable case. The first is the possibility of the PRs agreeing to distribute on a particular basis provided the recipient beneficiaries in return provide the PRs with suitable indemnities, possibly backed by security. Such indemnities would be designed to protect the PRs against the risk that they may be personally liable to disappointed beneficiaries if the basis on which they have distributed subsequently turns out to be wrong. The second is the possibility of obtaining insurance to provide the PRs with that same protection.

Whether either of these tools is a useful one will depend on all of the particular surrounding circumstances. As a rather crude rule of thumb, it is suggested that the greater the financial value of the construction problem, the less likely these tools are to provide a practical solution. This is because the greater the amount of money that turns on the construction problem, the greater the potential liability of the PRs, and thus the more nervous both the beneficiaries and any insurance company will be in providing PRs with adequate protection. Further, in high value cases there is less of a risk of the estate being significantly depleted by the costs involved in making a court application, which might also point towards a court application being the better option.

2.2.3 Professional negligence

If the will was professionally prepared, it may be possible to argue that the construction problem amounts to professional negligence by the draftsman. If so, a professional negligence claim against the draftsman is usually threatened, and sometimes issued, before a construction claim is brought.

Depending on the circumstances, if both the professional negligence claim and the construction claim have merit, the draftsman's insurers might agree to fund the construction claim, particularly if the costs involved in doing so are likely to be lower than their potential exposure in the event the professional negligence claim is successful.[28]

2.2.4 Court intervention: section 48 of the Administration of Justice Act 1985

A construction problem will usually be incapable of resolution by agreement without the court's intervention for one of two reasons (and sometimes both):

(a) all affected beneficiaries cannot reach an agreement; or

(b) all adult capacitous affected beneficiaries have reached an agreement, but the problem also affects beneficiaries who are minors, unborn, lack capacity and/or cannot be found.

Section 48 of the Administration of Justice Act 1985 ("AJA") contains a mechanism which can be useful in the latter situation (but not the former). The section provides:

> ***48.— Power of High Court to authorise action to be taken in reliance on counsel's opinion.***
>
> *(1) Where—*

28 See e.g. the will rectification case of *Re Bimson* [2010] EWHC 3679 (Ch) at [23].

(a) any question of construction has arisen out of the terms of a will or a trust; and

(b) an opinion in writing given by a person who has a 10 year High Court qualification, within the meaning of section 71 of the Courts and Legal Services Act 1990, has been obtained on that question by the personal representatives or trustees under the will or trust,

the High Court may, on the application of the personal representatives or trustees and without hearing argument, make an order authorising those persons to take such steps in reliance on the said opinion as are specified in the order.

(2) The High Court shall not make an order under subsection (1) if it appears to the court that a dispute exists which would make it inappropriate for the court to make the order without hearing argument.

There are two important points to note in relation to this mechanism. First, the procedure cannot be used where "*a dispute exists which would make it inappropriate for the court to make the order without hearing argument*" (section 48(2) AJA). That will be generally be the case where two or more affected beneficiaries are actively advancing two or more competing constructions, both of which are "*reasonably tenable*"[29]. However, it may also be the case where two conflicting opinions have been obtained from two different counsel as to the correct construction and the court feels it cannot resolve the conflict without hearing argument, as in *Greenwold v Pike.*[30]

Secondly, it is important to understand the nature of an order made under section 48 AJA and distinguish it from an order made at the conclusion of a contested construction claim (which is considered in the next section). An order made under section 48 AJA permits the PRs to

29 Paragraph 29.35 of the Chancery Guide. The paragraph, which is set out in full below, provides that the court may order a party who disagreed with the opinion when having "*no reasonably tenable argument [to the] contrary*" to pay "*all or part of any costs thrown away*".

30 [2007] EWHC 2202 (Ch).

proceed in accordance with counsel's opinion, and protects them from personal liability for *devastavit* if counsel's opinion later turns out to be wrong. However, it does not require the court to determine the construction problem itself, nor therefore to decide whether counsel's opinion is correct. It is therefore an order which is akin to a *Re Benjamin*[31] order (which authorises PRs to proceed on the footing that certain facts which cannot be established with certainty are correct).[32]

The significance of this is that an order made under section 48 AJA therefore leaves open the possibility that an affected beneficiary may subsequently[33] bring a contested construction claim and the court may at that stage determine that the opinion from counsel (in accordance with which the PRs have proceeded) is wrong. If this were to happen, the PRs will be protected from personal liability for *devastavit* because they have acted as authorised by the court's order (viz. in accordance with counsel's opinion). However, it would be open to the disappointed beneficiary to try to recover from the recipient beneficiaries any property which was distributed to them in accordance with the construction which the court has subsequently determined is wrong (subject to any applicable defences, such as laches and limitation).[34]

The question whether the mechanism provided by section 48 AJA should be used despite the fact that it carries this risk is generally answered by weighing up that risk against the costs saving in not having a fully contested construction claim. The mechanism provided by section 48 AJA is likely to be attractive if the estate is small and the capacitous adult beneficiaries are therefore keen to ensure that it is not depleted by a fully contested construction claim and/or the circum-

---

31 [1902] 1 Ch. 723.

32 The classic example is an order authorising PRs to distribute the estate on the footing that a beneficiary who cannot be found predeceased the testator (which were the circumstances in *Re Benjamin* itself).

33 E.g. after he has attained majority.

34 The leading authority on this difficult topic remains the House of Lords decision in *Ministry of Health v Simpson* [1951] AC 251. In relation to the limitation period applicable to this sort of claim, see *Davies v Sharples* [2006] EWHC 362 (Ch).

stances suggest that the risk of any beneficiary subsequently bringing a challenge is small or negligible. On the other hand, if the estate is large and/or it is thought that there is a serious risk that a beneficiary may subsequently bring a challenge, it may be worth incurring the extra cost of having a fully contested construction claim so as to have the construction problem resolved once and for all. For a rare example of a reported judgment which led to the making of an order under section 48 AJA, see *Re Duffy*.[35]

The CPR contain some procedural rules which apply to a claim for an order under section 48 AJA. Such a claim must be made in the High Court[36] and must be brought in the Chancery Division,[37] i.e. what has now become the Property, Trusts and Probate List (ChD) of the Business and Property Courts of England and Wales. It must be brought by the PRs or trustees[38] and can be brought either in the Rolls Building in London or in one of the District Registries (Birmingham, Bristol, Cardiff, Leeds, Liverpool, Manchester, Newcastle-upon-Tyne, Preston, Mold and Caernarfon).[39]

Rule 64.3 CPR requires such a claim to be made by way of a CPR Part 8 claim form.[40] Paragraph 5 of CPR Practice Direction 64A provides:[41]

---

35 [2013] EWHC 2395 (Ch).

36 This is required by section 48(1) AJA itself, which confers jurisdiction to make the relevant order on the High Court.

37 CPR rule 64.1(3).

38 This is required by section 48(1) AJA itself, which refers to "*the application of the personal representatives or trustees*".

39 Paragraph 30.1 of the Chancery Guide. Chapter 30 of the Chancery Guide contains helpful information regarding Chancery business outside London, including contact details of the various District Registries.

40 CPR rule 64.3 applies to claims under section 48 AJA as a result of CPR rule 64.2(a).

41 Consistently with this, CPR rule 64.4 expressly states that its provisions (which govern who should be a party to a claim) do not apply to a claim under section 48 AJA.

> *A Part 8 claim form for an application by trustees[42] under section 48 of the Administration of Justice Act 1985 (power of High Court to authorise action to be taken in reliance on legal opinion) may be issued without naming a defendant, under rule 8.2A. No separate application for permission under rule 8.2A need be made.*

Chapter 29 of the Chancery Guide provides the following detailed procedural guidance, which helpfully lists the topics which need to be addressed in the witness statement filed in support of the claim:[43]

> ***Applications under section 48 of the Administration of Justice Act 1985***
>
> *29.29 Applications under section 48 of the Administration of Justice Act 1985 should be made by Part 8 claim form without naming a defendant, under rule 8.2A. No separate application for permission under rule 8.2A need be made.*
>
> *29.30 The claim should be supported by a witness statement or affidavit to which are exhibited: (a) copies of all relevant documents;*
>
> *(b) instructions to a person with a 10-year High Court qualification within the meaning of the Courts and Legal Services Act 1990 ("the qualified person");*
>
> *(c) the qualified person's opinion; and*
>
> *(d) draft terms of the desired order.*
>
> *The application is for an order to authorise the trustees to act on the basis of a legal opinion, which may deal with construction issues; it should not seek a decision of the court itself on the construction of any instrument.*

---

42 CPR rule 64.1(2) makes it clear that "*where appropriate, references to trustees include executors and administrators*".

43 This derives (with necessary modifications) from *Practice Direction (Chancery: Construction Summons)* [1987] 1 WLR 251.

29.31 The witness statement or affidavit (or exhibits thereto) should state:

(a) the reason for the application;

(b) the names of all persons who are, or may be, affected by the order sought;

(c) all surrounding circumstances admissible and relevant in construing the document;

(d) the date of qualification of the qualified person and his or her experience in the construction of trust documents;

(e) the approximate value of the fund or property in question;

(f) whether it is known to the applicant that a dispute exists and, if so, details of such dispute; and

(g) what steps are proposed to be taken in reliance on the opinion.

29.32 When the file is placed before the Master he or she will consider whether the evidence is complete and, if it is, whether it is appropriate for the Master to deal with the matter, or to send the file to the Judge.

29.33 The Master or Judge will consider the papers and, if necessary, direct service of notices under CPR rule 19.8A or request further information. If the court is satisfied that the order sought is appropriate, it will be made and sent to the claimant.

29.34 If following service of notices under rule 19.8A any acknowledgment of service is received, the claimant must apply to the Master (on notice to the parties who have so acknowledged service) for directions. If the claimant desires to pursue the application to the court, the Master will ordinarily direct that the case proceeds as a Part 8 claim.

29.35 If on the hearing of the claim the court is of the opinion that any party who entered an acknowledgment of service has no reasonably tenable argument contrary to the qualified person's opinion, in the exercise of the court's discretion it may order such party to pay all or part of any costs thrown away.

Because applications pursuant to section 48 AJA are only suitable in non-contentious cases (as explained above), the incidence of the costs of the proceedings is also likely to be agreed in advance between the PRs and the adult capacitous affected beneficiaries. The usual agreement is likely to be that the costs of the proceedings will be borne by the estate as an administration expense. As the only active parties will be the PRs and the application must be uncontested (because the procedure is otherwise unsuitable), the costs should be relatively modest.

2.2.5 Court intervention: construction claim in the Chancery Division

If the affected beneficiaries cannot reach an agreement and the mechanism provided by section 48 AJA cannot be used or is considered undesirable,[44] the solution will be to ask the court to resolve the construction problem by way of a construction claim.

Starting the claim

A claim asking the court to resolve a construction problem is a claim "*for the court to determine [a] question arising in (i) the administration of the estate of a deceased person; or (ii) the execution of a trust*" within CPR rule 64.2(a). Indeed, it is highly likely to be one of the types of claims which are listed in paragraph 1(1) of CPR Practice Direction 64A as examples of claims which may be made under CPR rule 64.2(a), viz.:

(1) a claim for the determination of any of the following questions –

(a) any question as to who is included in any class of persons having –

44 E.g. because it is desirable to see the construction problem resolved once and for all.

(i) a claim against the estate of a deceased person;

(ii) a beneficial interest in the estate of such a person; or

(iii) a beneficial interest in any property subject to a trust;

(b) any question as to the rights or interests of any person claiming –

(i) to be a creditor of the estate of a deceased person;

(ii) to be entitled under a will or on the intestacy of a deceased person; or

(iii) to be beneficially entitled under a trust;

As a result, Section I of CPR Part 64 applies to such a claim, which in turn means the claim must be made by issuing a CPR Part 8 claim form.[45]

The claim is started by filing a CPR Part 8 claim form and accompanying evidence (considered below). No particulars of claim are required.[46] Claims brought by CPR Part 8 are automatically allocated to the multi-track.[47]

Claim form N208 should be used.[48] CPR rule 8.2 provides that the claim form must state:

(a) that CPR Part 8 applies;

(b) the question which the claimant wants the court to decide, or the remedy which the claimant is seeking and the legal basis for the claim to that remedy;

45 CPR rule 64.3.

46 CPR rule 8.9(a), which disapplies CPR Part 16; see also paragraph 9.4 of the Chancery Guide.

47 CPR rule 8.9(c); see also paragraph 9.4 of the Chancery Guide.

48 Paragraph 4.2 of CPR Practice Direction 8A; see also paragraph 9.5 of the Chancery Guide.

(c) if the claim is being made under an enactment, what that enactment is;

(d) if the claimant is claiming in a representative capacity, what that capacity is; and

(e) if the defendant is sued in a representative capacity, what that capacity is.

Although in some cases rectification will not be relevant, claims for construction and rectification are often brought in the alternative.[49] A construction problem may also arise in the context of another dispute, such as a claim pursuant to the Inheritance (Provision for Family and Dependants) Act 1975.[50] In these sorts of circumstances, the procedural rules governing any other claim must also be borne in mind. Where the construction problem is one of several aspects in dispute, it may be worth considering whether the court should be asked to deal with any aspect as a preliminary issue.[51]

Limitation

No limitation period applies to construction claims. However, a time limit or limitation period may be relevant if the dispute involves one or more other claims to which a time limit or limitation period does apply, such as a claim pursuant to the Inheritance (Provision for Family and Dependants) Act 1975 or a professional negligence claim, and/or if the intention is to ask the court to rectify the will.[52]

---

49 See e.g. *Burnard v Burnard* [2014] EWHC 340 (Ch), *Reading v Reading* [2015] EWHC 946 (Ch), *Re Harte* [2015] EWHC 2351 (Ch), *Guthrie v Morel* [2015] EWHC 3172 (Ch), *Slattery v Jagger* [2015] EWHC 3976 (Ch) and *Royal Society v Robinson* [2015] EWHC 3442 (Ch).

50 See e.g. *Burnard v Burnard* [2014] EWHC 340 (Ch) and *Tish v Olley* [2018] EWHC 1069 (Ch).

51 As in *Burnard v Burnard* [2014] EWHC 340 (Ch) (see [7]) and *Tish v Olley* [2018] EWHC 1069 (Ch) (see [1]).

52 In relation to which see chapter 3.

Which court

The County Court appears to have jurisdiction to determine a construction problem if the value of the estate or trust fund does not exceed £350,000.[53] However, in practice most construction claims are issued in the High Court, where they must be brought in the Chancery Division,[54] i.e. what has now become the Property, Trusts and Probate List (ChD) of the Business and Property Courts of England and Wales. If it is to be issued in the High Court, a construction claim can be issued either in the Rolls Building in London or in one of the District Registries (Birmingham, Bristol, Cardiff, Leeds, Liverpool, Manchester, Newcastle-upon-Tyne, Preston, Mold and Caernarfon).[55]

Evidence

The claimant must file the evidence on which he intends to rely when his claim form is issued[56] (unless the claimant only intends to rely on the evidence contained in the claim form itself, which it is suggested is unlikely to be the case in construction claims). This will generally be in the form of one or more witness statements.[57] The claimant's evidence must be served on the defendant with the claim form.[58]

---

53 Section 23 of the County Courts Act 1984 and article 3 of the County Court Jurisdiction Order 2014 (SI 2014/503). This assumes that the construction claim in question is a type of "*proceedings for the administration of the estate of a deceased person*" or "*proceedings for the execution of any trust*" within section 23(a) or (b) respectively.

54 CPR rule 64.1(3). See also Section 61 and paragraphs 1(c) and 1(d) of Schedule 1 to the Senior Courts Act 1981 and paragraphs 29.2(c) and 29.2(d) of the Chancery Guide.

55 Paragraph 30.1 of the Chancery Guide. Chapter 30 of the Chancery Guide contains helpful information regarding Chancery business outside London, including contact details of the various District Registries.

56 CPR rule 8.5(1) and paragraph 7.1 of CPR Practice Direction 8A; see also paragraph 9.6 of the Chancery Guide.

57 Paragraph 7.2 of CPR Practice Direction 8A.

58 CPR rule 8.5(2).

The contents of the witness statement(s) will of course depend on the circumstances of the particular case, and on whether the claimant is a neutral PR who is simply explaining the construction problem to the court, or an interested beneficiary who is advancing a particular construction. In general terms, the topics which one should consider covering in the evidence filed in support of the claim are likely to be:

(a) the claimant's role and the capacity in which he brings the claim;

(b) the factual background;

(c) the construction problem;

(d) how the will was prepared;

(e) if it is contended that section 21 AJA is engaged, extrinsic evidence of the testator's intention (e.g. the will file);

(f) the position of the other interested parties.

If the will was professionally prepared, some thought should be given as to whether evidence should be obtained from the draftsman responsible for preparing it (if available).

It should be borne in mind that the CPR requires witness statements to be in the witness's own words[59] and that construction problems are usually issues of law rather than fact. The temptation to include in a witness statement extensive legal submissions and references to case law should generally be resisted, particularly in witness statements of lay witnesses; these are properly a matter for skeleton arguments and submissions.[60]

59 Paragraph 18.1 of CPR Practice Direction 32; see also paragraph 19.2 of the Chancery Guide.

60 See paragraph 19.3 of the Chancery Guide.

Disclosure

CPR Practice Direction 51U contains a new 'disclosure pilot' which sets out detailed rules concerning disclosure that apply to claims in the Business and Property Courts of England and Wales. The pilot came into force on 1st January 2019 and applies to both existing claims and to new claims issued after that date.[61] It will remain in force for two years.[62]

A Practice Note by Chief Master Marsh dated 27th March 2019[63] clarifies that the pilot "*does not directly apply to Part 8 claims because Part 8 contains its own regime for the disclosure of documents that are relied on by the parties*".[64] In particular, the pilot's new concept of 'Initial Disclosure' does not apply to CPR Part 8 claims.[65] However, paragraph 5 of the Practice Note explains:

> "*The court has power to make an order for extended disclosure under the pilot in a case proceeding under Part 8. It will adopt such elements of the Practice Direction as are appropriate to the case and the scope of disclosure that is sought. The party requesting disclosure will need to identify the issues for disclosure and the Model or Models that apply. It is not expected that the full procedure for extended disclosure, including completion of all elements of the Disclosure Review Document, will normally be required.*"

Given the disclosure obligations already imposed by CPR Part 8, it is suggested that orders for extended disclosure pursuant to the pilot are likely to be rare in construction claims. Some support of this can be found in paragraph 17.74 of the Chancery Guide: "*It is rare for orders for disclosure to be made in a Part 8 claim because for most types of Part 8*

61 Paragraph 1.2 of CPR Practice Direction 51U.

62 Paragraph 1.2 of CPR Practice Direction 51U.

63 Available here: https://www.judiciary.uk/wp-content/uploads/2019/03/Practice-Note-27_03_19.pdf

64 Paragraph 3 of the Practice Note.

65 Paragraph 5.1 of CPR Practice Direction 51U; see also paragraph 4 of the Practice Note.

claim it should suffice for the parties to rely upon the documents they exhibit".

Prospective (or pre-emptive) costs orders

In some construction cases it may be appropriate to consider at an early stage of the proceedings whether a mechanism should be put in place for the costs of one or more of the parties to be paid out of the estate or trust fund in any event irrespective of the outcome.[66] This can be either by way of a contractual agreement by the PRs or by a so-called prospective (or pre-emptive) costs order by the court. This issue tends to arise primarily in pension cases, where an individual pension scheme member may be made a party to complex litigation as representative of other scheme members, and it may be unfair for him to have to bear his costs personally at least until the conclusion of the litigation, which can create a cash flow problem.[67] However, the issue is unlikely to arise in claims concerning the correct construction of a will.

Where the issue does arise, the eight sub-paragraphs of paragraph 6 of CPR Practice Direction 64A contain some detailed guidance about prospective costs orders, as do paragraphs 29.19 and 29.20 of the Chancery Guide, and a model form of prospective costs order is appended to CPR Practice Direction 64A.

Costs management

CPR rule 3.12 now makes it clear that costs management does not apply to CPR Part 8 claims unless the court orders that it should pursuant to CPR rule 3.12(1A).[68] Paragraph 5(e) of CPR Practice Direction 3E provides that an order for costs management may be "*particularly appropriate*" in "*any Part 8 or other claims or applications*

66 The costs orders which are likely to be made at the conclusion of the proceedings are considered at "*Costs*" below.

67 The principles governing the making of a prospective costs order have been considered in a line of pensions cases which includes *McDonald v Horn* [1995] 1 All ER 961 and *IBM United Kingdom Pensions Trust Ltd v Metcalfe* [2012] EWHC 125 (Ch).

68 In relation to which see also paragraph 2 of CPR Practice Direction 3E.

involving a substantial dispute of fact and/or likely to require oral evidence and/or extensive disclosure". A party seeking an order that costs management should apply to the proceedings should "*give notice to the other parties and the court well in advance of the directions hearing and explain, preferably in a witness statement, why such an order is sought*".[69]

In will construction claims an obligation to file and serve a costs budget may nonetheless be imposed by paragraph 5 of CPR Practice Direction 3F. Significantly, the obligation applies early on in the proceedings when the party files his evidence (as explained below).

Section II of Practice Direction 3F is entitled '*Costs Capping in Relation to Trust Funds*'; paragraph 5 is the Section's only paragraph. It supplements CPR rules 3.19 to 3.21 and paragraphs 1 to 4 of Practice Direction 3F,[70] which govern costs capping orders generally. Paragraph 5.1 makes it clear that references in it to "*trust fund*" includes the estate of a deceased person. The provisions of the paragraph are designed to "*enable the parties to consider whether to apply for, and the court to consider whether to make of its own initiative, a costs capping order in relation to proceedings relating to trust funds*".[71]

The obligation to file and serve a costs budget is imposed by paragraphs 5.4 and 5.5, which provide:

> *5.4 Any party to such proceedings who intends to apply for an order for the payment of costs out of the trust fund must file and serve on all other parties written notice of that intention together with a budget of the costs likely to be incurred by that party.*
>
> *5.5 The documents mentioned in paragraph 5.4 must be filed and served –*
>
> *[…]*

69 Paragraph 17.71 of the Chancery Guide.

70 Paragraph 5.3 of CPR Practice Direction 3F.

71 Paragraph 5.2 of CPR Practice Direction 3F.

> *(b) in a Part 8 claim, with the evidence (or, if a defendant does not intend to serve and file evidence, with the acknowledgement of service).*

Finally, paragraph 5.6 provides that when the proceedings first come before the court for directions, the court may make a costs capping order of its own initiative, whether or not any party has applied for such an order.

In most construction claims, all parties will seek an order that their costs of the proceedings be paid out of the estate or trust fund[72] – or at least will "*intend*" to apply for such an order when the proceedings are started and/or when the relevant party files his evidence. This appears to trigger the obligation (imposed by paragraph 5.4) to file and serve on all other parties both "*written notice of that intention*" and a budget "*of the costs likely to be incurred by that party*".

On the other hand, costs capping orders are rare in construction claims, and anecdotal evidence suggests that this provision is rarely (if ever) complied with or enforced in practice in such claims. It is also unclear what the sanction for non-compliance is (if any). However, the provision is there, and practitioners ought to be aware of it, at least unless and until it is amended by the Civil Procedure Rule Committee.

Parties

Determining who should be made a party to a construction claim often requires some careful thought. In general, it is useful to bear in mind that:

(a) the court will expect someone to argue in favour of each of the various possible constructions (which may be two or more);

(b) it is generally desirable to take steps to ensure that everyone affected by the construction problem will be bound by the court's order;

---

72 See further under "Costs" below.

(c) the PRs should generally remain neutral in their capacity as PRs and not argue in favour of one of the possible constructions;[73] and

(d) if the construction problem affects the amount of tax payable, it may be necessary to notify, and perhaps even join, HMRC.

As a starting point, CPR rule 64.4(1) provides the following rules in relation to who the parties should be:

> *(1) In a claim to which this Section applies, other than an application under section 48 of the Administration of Justice Act 1985 –*
>
> *(a) all the trustees[74] must be parties;*
>
> *(b) if the claim is made by trustees, any of them who does not consent to being a claimant must be made a defendant; and*
>
> *(c) the claimant may make parties to the claim any persons with an interest in or claim against the estate, or an interest under the trust, who it is appropriate to make parties having regard to the nature of the order sought.*

The claim can generally be brought either by the PRs, or by one or more of the beneficiaries.

All PRs must be parties (CPR rule 64.4(1)(a) and (b) above), which is unsurprising given that they need to be bound by the order. What may be less clear is how to ensure that all affected beneficiaries are joined or are otherwise bound by the court's order.

In cases involving a limited number of affected beneficiaries, the answer may be fairly straightforward. The simplest example is where there are two possible constructions and the affected beneficiaries are capacitous

73 See e.g. *Re Aspinall* [2017] EWHC 454 (Ch), in which the executors as claimants brought the proceedings and then let the rival beneficiaries (who had been joined as defendants) advance the two construction arguments (see [11]).

74 CPR rule 64.1(2) makes it clear that in Part 64 and its accompanying Practice Directions "*where appropriate, references to trustees include executors and administrators*".

adults, as in Example 1 above (assuming Alfredo is a capacitous adult). In such cases, either the PRs bring the claim and join the affected beneficiaries as defendants,[75] or one of the affected beneficiaries can bring the claim and join the PRs and the other affected beneficiaries as defendants.[76] In either case, the PRs should generally adopt a neutral position and let the two affected beneficiaries advance the two alternative construction arguments. Exceptionally, the particular circumstances may mean that it is convenient for the PRs to advance one of the construction arguments; if so, they should ensure that they do so without jeopardising their neutrality.[77]

Where one or more of the affected beneficiaries is a minor or lacks capacity and is to be a party to the claim, that beneficiary will need a litigation friend.[78] CPR Part 21 contains detailed guidance on the procedure for the appointment of a litigation friend.

On the other hand, the position may be more complicated where the construction problem affects a large number of beneficiaries (e.g. large classes) and/or where some of the affected beneficiaries are minors, unborn, lack capacity and/or cannot be found. In Example 3 above, the class of intestacy beneficiaries may be large and/or its members difficult to trace, and it may be difficult to ascertain all members of the other class. In these sorts of cases, there is likely to be a tension between ensuring on the one hand that everyone who has an interest is properly represented and has an opportunity to be heard, and trying on the other to avoid depleting the estate or trust by incurring significant costs tracing and communicating with large classes of beneficiaries.

How the balance should be struck will inevitably depend on the circumstances of the particular case. In complicated cases, the provisions of CPR rule 8.2A, rule 19.7 and/or 19.8A can be of considerable

---

75 As e.g. in *Re Aspinall* [2017] EWHC 454 (Ch) (see [11]).

76 As e.g. in *Guthrie v Morel* [2015] EWHC 3172 (Ch) (see [4]).

77 See e.g. *Re Wippell* [2018] EWHC 730 (Ch) at [8].

78 CPR rule 21.2(1).

assistance.[79] These govern respectively the circumstances in which a CPR Part 8 claim may be issued without naming a defendant, the appointment of a party to represent the interests of others, and the service of proceedings and/or orders on non-parties so as to bind them.

CPR rule 8.2A provides:

> *Issue of claim form without naming defendants*
>
> *(1) A practice direction may set out circumstances in which a claim form may be issued under this Part without naming a defendant.*
>
> *(2) The practice direction may set out those cases in which an application for permission must be made by application notice before the claim form is issued.*
>
> *(3) The application notice for permission –*
>
> *(a) need not be served on any other person; and*
>
> *(b) must be accompanied by a copy of the claim form that the applicant proposes to issue.*
>
> *(4) Where the court gives permission it will give directions about the future management of the claim.*

In fact, neither of the two Practice Directions to CPR Part 8[80] deal with the circumstances in which a claim form may be issued without naming a defendant. However, paragraphs 7.15 and 7.16 of the Chancery Guide provide the following guidance:

> *Application to issue the claim form without naming defendants*

---

79 The relevance of these rules to claims concerning estates and trusts is highlighted by paragraphs 29.12, 29.15 and 29.16 of the Chancery Guide, considered below. Note that CPR rule 19.6, which is entitled "*Representative parties with same interest*", does not apply to claims "*about (a) the estate of a deceased person, (b) property subject to a trust, or (c) the meaning of a document, including a statute*": see CPR rules 19.6(5) and 19.7(1).

80 viz. Practice Directions 8A and 8B.

> *7.15 CPR rule 8.2A permits the court to make an order in relation to a Part 8 claim (not a Part 7 claim) entitling the claimant to issue the claim without naming defendants. An order might be appropriate, for example, where the court is asked to make an order to assist executors who are unable to locate beneficiaries named in a will.*
>
> *7.16 The application is made by application notice issued at Chancery Chambers. It will then be placed before the assigned Master. Alternatively in a simple case the Master may be willing to deal with it at 10.30 or 2.00 as an Application without Notice ("AWN").*

Similarly, paragraph 29.12 of the Chancery Guide provides:

> *29.12 Rule 8.2A (issue of claim form without naming a defendant) can also be relevant [to applications by PRs for directions in relation to a deceased person's estate]. Normally, permission to issue the claim form under rule 8.2A is required (see Chapter 7 paragraphs 15-16 above). In urgent cases this can be obtained on an application without notice. But in some cases the claim form may be issued under rule 8.2A without first seeking permission.*

Paragraph 29.13 of the Chancery Guide explains that it may be appropriate to adopt this procedure where, for example, "*the only possible defendant(s) cannot be located (eg no address can be given, or it is unknown if they survive), or there are too many possible defendants*".[81] Paragraph 15.8 of the Chancery Guide indicates that such applications are generally considered by the Master as part of file work and that the application should "*explain carefully why the order is appropriate*".

---

81 In so far as relevant, the paragraph provides: "*One example [of cases in which the claim form may be issued under rule 8.2A without first seeking permission] is where the only possible defendant(s) cannot be located (eg no address can be given, or it is unknown if they survive), or there are too many possible defendants. The Master will then give any directions required. Applications for Benjamin orders may also fall into this category, as well as applications for permission to distribute the estates of deceased Lloyds' names (see below). [...]*"

CPR rule 19.7(2) provides:

> *The court may make an order appointing a person to represent any other person or persons in the claim where the person or persons to be represented –*
>
> *(a) are unborn;*
>
> *(b) cannot be found;*
>
> *(c) cannot easily be ascertained; or*
>
> *(d) are a class of persons who have the same interest in a claim and –*
>
> > *(i) one or more members of that class are within sub-paragraphs (a), (b) or (c); or*
> >
> > *(ii) to appoint a representative would further the overriding objective.*

This caters for several different scenarios:

(a) is self-explanatory;

(b) covers situations in which it is clear who the affected beneficiary is, but (reasonable) attempts to find him have proved unsuccessful;

(c) covers situations in which it is not clear who the affected beneficiary is, nor can this be easily clarified;

(d) covers two alternative situations where a class of persons has the same interest in the claim:

   (i) is self-explanatory;

   (ii) is potentially wide and flexible. It can be used, for example, where there is a large class of affected beneficiaries scattered around the world, all of whom have the same interest, and it would further the overriding objective to appoint one of them to represent the whole class (e.g. by reducing procedural delay and costs) – ideally one who can be served within the jurisdiction.[82]

CPR rule 19.7(3) provides that an application for a representation order under CPR rule 19.7(2) may be made "*by any person who seeks to be appointed under the order or any party to the claim*", and may be made "*at any time before or after the claim has started*". CPR rule 19.7(4) provides that the application notice for such an order must be served on:

(a) all parties to the claim, if the claim has started;

(b) the person sought to be appointed, if that person is not the applicant or a party to the claim; and

(c) any other person as directed by the court.

It is important to note that where the court has made a representation order under CPR rule 19.7, the court's approval is required to settle the claim.[83] This is to safeguard the position of the represented parties and to ensure their representative does not enter into a compromise which is disadvantageous to them: CPR rule 19.7(6) gives the court jurisdiction to approve a settlement "*where it is satisfied that the settlement is for the benefit of all represented persons*".

Finally, CPR rule 19.8A provides:

Power to make judgements binding on non-parties

(1) This rule applies to any claim relating to –

(a) the estate of a deceased person;

(b) property subject to a trust; or

---

82 For an example, see the trust case of *Public Trustee v Harrison* [2018] EWHC 166 (Ch) at [8].

83 CPR rule 19.7(5).

(c) the sale of any property.

(2) The court may at any time direct that notice of –

(a) the claim; or

(b) any judgment or order given in the claim,

be served on any person who is not a party but who is or may be affected by it.

(3) An application under this rule –

(a) may be made without notice; and

(b) must be supported by written evidence which includes the reasons why the person to be served should be bound by the judgment in the claim.

(4) Unless the court orders otherwise –

(a) a notice of a claim or of a judgment or order under this rule must be –

(i) in the form required by the practice direction;

(ii) issued by the court; and

(iii) accompanied by a form of acknowledgment of service with any necessary modifications;

(b) a notice of a claim must also be accompanied by –

(i) a copy of the claim form; and

(ii) such other statements of case, witness statements or affidavits as the court may direct; and

(c) a notice of a judgment or order must also be accompanied by a copy of the judgment or order.

(5) If a person served with notice of a claim files an acknowledgment of service of the notice within 14 days he will become a party to the claim.

(6) If a person served with notice of a claim does not acknowledge service of the notice he will be bound by any judgment given in the claim as if he were a party.

(7) If, after service of a notice of a claim on a person, the claim form is amended so as substantially to alter the relief claimed, the court may direct that a judgment shall not bind that person unless a further notice, together with a copy of the amended claim form, is served on him.

(8) Any person served with a notice of a judgment or order under this rule –

(a) shall be bound by the judgment or order as if he had been a party to the claim; but

(b) may, provided he acknowledges service –

(i) within 28 days after the notice is served on him, apply to the court to set aside or vary the judgment or order; and

(ii) take part in any proceedings relating to the judgment or order.

(9) The following rules of Part 10 (acknowledgment of service) apply –

(a) rule 10.4; and

(b) rule 10.5, subject to the modification that references to the defendant are to be read as references to the person served with the notice.

(10) A notice under this rule is issued on the date entered on the notice by the court.

The procedure in CPR rule 19.8A can be useful to bind interested beneficiaries who do not want to take an active role in the proceedings, such as the adult children of an 'active' interested beneficiary who are content to simply support their parent's position. However, it suggests that it is unlikely to be a good idea to press on with the proceedings and to then try to rely on CPR rule 19.8A to serve a judgment or order on an interested beneficiary who it is thought will want to actively have a say. In such cases there is a risk that such a beneficiary will then apply to set aside the judgment or order (pursuant to CPR rule 19.8A(8)(b)) to, in effect, re-open the case to advance his argument, and this could significantly increase the overall costs. In this sort of situation it is likely to be preferable to ensure that such a beneficiary is able to actively participate from the outset.

It should be borne in mind that the issue of representation is likely to be considered by the court at the first directions hearing, at which creative and pragmatic solutions can be considered with the Master, particularly in complex cases.[84]

Service

The usual rules for service contained in the CPR – mostly in CPR Part 6 – apply to claims for the construction of a will. If it is necessary to seek the court's permission to serve the claim form out of the jurisdiction pursuant to CPR rule 6.36, the grounds listed in paragraph 3.1 of CPR Practice Direction 6B which are likely to be relevant are grounds (11) to (13):

> *Claims about property within the jurisdiction*
>
> *(11) The subject matter of the claim relates wholly or principally to property within the jurisdiction, provided that nothing under this*

84 See e.g. *Re Harte* [2015] EWHC 2351 (Ch), in which the PRs were initially given permission to issue the construction and rectification claims without naming a defendant (pursuant to CPR rule 8.2A), and were then given directions as to the steps they should take to ascertain the intestacy beneficiaries (including by advertisement) and as to the parties to whom they should give notice of the proceedings pursuant to CPR rule 19.8A (see [3]-[4]).

> *paragraph shall render justiciable the title to or the right to possession of immovable property outside England and Wales.*
>
> *Claims about trusts etc.*
>
> *(12) A claim is made in respect of a trust which is created [...] by a written instrument, or created orally and evidenced in writing, and which is governed by the law of England and Wales.*
>
> *(12A) A claim is made in respect of a trust which is created [...] by a written instrument, or created orally and evidenced in writing, and which provides that jurisdiction in respect of such a claim shall be conferred upon the courts of England and Wales.*
>
> *(13) A claim is made for any remedy which might be obtained in proceedings for the administration of the estate of a person who died domiciled within the jurisdiction or whose estate includes assets within the jurisdiction.*

Responding to the claim

A defendant who wishes to respond to the claim must file an acknowledgment of service in the relevant practice form (viz. form N210)[85] not more than 14 days after service of the claim form on him.[86] At the same time he must also serve his acknowledgment of service on the claimant and on any other party.[87] If he fails to do so, the defendant may attend the hearing of the claim but may not take part in the hearing unless the court gives permission.[88] The defendant must indicate in his acknowledgment of service whether he contests the claim, and if he seeks a different remedy from that set out in the claim form, what that remedy is.[89] If he wishes to object to the use of the CPR Part 8 procedure, he

---

85 Paragraph 5.2 of CPR Practice Direction 8A.

86 CPR rule 8.3(1); see also paragraph 9.5 of the Chancery Guide. Note that different (longer) periods apply if the proceedings have been served on the defendant out of the jurisdiction: see CPR rules 8.3(3) and 10.3(2).

87 CPR rule 8.3(1).

88 CPR rule 8.4(2).

89 CPR rule 8.3(2).

should also say so in his acknowledgment of service[90] – although this is likely to be rare in construction claims, as such claims must be started by issuing a Part 8 claim form[91] and tend not to involve substantial disputes of fact. There is no need to file a defence, as CPR Part 15 does not apply to claims brought pursuant to CPR Part 8.[92]

A defendant who wishes to rely on written evidence must file it when he files his acknowledgment of service,[93] and must at the same time serve a copy of his evidence on the other parties.[94] As the time limit for the defendant to do this is quite short (viz. 14 days from service of the claim on him), paragraph 7.5 of CPR Practice Direction 8A allows the parties to agree in writing to extend that time limit by up to "*14 days after the defendant files his acknowledgment of service*".[95] Such an agreement must be filed at court by the defendant at the same time as he files his acknowledgment of service.[96] Because of the somewhat awkward wording of paragraph 7.5(2)(b), it seems that in order to obtain the maximum time of 28 days from service of the claim form to file his evidence, a defendant must:

(a) first, agree in writing with the other parties that he may file his evidence 14 days after he files his acknowledgment of service; and then

(b) wait until the 14th day after he was served with the claim form, and on that day file both his acknowledgment of service and the written agreement.

---

90 CPR rule 8.8(1); see also paragraph 9.5 of the Chancery Guide.

91 CPR rule 64.3.

92 CPR rule 8.9(a) and paragraph 5.1 of CPR Practice Direction 8A; see also paragraph 9.6 of the Chancery Guide.

93 CPR rule 8.5(3) and paragraph 7.3 of CPR Practice Direction 8A; see also paragraph 9.6 of the Chancery Guide.

94 CPR rule 8.5(4).

95 Paragraph 7.5(2)(b) of CPR Practice Direction 8A; see also paragraph 9.6 of the Chancery Guide.

96 Paragraph 7.5(2)(a) of CPR Practice Direction 8A; see also paragraph 9.6 of the Chancery Guide.

This is because the 14-day extension runs from the date on which the defendant files his acknowledgment of service, as opposed to extending the period for filing of the defendant's evidence to 28 days from the date of service of the claim form on him.[97] The defendant may not rely on any written evidence which has not been served in accordance with the rules described above at the hearing of the claim unless the court gives permission.[98]

If a defendant requires more time to file his evidence, he should apply to the court for an extension of time by way of an application pursuant to CPR Part 23.[99] The Chancery Guide recognises that in substantial matters the time limits for evidence imposed by CPR Part 8 "*may be burdensome upon defendants*" and indicates that in such matters the court will normally be willing to grant a reasonable extension.[100] If the parties are in agreement that such an extension should be granted, the application should be made by filing a consent order.[101] If there is no agreement an application notice must be issued and listed for hearing unless the Master considers that the application may be dealt with without a hearing.[102] The Chancery Guide requires parties to "*at all times act co-operatively and agree reasonable requests for additional time*" and indicates that the court is "*likely to order the opposing party to pay the costs of a contested application for additional time where the opposition is unreasonable*".[103]

As for the claimant's evidence, the contents of any witness statement(s) adduced by a defendant will of course depend on the circumstances of

97 Contrast the effect of filing an acknowledgment of service in CPR Part 7 claims, which is to extend the period within which the defendant must file his defence to 28 days from the date of service on him of the particulars of claim: CPR rule 15.4(1)(b).

98 CPR rule 8.6(1).

99 Paragraph 7.4 of CPR Practice Direction 8A; and see paragraph 9.7 of the Chancery Guide of the Chancery Guide.

100 Paragraph 9.7 of the Chancery Guide of the Chancery Guide.

101 *Ibid.*

102 *Ibid.*

103 *Ibid.*

the particular case. In general terms, the topics one should consider covering are likely to be the same as those to be covered by the claimant in his evidence (discussed above). An aspect which can give rise to conflicting factual evidence is the extrinsic evidence of the testator's intention (which may be relevant if section 21 AJA is engaged). This might be the case for example where that evidence consists of conversations the testator had with different people at different times about his will, which are inconsistent with one another.[104]

It is generally not possible to obtain judgment in default in a claim commenced by pursuant to CPR Part 8[105] or a claim which seeks declaratory relief,[106] and construction claims are usually both.

If the claim is unopposed and is brought by way of CPR Part 8 proceedings, it will generally be unnecessary to apply for summary judgment, and the claimant can instead ask the court to list the claim for a disposal hearing, as Chief Master Marsh explained in *Sovereign Trustees Ltd v Lewis*:[107]

> "*Part 8 claims are markedly different to Part 7 claims. Although there is no bar to issuing a Part 24 application [i.e. an application for summary judgment] in a Part 8 claim, it will rarely be necessary*

---

104 See for example *Hives v Machin* [2017] EWHC 1414 (Ch), in which the judge heard and analysed conflicting oral evidence as to the testatrix's intentions, but ultimately concluded that section 21 AJA was not engaged and such evidence was therefore inadmissible (see in particular [39] to [59]).

105 CPR rules 8.1(5) and 12.2(b); see also paragraph 9.4 of the Chancery Guide.

106 Paragraph 12.3 of the Chancery Guide provides "*If the claimant seeks discretionary relief such as a declaration, rectification, an injunction or other similar relief the Master will usually require to be satisfied that such relief is necessary, and if so ought to be granted, and a full witness statement will usually be required. In cases of complexity the application notice may need to be listed. Declaratory relief and relief by way of rectification will not be granted without evidence and will not ordinarily be appropriate for resolution by way of judgment in default*"; see also paragraph 29.69 of the Chancery Guide.

107 [2016] EWHC 2593 (Ch) at [3]. However, see also *Guthrie v Morel* [2015] EWHC 3172 (Ch), where summary judgment was granted in a contested will construction claim.

> *for the claimant to do so where it is seeking judgment on the whole of the claim. In part this is because the second limb of CPR 24.2 will normally have no application because there will be no 'trial' as such. Part 8 claims are normally resolved at a 'disposal hearing'. This is made clear by paragraph 8.1 of Practice Direction 8A which states:*
>
> *'8.1 The court may on the hearing date –*
>
> *(i) proceed to hear the case and dispose of the claim;*
>
> *(ii) give case management directions.'*
>
> *It follows that in most Part 8 claims, where the relief sought is unopposed, or cannot realistically be opposed, it will suffice for the claimant to ask the court to fix a disposal hearing at which the court may determine whether or not the relief sought by the claimant should be granted."*

Claimant's evidence in reply

If the claimant wishes to rely on further written evidence in reply to the defendant's evidence, he must file it within 14 days of service of the defendant's evidence on him,[108] and he must also serve a copy of it on the other parties "*within the same time limit*".[109] As that time limit is also quite short, paragraph 7.5 of CPR Practice Direction 8A also allows the parties to agree in writing to extend it by up to 14 days; i.e. the maximum period which the parties can agree is that the claimant shall file his evidence in reply 28 days after service of the defendant's evidence on him.[110] Any such agreement should similarly be filed at court.[111] In the same way as a defendant, a claimant may not rely on any written evidence which has not been served in accordance with the rules

108 CPR rule 8.5(5); and see paragraph 9.6 of the Chancery Guide.

109 CPR rule 8.5(6).

110 Paragraph 7.5(2)(b) of CPR Practice Direction 8A; and see paragraph 9.6 of the Chancery Guide.

111 Although the CPR does not appear to require this, paragraph 9.7 of the Chancery Guide does.

described above at the hearing of the claim unless the court gives permission.[112]

If a claimant requires more time to file his evidence in reply to the defendant's, he too should apply to the court for an extension of time by way of an application pursuant to CPR Part 23.[113] The guidance contained in paragraph 9.7 of the Chancery Guide – which is considered above in the context of the defendant's evidence – applies equally to applications for extensions of time by claimants. In particular, parties should bear in mind that the court is likely to grant reasonable requests for extensions of time and expects parties to "*at all times act co-operatively and agree reasonable requests for additional time*" and may punish in costs a party who unreasonably opposes an application.[114]

Directions hearing

In some cases the court may give directions immediately after the claim has been issued, either on the application of a party or of its own initiative, which may include fixing a hearing date.[115] This is likely to happen particularly in cases which have been issued without naming a defendant pursuant to CPR rule 8.2A.[116] However, it is more usual for the claim to be referred to the Master[117] only after an acknowledgment of service has been filed or after the period for doing so has expired.[118]

At that stage the Master will consider whether the claim may be capable of being dealt with 'on the file', i.e. on the papers without a hearing.[119]

---

112 CPR rule 8.6(1).

113 Paragraph 7.4 of CPR Practice Direction 8A.

114 Paragraph 9.7 of the Chancery Guide.

115 Paragraph 6.1 of CPR Practice Direction 8A.

116 Paragraph 29.14 of the Chancery Guide.

117 Or to a District Judge of the High Court if the claim is in one of the District Registries.

118 Paragraph 6.2 of CPR Practice Direction 8A; see also paragraphs 9.10, 15.9 and 17.65 of the Chancery Guide.

119 Paragraph 17.65 of the Chancery Guide.

This might be appropriate if the claim is undefended,[120] but in practice it is rare for contested construction claims to be dealt with in this way.

Instead, if no acknowledgment of service has been filed, the Master may "*sometimes override the provisions of Part 8 by directing that the defendant must file and serve an acknowledgment and evidence by a specified date failing which the defendant will not be entitled to play any part in the disposal hearing*".[121] Doing so is "*intended to make explicit for a [litigant in person] what is already set out in the CPR*".[122] If this route is taken, directions may be given to lead straight to disposal hearing (without a directions hearing being held first).

On the other hand, if an acknowledgment of service has been filed, the claim is likely to be listed for a directions hearing in the first instance,[123] and some directions may be given as to how the parties should prepare for it.

At a directions hearing, the issues which the court is likely to consider are:[124]

(a) Evidence, including whether directions should be given for the filing of any further evidence (in addition to the evidence which will already have been filed by that point) and whether any witnesses should be required to attend to give oral evidence and be cross-examined at the disposal hearing.[125] In general, the CPR Part 8 procedure is designed for claims which do not involve substantial disputes of fact, and the starting point in CPR Part 8 claims seems to be that there should be no oral evidence at the

120 Paragraph 15.11 of the Chancery Guide.

121 Paragraph 15.09 of the Chancery Guide.

122 *Ibid.*

123 Paragraphs 15.10 and 17.66 of the Chancery Guide.

124 See paragraph 17.74 of the Chancery Guide.

125 CPR rule 8.6(2) provides "*The court may require or permit a party to give oral evidence at the hearing*" and CPR rule 8.6(3) provides "*The court may give directions requiring the attendance for cross-examination of a witness who has given written evidence*".

disposal hearing unless the court orders otherwise.[126] However, as indicated above, an aspect which can give rise to conflicting factual evidence is the extrinsic evidence of the testator's intention, which may be relevant if section 21 AJA is engaged.[127] This might be the case for example where that evidence consists of conversations the testator had with different people at different times about his will, which are inconsistent with one another. In cases in which this sort of factual conflict arises, directions may be given for witnesses to attend the disposal hearing to give oral evidence and be cross-examined.[128]

(b) Representation of the parties, such as whether any litigation friend needs to be appointed and/or whether any representation order should be made and/or notice given pursuant to CPR rule 19.8A (as to which, see Parties above).

(c) Directions in relation to the disposal hearing, such as directions about when and how the disposal hearing should be listed,[129] its time estimate, and the level of judge required. As regards time estimate, this is likely to depend in particular on the number and complexity of the construction arguments which are being advanced, and on whether extrinsic evidence is admissible pursuant to section 21 AJA and, if so, whether that evidence consists of live oral evidence from witnesses who will be cross-examined. As regards level of judge, CPR rule 2.4 provides that in proceedings in the High Court, any act which may be performed by

126 See paragraph 9.3 of the Chancery Guide: "*Part 8 claims will generally be disposed of on written evidence without cross-examination. The witness statements with the claim form should be sufficient in most cases to define the issues*".

127 This can be contrasted with claims for the construction of other trust instruments, where such evidence is inadmissible.

128 See for example *Hives v Machin* [2017] EWHC 1414 (Ch), in which the judge heard and considered conflicting oral evidence as to the testatrix's intentions, but ultimately concluded that section 21 AJA was not engaged and that such evidence was therefore inadmissible (see in particular [39] to [59]).

129 Unless oral evidence is envisaged, CPR Part 8 proceedings are usually entered in the General List: see paragraphs 21.5 and 21.6 of the Chancery Guide.

the court may be performed "*by any judge, Master, Registrar in Bankruptcy or District Judge*".[130] Section II of CPR Practice Direction 2B does not impose any restriction on the jurisdiction of Masters or District Judges in relation to construction claims. On the contrary, sub-paragraph 3 of paragraph 14.2 of the Chancery Guide lists "*Declarations*" as one of the "*non-excluded matters*" which paragraph 14.3 indicates "*should normally be listed before a Master*", "*whether for case management, interim relief or disposal*". Paragraph 14.3 goes on to provide: "*If it is considered that exceptionally the application should be heard by a High Court Judge the Master should be requested to release it.*"[131] Construction claims can therefore be heard either by a Master (or a District Judge in a District Registry), or by a High Court Judge. In practice, the factors which are likely to determine whether the claim will be released to a High Court Judge are likely to include the complexity and significance of the construction issue, and the amount at stake.

(d) 'Housekeeping' directions to prepare the case for the disposal hearing, such as directions relating to the hearing bundle,[132] skeleton arguments,[133] and other documents such as dramatis personae, chronologies, case summaries, lists of issues,[134] reading lists[135] and bundles of authorities.[136] As regards the latter, it is

---

130 Note the reference to 'District Judge' here is to a District Judge of the High Court (who is broadly the equivalent in the District Registries of a Master in London), not to a District Judge of the County Court.

131 Paragraph 29.10 of the Chancery Guide echoes this: "*Most applications relating to trusts will be dealt with by a Master and should therefore be listed before a Master. They will only be heard by a High Court Judge if, exceptionally, the application is released to the Judge.*"

132 Detailed rules in relation to hearing bundles are contained in paragraph 3 of CPR Practice Direction 39A and are supplemented by the guidance contained in paragraphs 21.34 to 21.72 of the Chancery Guide.

133 In relation to which see paragraphs 21.73 to 21.81 of the Chancery Guide.

134 In relation to which see paragraphs 21.75, 21.76 and 21.83 of the Chancery Guide.

135 In relation to which see paragraph 21.82 of the Chancery Guide.

136 In relation to which see paragraph 21.85 to 21.87 of the Chancery Guide.

important to bear in mind that the court is being asked to construe the particular will in question (or one of its provisions) in the circumstances in which it was made, and is therefore unlikely to be assisted by the citation of numerous authorities which have construed similar provisions in different wills made in different circumstances. The Privy Council made this clear in *Sammut v Manzi*:[137]

> *There were placed before their Lordships no less than 17 decided cases, some of which involved decisions on wording that bore some similarity with that used in the present case. Little assistance in construing a will is likely to be gained by consideration of how other judges have interpreted similar wording in other cases. Counsel rightly recognised that the starting point must be to look at the natural meaning of the wording of the will to be construed without reference to other decisions or to prima facie principles of construction.*

(e) Whether the court should make a costs capping order of its own initiative pursuant to CPR rules 3.19 to 3.21. These are rare in practice in construction claims.

Disposal hearing

At the disposal hearing, the court will hear the competing construction arguments, which may be two or, sometimes, more.

Disposal hearings in construction claims are generally listed in public, i.e. in a court which is open to members of the public.[138] Whilst it may be possible in some cases to persuade a court to list the claim in private pursuant to CPR rule 39.2(3),[139] or to impose some other less extensive

137 [2009] 1 WLR 1834 at [3]-[4].

138 Under the general rule in CPR rule 39.2(1).

139 The sub-rules of CPR rule 39.2(3) which may be engaged in construction claims are (c), (d) and (g), viz.:

> *(c) [the hearing] involves confidential information (including information relating to personal financial matters) and publicity would damage that confidentiality;*

reporting restriction, a party seeking such an order is likely to have to show compelling reasons why the court should depart from the principle of open justice.[140]

Judgment

The Master or judge will decide how, when and where to deliver judgment. Judgment may be delivered orally immediately at the conclusion of the hearing (a so-called '*ex tempore*' judgment),[141] or may be reserved. A reserved judgment may be delivered orally at a later date or, more commonly, may be circulated in written draft to the parties and then formally handed down at a subsequent date.

Costs

In *Re Buckton*,[142] Kekewich J identified the following two classes of cases in which he considered it appropriate to order that all parties' costs be paid out of the estate or trust (instead of following the general rule, now contained in CPR rule 44.2.(2)(a), that the unsuccessful party will be ordered to pay the costs of the successful party):

> *In a large proportion of the summonses adjourned into Court for argument the applicants are trustees of a will or settlement who ask the Court to construe the instrument of trust for their guidance, and in order to ascertain the interests of the beneficiaries, or else ask to*

> *(d) a private hearing is necessary to protect the interests of any child or protected party;*
>
> *[...]*
>
> *(g) the court considers [a hearing in private] to be necessary, in the interests of justice.*"

On the other hand, sub-rule (f) is unlikely to be engaged where the correct construction is in dispute, as that sub-rule is engaged in relation to hearings involving "*uncontentious matters arising in the administration of trusts or in the administration of a deceased person's estate*" (emphasis added).

140 See in this regard the Court of Appeal's guidance in *MN v OP* [2019] EWCA Civ 679 regarding privacy and reporting restrictions in the context of applications pursuant to the Variation of Trusts Act 1958.

141 See e.g. *Slattery v Jagger* [2015] EWHC 3976 (Ch) and *Jump v Lister* [2016] EWHC 2160 (Ch).

142 [1907] 2 Ch 406.

> *have some question determined which has arisen in the administration of the trusts. In cases of this character I regard the costs of all parties as necessarily incurred for the benefit of the estate, and direct them to be taxed as between solicitor and client and paid out of the estate. It is, of course, possible that trustees may come to the Court without due cause. A question of construction or of administration may be too clear for argument, or it may be the duty of trustees to inform a claimant that they must administer their trust on the footing that his claim is unfounded, and leave him to take whatever course he thinks fit. But, although I have thought it necessary sometimes to caution timid trustees against making applications which might with propriety be avoided, I act on the principle that trustees are entitled to the fullest possible protection which the Court can give them, and that I must give them credit for not applying to the Court except under advice which, though it may appear to me unsound, must not be readily treated as unwise. I cannot remember any case in which I have refused to deal with the costs of an application by trustees in the manner above mentioned.*
>
> *There is a second class of cases differing in form, but not in substance, from the first. In these cases it is admitted on all hands, or it is apparent from the proceedings, that although the application is made, not by trustees (who are respondents), but by some of the beneficiaries, yet it is made by reason of some difficulty of construction, or administration, which would have justified an application by the trustees, and it is not made by them only because, for some reason or other, a different course has been deemed more convenient. To cases of this class I extend the operation of the same rule as is observed in cases of the first class. The application is necessary for the administration of the trust, and the costs of all parties are necessarily incurred for the benefit of the estate regarded as a whole.*

Construction claims generally fall in either the first or the second class of cases identified in *Re Buckton* (depending on whether the claim is brought by the PRs or a beneficiary). As a result, the general starting point is that the costs of all of the parties will be payable out of the estate or trust.

Costs are however ultimately in the discretion of the court,[143] and the court may therefore decide to depart from that starting point and make a different costs order. It may decide to do so, for example, if it considers that the unreasonable conduct of one of the parties has materially increased costs unnecessarily,[144] or that the construction problem was not in fact a problem at all because one of the possible constructions was unarguable.[145] As indicated at 2.2.3 above, in cases involving professional negligence, the draftsman's insurers may have agreed in advance to pay the costs of the construction claim.[146]

In general terms, in deciding costs the court will try to ensure that the costs are in fact borne by the negligent draftsman and/or (in a contested case) by the party who has lost, and not by the successful party. In deciding precisely how this should be achieved, the court will have to take into account all of the circumstances, including the parties' respective interests under the will and who would in fact bear the costs if the costs are ordered to be paid out of the estate.[147]

Order

In construction claims the order which gives effect to the judgment will generally consist of two parts:

---

143 Section 51(1) of the Senior Courts Act 1981.

144 See *Harrison-Mills v Public Trustee* [2019] EWCA Civ 966 at [66].

145 In *Re Buckton* [1907] 2 Ch 406 Kekewich J acknowledged the possibility that trustees "*may come to the Court without due cause*". However, his subsequent comments suggest that cases in which PRs or trustees will be deprived of their costs as a result will be rare: "*although I have thought it necessary sometimes to caution timid trustees against making applications which might with propriety be avoided, I act on the principle that trustees are entitled to the fullest possible protection which the Court can give them, and that I must give them credit for not applying to the Court except under advice which, though it may appear to me unsound, must not be readily treated as unwise.*" See also *Harrison-Mills v Public Trustee* [2019] EWCA Civ 966 at [59].

146 See e.g. *Slattery v Jagger* [2015] EWHC 3976 (Ch) at [103]-[112] (which involved both a construction and a rectification claim).

147 See e.g. *Marley v Rawlings (costs)* [2014] UKSC 51 and *Slattery v Jagger* [2015] EWHC 3976 (Ch) at [103]-[112].

(a) a declaration by which the court formally declares the correct meaning of the will, or of one or more of its provisions; and

(b) an order directing the PRs or trustees to administer and distribute the estate or trust in question in accordance with the declaration.

Chapter 22 of the Chancery Guide contains guidance in relation to the drafting, filing and sealing of orders.

<u>Appeals</u>

A party who is dissatisfied with the court's decision must obtain the court's permission in order to appeal it.[148] The court will only grant permission to appeal if it considers that the appeal would have a real prospect of success, or that there is some other compelling reason for the appeal to be heard.[149]

Although this is not strictly required, it is generally sensible for a party who wishes to appeal to first seek permission from the lower court.[150] This is usually done when judgment is delivered or handed down and consequential issues, such as the terms of the order giving effect to the judgment and costs, are decided.

If the lower court refuses permission, or if permission was not sought from it, permission must be sought from the appeal court by filing an Appellant's Notice.[151] Unless the court orders otherwise, the time limit for doing so is "*21 days after the date of the decision of the lower court*".[152] That is a relatively short time limit, which cannot be extended by agreement between the parties,[153] and it must be borne in mind that the period starts to run from the date of the decision of the lower court and

---

148 CPR rule 52.3(1).

149 CPR rule 52.6(1).

150 Pursuant to CPR rule 52.3(2)(a); see e.g. *In re T (A Child)* [2002] EWCA Civ 1736 at [12]-[13].

151 CPR rules 52.3(2)(b) and 52.12(1).

152 CPR rule 52.12(2)(b).

153 CPR rule 52.15(2).

not, if later, the date on which consequential matters are decided or the date on which the order giving effect to the decision is approved and sealed.[154] If – as is quite common – the lower court's judgment is circulated to the parties in draft and then formally handed down in the absence of the parties, and a hearing to decide consequential matter is arranged at a later date, the lower court should be asked to direct[155] that the 21-day period will only start to run from the date of the later hearing, rather than from the date on which judgment was handed down.[156]

Compromise

In some cases it may be possible to compromise a construction claim after proceedings have been issued.[157] The mechanism by which the compromise should be implemented will inevitably depend on its terms and on the particular circumstances of the case. In most cases, the following will have to be considered:

(a) Whether the compromise has any tax implications and, if so, whether it is desirable to implement it by way of a deed of variation which can be 'read back' for IHT and/or CGT purposes.[158]

(b) Whether a declaration by the court as to the correct construction of the will, or of one or more of its provisions, is required or desirable, and if so whether the court can be asked to make it by consent without hearing full argument in accordance with the principles in *Hayim v Couch*,[159] *Pavilion Property Trustees Ltd v*

154 See e.g. *Sayers v Clarke Walker (A Firm)* [2002] EWCA Civ 645 at [8]-[9] and *Owusu v Jackson* [2002] EWCA Civ 877 at [24]-[27].

155 Pursuant to CPR 52.12(2)(a).

156 See e.g. *Jackson v Marina Homes Ltd* [2007] EWCA Civ 1404 at [8].

157 The circumstances in which it may be possible to resolve a construction issue without the need for court proceedings are considered at 2.2.2 above.

158 See section 142 of the Inheritance Tax Act 1984 and section 62 of the Taxation of Chargeable Gains Act 1992.

159 [2009] EWHC 1040 (Ch) at [12]-[18].

Permira Advisers LLP[160] and *Singh v Singh*.[161] It should be borne in mind that this jurisdiction tends to be exercised sparingly.

(c) Whether the court's approval of the compromise is required, which will be the case where one or more of the parties is a minor,[162] an adult who lacks capacity to conduct litigation[163] and/or a party who has been appointed to represent others pursuant to CPR rule 19.7.[164]

Paragraphs 22.9 to 22.13 of the Chancery Guide contain guidance in relation to consent orders.

---

160 [2014] EWHC 145 (Ch) at [9]-[10].

161 [2014] EWHC 2762 (Ch) at [5]-[9].

162 CPR rule 21.10.

163 *Ibid.*

164 CPR rule 19.7(5).

CHAPTER THREE
RECTIFICATION OF WILLS

3.1 The law

Until 1982 there was limited scope to correct the wording of a will which appeared to contain an error, or to insert words which appeared to have been accidentally omitted from a will. However, that position was changed by the enactment of section 20 of the Administration of Justice Act 1982 ("AJA"). Section 20(1) AJA grants the court a statutory jurisdiction to rectify wills. It provides:

> *(1) If a court is satisfied that a will is so expressed that it fails to carry out the testator's intentions, in consequence—*
>
> *(a) of a clerical error; or*
>
> *(b) of a failure to understand his instructions,*
>
> *it may order that the will shall be rectified so as to carry out his intentions.*

In *Re Segleman*,[1] Chadwick J (as he then was) explained that the court will approach a claim for a rectification of a will in three stages:

> *The subsection requires the court to examine three questions. First, what were the testator's intentions with regard to the dispositions in respect of which rectification is sought. Secondly, whether the will is so expressed that it fails to carry out those intentions. Thirdly, whether the will is expressed as it is in consequence of either (a) a clerical error or (b) a failure on the part of someone to whom the testator has given instructions in connection with his will to understand those instructions.*

1 [1996] Ch 171.

The judge also made it clear that in order to answer the first of those questions, the court must admit extrinsic evidence of the testator's intentions with regard to the relevant dispositions.

Several cases involving claims for the rectification of wills have emphasised that the court will require cogent evidence before being persuaded that the will does indeed need rectifying, given that the court is being asked to correct a document made by a person who cannot himself give evidence as to his intentions. For example, in *Re Segelman*[2] itself Chadwick J (as he then was) pointed out: "*although the standard of proof required in a claim for rectification made under section 20(1) of the Act of 1982 is that the court should be satisfied on the balance of probability, the probability that a will which a testator has executed in circumstances of some formality reflects his intentions is usually of such weight that convincing evidence to the contrary is necessary*". Norris J cited this passage in *Sprackling v Sprackling*[3] and commented:[4] "*This emphasises that speculation is no basis upon which to interfere with a formal expression of testamentary intentions. One must be confident that the will as expressed does not record the instructions given because of error or misunderstanding, "confident" in the sense of being satisfied on the balance of probabilities by evidence of a quality commensurate with the inherent probabilities of the case itself.*" Similarly, in *Goodman v Goodman*[5] Evans-Lombe J accepted the submission that the court's conclusion is "*to be arrived at on the balance of probabilities but bearing in mind a strong bias in favour of the conclusion that a duly executed will evidences the intention of the testator*".[6]

In *Marley v Rawlings*[7] the Supreme Court explained: "*As a general proposition, there may be force in the point that the greater the extent of the correction sought, the steeper the task for a claimant who is seeking rectific-*

2 *Ibid.*

3 [2008] EWHC 2696 (Ch).

4 [2008] EWHC 2696 (Ch) at [15].

5 [2006] EWHC 1757 (Ch).

6 [2006] EWHC 1757 (Ch) at [18].

7 [2014] UKSC 2.

ation. However, I can see no reason in principle why a wholesale correction should be ruled out as a permissible exercise of the court's power to rectify, as a matter of principle. On the contrary: to impose such a restriction on the power of rectification would be unprincipled — and it would also lead to uncertainty".[8]

It is generally relatively straightforward to determine whether an error in a will is the result of a failure to understand the testator's instructions (for the purposes of section 20(1)(b) AJA).[9]

On the other hand, the expression "*clerical error*" (contained in section 20(1)(a) AJA) has proved more controversial. It is now clear that the expression should be given a wide rather than a narrow meaning.[10] One of the reasons for this is that section 20 AJA is one of the provisions of the AJA "*aimed at making the law on wills more flexible and rendering it easier to validate or "save" a will than previously*"[11] (the others being sections 17, 18, 19 and 21 AJA). The expression "*is not one with a precise or well-established, let alone a technical, meaning*".[12] Lord Neuberger identified the expression's wider meaning as "*a mistake arising out of office work of a relatively routine nature, such as preparing, filing, sending, organising the execution of, a document (save, possibly, to the extent that the activity involves some special expertise).*"[13] The omission of an entire clause from a will can be a clerical error.[14]

Importantly, a line of authorities makes it clear that rectification will not be available in cases in which the draftsman has correctly understood the testator's intentions and has then considered how to give

8 [2014] UKSC 2 at [53].

9 For some examples, see *Lilly v Pegram* [2002] EWHC 2817 (Ch), *Foster-Orr v Colliss* [2005] EWHC 2600 (Ch), *Goodman v Goodman* [2006] EWHC 1757 (Ch) and *Royal Society v Robinson* [2015] EWHC 3442 (Ch).

10 *Marley v Rawlings* [2014] UKSC 2 at [76].

11 *Marley v Rawlings* [2014] UKSC 2 at [79].

12 *Marley v Rawlings* [2014] UKSC 2 at [75].

13 *Ibid.*

14 *Wordingham v Royal Exchange Trust Co Ltd* [1992] Ch 412.

effect to them, but has (advertently) chosen inapposite words.[15] These cases fall outside of the scope of section 20 AJA altogether: the error is not a "*clerical error*" (within section 20(1)(a) AJA), and there is also no failure to understand instructions (within section 20(1)(b) AJA). Rather, the error is one which might be described as a conscious drafting error, and thus falls outside the scope of the statutory jurisdiction to rectify contained in section 20 AJA. In these sorts of situations, the only possible recourse may be to pursue professional negligence proceedings against the draftsman.

Section 20(2) AJA contains an important statutory time limit which applies to rectification claims: "*An application for an order under this section shall not, except with the permission of the court, be made after the end of the period of six months from the date on which representation with respect to the estate of the deceased is first taken out.*"[16]

The statute itself contains no guidance on how the court should decide whether to grant the claimant permission to bring a rectification claim more than 6 months from the date on which representation was first taken out. In *Chittock v Stevens*[17] the court held that the approach to be adopted is the same as that adopted when deciding whether to grant a claimant permission to bring a claim pursuant to the Inheritance (Provision for Family and Dependants) Act 1975 more than 6 months after representation in respect of the estate was first taken out. In summary, the court will approach an application for permission by considering the following factors:[18]

15 *Kell v Jones* [2013] WTLR 507, *Reading v Reading* [2015] EWHC 946 (Ch)

16 Sections 20(4) and (5) AJA provide that certain types of limited grants of representations are to be left out of account in calculating the 6-month period prescribed by section 20(2) AJA.

17 [2000] WTLR 643.

18 The seven factors are taken from the jurisprudence concerning applications for permission to bring a late claim under the Inheritance (Provision for Family and Dependants) Act 1975, and have been adapted to fit rectification claims. The leading authorities in the jurisprudence concerning Inheritance (Provision for Family and Dependants) Act 1975 claims are *Re Salmon* [1981] Ch 167, *Re Dennis* [1981] 2 All ER 140, *Berger v Berger* [2013] EWCA Civ 1305 (where the seven factors are referred to at [44]), *Cowan v Foreman* [2019] EWCA Civ 1336

(1) The court's discretion is unfettered but must be exercised judicially in accordance with what is right and proper.

(2) The onus is on the applicant to show sufficient grounds for the granting of permission to apply out of time.

(3) The court must consider whether the Applicant has acted promptly and the circumstances in which he applied for an extension of time after the expiry of the time limit.

(4) Were negotiations begun within the time limit?

(5) Has the estate been distributed before the claim was notified to the defendants?

(6) Would dismissal of the claim leave the applicant without recourse to other remedies?

(7) Looking at the position as it is now, has the applicant an arguable rectification claim if the claim is allowed to proceed?

In *Fielden v Christie-Miller*[19] the court suggested that it might have been prepared to grant the claimant permission to bring a rectification claim over 15 years after representation in respect of the estate was first taken out had the claim been more meritorious.

Section 20(3) AJA provides PRs with protection against personal liability for having distributed the estate after the end of the period of six months from the date on which representation was first taken out, on the ground that they ought to have taken into account the possibility that the court might grant permission to bring a late rectification claim. However, the subsection does not affect the ability to recover any distribution from the recipient if the will is rectified.

(where the seven factors are referred to at [32]) and *Begum v Ahmed* [2019] EWCA Civ 1794 .

19 [2015] EWHC 2940 (Ch) at [45].

In cases involving professionally prepared wills in which professional negligence proceedings are likely to be relevant, regard must also be had to the limitation period which applies to those proceedings.

3.2 Practice and procedure

3.2.1 Who is affected?

The first question PRs should ask themselves when faced with a rectification problem is: who is affected by it?

The main concern for PRs faced with a possible rectification problem is to ensure that before they take any step based on a particular provision of the will, they protect themselves from potential personal liability for *devastavit*, which they can do by obtaining either the binding consent of all affected beneficiaries or authorisation from the court. To get to that position, the PRs will first have to establish who the affected beneficiaries are.

Needless to say, the answer to this will depend on the particular circumstances, and can vary widely. In simple terms, the way to go about ascertaining the affected beneficiaries is to consider the different possible outcomes depending on whether the will is or is not rectified (which may be two or more) and then consider who would benefit in each situation, as illustrated by the following examples.

Example 4

In 2005 Manrico made a professionally prepared will by which he appointed two partners in the firm of Di Luna & Co as his executors and trustees and gave a legacy of £500,000 to Azucena and the residue of his estate to Leonora. He subsequently fell out with his solicitors and in 2010 he instructed a different firm to prepare his last will. The will file indicates that he told his new solicitors that the only changes he wanted to make were to appoint his friend Ruiz as his executor and trustee in the place of Di Luna & Co, and to give Ruiz a legacy of £10,000. Manrico's last will includes that appointment and legacy and leaves the residuary estate to Leonora, but it omits the legacy of £500,000 to Azucena.

The issue is whether the 2010 will should be rectified to include the legacy of £500,000 to Azucena.

Assuming Manrico's estate is worth over £510,000 (and that Ruiz's legacy will therefore be paid in any event), the affected beneficiaries are Azucena and Leonora.

Example 5

By clause 5 of his will Tristan gave his castle, Kareol, to "*my trusted servant Brangäne who has been loyal to me for over 20 years*"; he then gave the residue of his estate to his wife Isolde.

In fact, Tristan's long-term loyal servant is Kurwenal, and Brangäne is Isolde's maid, whom Tristan had only known for 3 years when he made his will.

The issue is whether clause 5:

(a) takes effect as a gift to Brangäne;

(b) should be rectified by replacing "*Brangäne*" with "*Kurwenal*"; or

(c) fails, with the result that Kareol falls into residue and passes to Isolde.

The affected beneficiaries are therefore:

(a) Brangäne;

(b) Kurwenal; and

(c) Isolde.

Example 6

The will file relating to Simon Boccanegra's will indicates that his instructions to his solicitor were that he wished to leave his residuary estate to the people of Genoa. However, the gift of residue in his will reads: "*for the patricians of Genoa alive at the date of my death, if more than one in equal shares absolutely*".

The issue is whether the gift should be rectified by replacing the word "*patricians*" with "*people*".

The affected beneficiaries are therefore:

(a) the patricians of Genoa;

(b) the people of Genoa; and

(c) possibly Simon Boccanegra's intestacy beneficiaries who may argue that the gift is void for uncertainty and therefore gives rise to a partial intestacy.

If the rectification problem affects the amount of tax payable, some thought should be given to whether it is also necessary to involve HMRC.[20]

The corollary to the above is that PRs should bear in mind that they have no personal interest in how the rectification problem is resolved between the affected beneficiaries. It is not for the PRs to try to second guess what the testator might have intended, nor to form a view as to which of the affected beneficiaries is more 'worthy' or 'deserving'. The PRs should remain neutral and impartial, and simply do what they are told, either by a unanimous binding agreement reached by all of the affected beneficiaries, or by the court.

20 Paragraph 29.70 of the Chancery Guide.

3.2.2 Can the problem be resolved by agreement?

Some rectification problems can be resolved by the unanimous agreement of all of the beneficiaries affected by it. Therefore, once the PRs have identified all of the affected beneficiaries, the next question they should ask themselves is: can the problem be resolved by agreement?

Suppose that in Example 4 above, Azucena and Leonora agree that Azucena should receive a legacy of £500,000. Azucena and Leonora are the only two individuals affected by the uncertainty.[21] If they are both capacitous adults and agree what should happen to the property, they can resolve the construction problem between themselves without having to go to court. The PRs' only concern will be to ensure that the agreement is properly documented so that they cannot later be criticised by Azucena or Leonora for acting in accordance with it.

Resolving the problem by agreement is usually significantly cheaper and quicker than asking the court to do so. Moreover, if an agreement is reached within two years of the deceased's death, it may be possible for the agreement to be 'read back' for IHT and/or CGT purposes if doing so is advantageous.[22]

As indicated above, if the rectification problem affects the amount of tax payable, some thought should be given to whether it is also necessary to obtain the agreement of HMRC. Typical examples are cases in which the problem concerns whether property passes to an IHT-exempt beneficiary (such as a surviving spouse or charity). HMRC's involvement will generally not be required if an agreement is reached and implemented by an instrument which is executed within two years of the testator's death, because in such cases it should be possible for the affected beneficiaries to determine the tax consequences.[23]

21 This assumes the estate is sufficiently solvent for there to be residue.

22 See section 142 of the Inheritance Tax Act 1984 and section 62 of the Taxation of Chargeable Gains Act 1992.

23 By availing themselves of the 'reading back' mechanisms in section 142 of the Inheritance Tax Act 1984 and/or section 62 of the Taxation of Chargeable Gains

However, if an agreement is only reached or implemented more than two years after the testator's death and affects (or purports to affect) the amount of tax payable, HMRC's agreement is likely to be required.

Suppose that in Example 5 above, Brangäne, Kurwenal and Isolde agree that Kareol should pass as part of residue to Isolde. As Isolde is the surviving spouse and thus an IHT-exempt beneficiary, whereas Brangäne and Kurwenal are not, this could affect the amount of IHT payable. It may therefore be necessary to involve HMRC.

In practice, rectification problems are generally only resolved by agreement in the most straightforward cases. Two reasons can be identified for this. First, beneficiaries often have different views about what the testator did or did not intend, and are therefore simply unable to reach an agreement. Secondly, to avoid exposing themselves to potential personal liability to disappointed beneficiaries, PRs must obtain the binding consent of all of the beneficiaries who are affected by the problem. This will not be possible if the problem affects beneficiaries who are minors, unborn, lack capacity and/or cannot be found. As those types of beneficiaries are unable to give the PRs their binding consent, in cases in which they are affected, the court's intervention will be necessary.

A useful way to explore whether the rectification problem can be resolved by agreement is for the PRs, who are often the first to spot the problem, to obtain advice from counsel on the rectification problem and then share that advice with all affected beneficiaries and canvass their views. If the will incorporates clause 12.3 of the STEP Standard Provisions (2nd edition), the PRs should consider obtaining the advice of counsel of "*at least five years' standing*" if they want to rely on the protection from liability afforded by that clause.[24]

Act 1992.

24 Clause 12.3 and the following two clauses provide:

12.3 A Trustee shall not be liable for acting in accordance with the advice of counsel, of at least five years' standing, with respect to the Trust. The Trustees may in particular conduct legal proceedings in accordance with such advice without obtaining a court order. A Trustee may recover from the Trust Fund any expenses

This process should help both the PRs and all affected beneficiaries understand their respective positions, which in turn should inform all involved whether there is any hope of the rectification problem being resolved by agreement and, if so, how this might be achieved. Depending on the circumstances, the affected beneficiaries may wish to try to reach an agreement by, for example, negotiating in correspondence, at a round-table meeting or at a mediation.

As indicated above, PRs should bear in mind that they have no personal interest in how the rectification problem is resolved between the affected beneficiaries. The focus of the PRs should be to ensure:

(a) that they obtain the binding consent of all affected beneficiaries so they are protected from potential personal liability for *devastavit* (i.e. for having distributed to the wrong person); and

(b) that the agreement is one which the PRs can in fact implement. For example, the PRs should consider whether the agreement has tax consequences and, if so, how these should be addressed.

However, if all affected beneficiaries manage to reach a binding agreement which the PRs can implement, it is not for the PRs to 'approve' or 'disapprove' of it in any moral or ethical sense, e.g. on the basis that they think the testator would or would not have liked it. It also follows from this that PRs are generally not required to actively participate in any negotiations between the affected beneficiaries;

---

where he has acted in accordance with such advice.

12.4 Clause 12.3 does not apply:

12.4.1 in relation to a Trustee who knows or has reasonable cause to suspect that the advice was given in ignorance of material facts;

12.4.2 if proceedings are pending to obtain the decision of the court on the matter;

12.4.3 in relation to a Trustee who has a personal interest in the subject matter of the advice; or

12.4.4 in relation to a Trustee who has committed a breach of trust relating to the subject matter of the advice.

12.5 Clause 12.3 does not prejudice any right of any Person to follow property or income into the hands of any Person, other than a purchaser, who may have received it.

indeed, PRs should ensure they do not incur unnecessary costs by doing so.

In cases in which professional negligence proceedings against the draftsman have also been threatened or are on foot, it may be sensible to try to compromise the professional negligence at the same time.

There are two further tools which can help achieve a pragmatic solution without the court's intervention in a suitable case. The first is the possibility of the PRs agreeing to distribute on a particular basis provided the recipient beneficiaries in return provide the PRs with suitable indemnities, possibly backed by security. Such indemnities would be designed to protect the PRs against the risk that they may be personally liable to disappointed beneficiaries if the basis of which they have distributed subsequently turns out to be wrong. The second is the possibility of obtaining insurance to provide the PRs with that same protection.

Whether either of these tools is a useful one will depend on all of the particular surrounding circumstances. As a rather crude rule of thumb, it is suggested that the greater the financial value of the rectification problem, the less likely these tools are to provide a practical solution. This is because the greater the amount of money that turns on the rectification problem, the greater the potential liability of the PRs, and thus the more nervous both the beneficiaries and any insurance company will be in providing PRs with adequate protection. Further, in high value cases there is less of a risk of the estate being significantly depleted by the costs involved in making a court application, which might also point towards a court application being the better option.

3.2.3 **Professional negligence**

If the will was professionally prepared, it may be possible for a disappointed beneficiary to argue that the rectification problem amounts to professional negligence of the draftsman and seek damages on the basis of *White v Jones*.[25] In these sorts of circumstances, the disappointed

25 [1995] 2 AC 207.

beneficiary is usually under a duty to mitigate his loss by seeking to rectify the will before pursuing professional negligence proceedings against the draftsman[26] (although the professional negligence claim may have to be issued protectively and stayed, or a limitation standstill agreed, if limitation is a concern).

Depending on the circumstances, if both the professional negligence claim and the rectification claim have merit, the draftsman's insurers might agree to fund the rectification claim, particularly if the costs involved in doing so are likely to be lower than their potential exposure in the event the professional negligence claim is successful.[27]

3.2.4 Court intervention: rule 55 of the Non-Contentious Probate Rules 1987

In cases in which it is necessary to rectify a will and the proposed rectification is not opposed by those who might be prejudiced by it, it may be possible to apply to a district judge of the Principal Registry of the Family Division (in London) or a district probate registrar in one of the District Probate Registries to rectify the will pursuant to rule 55 of the Non-Contentious Probate Rules 1987 ("NCPR"). This procedure is likely to be cheaper and quicker than bringing a rectification claim in the Chancery Division[28] (considered below).

Rule 55 NCPR provides:

---

26 See e.g. *Walker v Geo H Medlicott & Son* [1999] 1 WLR 727 and *Horsfall v Haywards* [1999] 1 FLR 1182. See also *Grattan v McNaughton* [2001] WTLR 1305 in which the claimant was criticised for pursuing the professional negligence claim first up to and including trial, and only once that claim had been dismissed, pursuing a rectification claim based on the same evidence which she had issued only 14 days before the trial of the professional negligence claim. Although no application to strike out the rectification claim on the grounds that it was an abuse of process was pursued, the judge indicated that he would have been "*provisionally very attracted to it*" as it could not be "*in the public interest to permit virtually the same issues in relation to the drafting of the will to be litigated twice*".

27 See e.g. *Re Bimson* [2010] EWHC 3679 (Ch) at [23].

28 i.e. what has now become the Property, Trusts and Probate List (ChD) of the Business and Property Courts of England and Wales.

55.— Application for rectification of a will

(1) An application for an order that a will be rectified by virtue of section 20(1) of the Administration of Justice Act 1982 may be made to a district judge or registrar, unless a probate action has been commenced.

(2) The application shall be supported by an affidavit, setting out the grounds of the application, together with such evidence as can be adduced as to the testator's intentions and as to whichever of the following matters as are in issue:–

(a) in what respects the testator's intentions were not understood; or

(b) the nature of any alleged clerical error.

(3) Unless otherwise directed, notice of the application shall be given to every person having an interest under the will whose interest might be prejudiced, or such other person who might be prejudiced by the rectification applied for and any comments in writing by any such person shall be exhibited to the affidavit in support of the application.

(4) If the district judge or registrar is satisfied that, subject to any direction to the contrary, notice has been given to every person mentioned in paragraph (3) above, and that the application is unopposed, he may order that the will be rectified accordingly.

This procedure will not be appropriate where:

(a) a probate action has been commenced (rule 55(1) NCPR); or

(b) the application is opposed (rule 55(4) NCPR).

The first step is to give notice of the intended application to every person "*having an interest under the will whose interest might be prejudiced*", or such other person "*who might be prejudiced by the rectification applied for*" (rule 55(3) NCPR). This can be done by writing to the relevant person(s) explaining the problem, indicating that it is proposed to resolve the problem by asking the court to rectify the will, and asking the notified person to indicate whether they oppose the intended application for rectification. This first step is likely to be necessary in almost all cases, and will also help determine whether there is scope to resolve the rectification problem by agreement (as discussed above).

Although the position is not entirely clear, it is suggested that the requirement to notify imposed by rule 55(3) NCPR means that this procedure will not be appropriate where the affected beneficiaries who are to be notified include minors, unborns, individuals who lack capacity and/or individuals who cannot be found. In such cases an application for rectification should be made to the Chancery Division instead (considered at 3.2.5. below).

If none of the notified persons opposes the application, the next step will be to draft an affidavit "*setting out the grounds of the application, together with such evidence as can be adduced as to the testator's intentions and as to […] in what respects the testator's intentions were not understood or the nature of any alleged clerical error*". If the will was professionally prepared and the draftsman can be located and contacted, it is likely to be sensible for the draftsman to swear such affidavit, as he will be best placed to explain first-hand how the error occurred.

Once the affidavit has been prepared in draft, it should be submitted to a district judge/probate registrar for settling before it is actually sworn. This is a helpful way of ensuring that the affidavit is in order before it is sworn and is well worth the small fee charged by the Probate Registry for the service (currently £12).[29]

The settled affidavit should then be finalised (including by exhibiting any relevant documents) and sworn by the deponent. The sworn affidavit can then be submitted to the Probate Registry. As the affidavit itself seeks rectification, no separate application notice is required.

As explained above, the application should be made – i.e. the sworn affidavit submitted to the Probate Registry – within 6 months of the date on which representation in respect of the estate was first taken out,

29 Article 2 of, and item 11 in the table in paragraph 1 of the Schedule to, the Non-Contentious Probate Fees Order 2004 (SI 2004/3120) (as amended).

failing which the claimant will require the court's permission. If the court's permission is required, the deponent should explain this in the affidavit and should provide evidence which addresses the seven factors referred to above.

If the district judge/probate registrar is satisfied that the will should be rectified, he make an order to that effect. Where a will has been ordered to be rectified by virtue of section 20 AJA, an engrossment of the will in the form in which it is to be proved must be lodged at the Probate Registry.[30]

Because applications pursuant to rule 55 NCPR are only suitable in unopposed cases (as explained above), the incidence of the costs of the application is also likely to be agreed in advance. If the will was professionally drafted and the circumstances strongly suggest that the draftsman was responsible for the error, it is fairly common for the draftsman's insurers to agree to pay the costs of the rectification application, which are likely to be relatively modest if the application is unopposed and can be made pursuant to rule 55 NCPR.

3.2.5 Court intervention: rectification claims in the Chancery Division

Where the procedure provided by rule 55 NCPR cannot be used, for example because the rectification is opposed or because the affected beneficiaries include individuals who lack capacity, are minors and/or are unborn, the appropriate procedure will be to bring a rectification claim in the Chancery Division.

Starting the claim

In many cases rectification claims are brought by way of CPR Part 8 proceedings. This may be because the claim is not opposed by the beneficiaries who are capacitous adults, but it also affects beneficiaries who are minors, unborn, lack capacity and/or cannot be found, and/or it is necessary to obtain a court order granting rectification because the

30 Rule 11(2) NCPR.

drafting problem has tax consequences.[31] This may also be done because the rectification claim is being brought together with one or more other claims – typically a construction claim[32] – which must be brought by way of a CPR Part 8 claim (see 2.2.5.). In this sort of situation, the procedural rules governing the other claim(s) must also be borne in mind. Some thought should also be given as to whether the court should be asked to deal with any aspects in dispute as a preliminary issue.[33]

On the other hand, if the rectification claim is brought on its own and is opposed, it is likely to involve a substantial dispute of fact, and it is therefore likely to be more appropriate for the claim to be brought as a CPR Part 7 claim rather than a CPR Part 8 claim.[34]

Lodging the grant

If the claimant is the person to whom the grant was made in respect of the will of which rectification is sought, he must, unless the court orders otherwise, lodge the probate or letters of administration with the will annexed with the court when the claim form is issued.[35]

Limitation

If a rectification claim is brought within 6 months of the date on which representation in respect of the estate was first taken out, the court's permission is not required; otherwise, the claimant will have to obtain the court's permission. This is considered in more detail at 3.1 above.

---

31 See e.g. the trust instrument cases of *Racal Group Services Ltd v Ashmore* [1995] STC 1151 and *Allnutt v Wilding* [2007] EWCA Civ 412.

32 See e.g. *Reading v Reading* [2015] EWHC 946 (Ch), *Re Harte* [2015] EWHC 2351 (Ch) and *Guthrie v Morel* [2015] EWHC 3172 (Ch).

33 As in *Burnard v Burnard* [2014] EWHC 340 (Ch) (see [7]) and *Tish v Olley* [2018] EWHC 1069 (Ch) (see [1]).

34 CPR rule 8.1(2)(a).

35 Paragraph 10.1 of CPR Practice Direction 57.

Which court

The County Court appears to have jurisdiction to determine a claim for the rectification of a will if the value of the estate or trust fund does not exceed £350,000.[36] However, in practice rectification claims are invariably issued in the Chancery Division of the High Court,[37] i.e. what has now become the Property, Trusts and Probate List (ChD) of the Business and Property Courts of England and Wales. A rectification claim can be issued either in the Rolls Building in London or in one of the District Registries (Birmingham, Bristol, Cardiff, Leeds, Liverpool, Manchester, Newcastle-upon-Tyne, Preston, Mold and Caernarfon).[38]

Evidence/Pleadings

A distinction needs to be drawn between rectification claims brought by way of a CPR Part 8 claim and those brought by way of a CPR Part 7 claim.[39]

CPR Part 8 claims: evidence

If the rectification claim is brought by way of a CPR Part 8 claim, the claimant must file the evidence on which he intends to rely when his claim form is issued[40] (unless the claimant only intends to rely on the evidence contained in the claim form itself, which it is suggested is unlikely to be the case in rectification claims). This will generally be in

---

36 Section 23 of the County Courts Act 1984 and article 3 of the County Court Jurisdiction Order 2014 (SI 2014/503). This assumes that the rectification claim in question is a type of "*proceedings for relief against [...] mistake*" within section 23(g).

37 Section 61 and paragraph 1(g) of Schedule 1 to the Senior Courts Act 1981.

38 Paragraph 30.1 of the Chancery Guide. Chapter 30 of the Chancery Guide contains helpful information regarding Chancery business outside London, including contact details of the various District Registries.

39 See "Starting the claim" above.

40 CPR rule 8.5(1) and paragraph 7.1 of CPR Practice Direction 8A; see also paragraph 9.6 of the Chancery Guide.

the form of one or more witness statements.[41] The claimant's evidence must be served on the defendant with the claim form.[42]

The contents of the witness statement(s) will of course depend on the circumstances of the particular case. In general terms, the topics which one should consider covering in the evidence filed in support of the claim are likely to be:

(a) the claimant's role and the capacity in which he brings the claim;

(b) the factual background;

(c) the current drafting of the will and its construction;

(d) what the testator's intentions are alleged to have been;

(e) how the current drafting of the will fails to give effect to the testator's intentions, and whether this is due to a clerical error and/or a failure to understand the testator's instructions;

(f) how the court is being asked to rectify the will;

(g) the position of the other interested parties.

If the will was professionally prepared, some thought should be given as to whether evidence should be obtained from the draftsman responsible for preparing it (if available).

It should be borne in mind that the CPR requires witness statements to be in the witness's own words.[43] Furthermore, the temptation to include in a witness statement extensive legal submissions and references to case law should generally be resisted, particularly in witness state-

41 Paragraph 7.2 of CPR Practice Direction 8A.

42 CPR rule 8.5(2).

43 Paragraph 18.1 of CPR Practice Direction 32; see also paragraph 19.2 of the Chancery Guide.

ments of lay witnesses; these are properly a matter for skeleton arguments and submissions.[44]

CPR Part 7 claims: particulars of claim

If the rectification claim is brought by way of a CPR Part 7 claim,[45] the particulars of claim must either be contained in or served with the claim form, or be served on the defendant within 14 days after service of the claim form, subject to them being served no later than the latest time for serving the claim form.[46] The contents of the particulars of claim will of course depend on the circumstances of the particular case. In general terms, the topics which the party seeking rectification should consider covering in the particulars of claim are likely to be the same as those the claimant's evidence should over in CPR Part 8 claims, viz.:

(a) the claimant's role and the capacity in which he brings the claim;

(b) the factual background;

(c) the current drafting of the will and its construction;

(d) what the testator's intentions are alleged to have been;

(e) how the current drafting of the will fails to give effect to the testator's intentions, and whether this is due to a clerical error and/or a failure to understand the testator's instructions;

(f) how the court is being asked to rectify the will;

(g) the position of the other interested parties.

As well as the rules in CPR rule 16.4 and CPR Practice Direction 16, the drafting guidelines contained in paragraphs 10.5 to 10.17 of the Chancery Guide apply to particulars of claim.

---

44 See paragraph 19.3 of the Chancery Guide.

45 See "Starting the claim" above.

46 CPR rule 7.4.

Disclosure – CPR Part 8 claims

This section considers disclosure in claims which are brought pursuant to CPR Part 8. Disclosure in CPR Part 7 claims is considered below.

CPR Practice Direction 51U contains a new 'disclosure pilot' which sets out detailed rules concerning disclosure that apply to claims in the Business and Property Courts of England and Wales. The pilot came into force on 1st January 2019 and applies to both existing claims and to new claims issued after that date.[47] It will remain in force for two years.[48]

A Practice Note by Chief Master Marsh dated 27th March 2019[49] clarifies that the pilot "*does not directly apply to Part 8 claims because Part 8 contains its own regime for the disclosure of documents that are relied on by the parties*".[50] In particular, the pilot's new concept of 'Initial Disclosure' does not apply to CPR Part 8 claims.[51] However, paragraph 5 of the Practice Note explains:

> "*The court has power to make an order for extended disclosure under the pilot in a case proceeding under Part 8. It will adopt such elements of the Practice Direction as are appropriate to the case and the scope of disclosure that is sought. The party requesting disclosure will need to identify the issues for disclosure and the Model or Models that apply. It is not expected that the full procedure for extended disclosure, including completion of all elements of the Disclosure Review Document, will normally be required.*"

Given the disclosure obligations already imposed by CPR Part 8, it is suggested that orders for extended disclosure pursuant to the pilot are

---

47 Paragraph 1.2 of CPR Practice Direction 51U.

48 Paragraph 1.2 of CPR Practice Direction 51U.

49 Available here: https://www.judiciary.uk/wp-content/uploads/2019/03/Practice-Note-27_03_19.pdf

50 Paragraph 3 of the Practice Note.

51 Paragraph 5.1 of CPR Practice Direction 51U; see also paragraph 4 of the Practice Note.

likely to be rare in construction claims. Some support of this can be found in paragraph 17.74 of the Chancery Guide: "*It is rare for orders for disclosure to be made in a Part 8 claim because for most types of Part 8 claim it should suffice for the parties to rely upon the documents they exhibit*".

Costs management

CPR Part 8 claims

CPR rule 3.12 now makes it clear that costs management does not apply to CPR Part 8 claims unless the court orders that it should pursuant to CPR rule 3.12(1A).[52] Paragraph 5(e) of CPR Practice Direction 3E provides that an order for costs management may be "*particularly appropriate*" in "*any Part 8 or other claims or applications involving a substantial dispute of fact and/or likely to require oral evidence and/or extensive disclosure*". A party seeking an order that costs management should apply to the proceedings should "*give notice to the other parties and the court well in advance of the directions hearing and explain, preferably in a witness statement, why such an order is sought*".[53]

CPR Part 7 claims

If a rectification claim is brought by way of CPR Part 7 proceedings, it is likely to be a multi-track claim and costs management is likely to apply to it, unless the court dispenses with costs management pursuant to CPR rule 3.12(e). It seems likely that the court will only do so if it is satisfied that the litigation can be conducted justly and at proportionate cost in accordance with the overriding objective without costs management.[54] Costs budgets and budget discussion reports will have to be

52 In relation to which see also and paragraph 2 of CPR Practice Direction 3E.

53 Paragraph 17.71 of the Chancery Guide.

54 This is the basis on which the court can decide (pursuant to CPR rule 3.15(2)) not to make a costs management order even where costs budgets have been filed. Paragraph 17.4 of the Chancery Guide makes it clear that "*[t]he fact that none of the parties wish the claim to be subject to costs management is a material factor but it is not determinative because the court must consider the broader test in CPR 3.15(2) in each case*".

filed and exchanged in accordance with the procedure contained in Section II of CPR Part 3.

Parties

Determining who should be made a party to a rectification claim often requires some careful thought. In general, it is useful to bear in mind that:

(a) if the rectification problem is being resolved by way of a contested rectification claim, it should be clear that there are at least two opposing parties, and who they are; they will need to be joined;

(b) the court will want to ensure that everyone affected by the rectification problem has an opportunity to be heard;

(c) in a contentious situation, the PRs should generally remain neutral in their capacity as PRs and not advocate in favour or against rectification, and should instead let the opposing beneficiaries fight it out; and

(d) if the rectification problem affects the amount of tax payable, it may be necessary to notify, and perhaps even join, HMRC.[55]

CPR rule 57.12(2) requires every PR of the estate to be joined as a party to a rectification claim, which is unsurprising given that the PRs need to be bound by the order. What may be less clear is how to ensure that all affected beneficiaries are joined and are able to have their say.

In cases involving a limited number of affected beneficiaries, the answer may be fairly straightforward. The simplest example is where there are two possible outcomes and the only affected beneficiaries are capacitous adults, as in Example 4 above (assuming both Azucena and Leonora are capacitous adults). In such cases, it may be sensible for the PRs to leave it to the beneficiary who would benefit from the rectification to bring the claim, and to join both the PRs and the other affected beneficiaries as defendants. As the contest is in substance between the affected bene-

55 See paragraph 29.70 of the Chancery Guide.

ficiaries, the PRs should adopt a neutral position and let the affected beneficiaries advance the two alternative arguments.

Where one or more of the affected beneficiaries is a minor or lacks capacity and is to be a party to the claim, that beneficiary will need a litigation friend.[56] CPR Part 21 contains detailed guidance on the procedure for the appointment of a litigation friend.

On the other hand, the position may be more complicated where the rectification problem affects a large number of beneficiaries (e.g. large classes) and/or where some of the affected beneficiaries are minors, unborn, lack capacity and/or cannot be found. In Example 6 above, the various classes may present several – and possibly all – of these problems. In these sorts of cases, there is likely to be a tension between ensuring on the one hand that everyone who has an interest is properly represented and has an opportunity to be heard, and trying on the other to avoid depleting the estate or trust by incurring significant costs tracing and communicating with large classes of beneficiaries.

How the balance should be struck will inevitably depend on the circumstances of the particular case. In complicated cases, the provisions of CPR rule 8.2A, rule 19.7 and/or 19.8A can be of considerable assistance.[57] These govern respectively the circumstances in which a CPR Part 8 claim may be issued without naming a defendant, the appointment of a party to represent the interests of others, and the service of proceedings and/or orders on non-parties so as to bind them.

CPR rule 8.2A provides:

Issue of claim form without naming defendants

56 CPR rule 21.2(1).

57 The relevance of these rules to claims concerning estates and trusts is highlighted by paragraphs 29.12, 29.15 and 29.16 of the Chancery Guide, considered below. Note that CPR rule 19.6, which is entitled "*Representative parties with same interest*", does not apply to claims "*about (a) the estate of a deceased person, (b) property subject to a trust, or (c) the meaning of a document, including a statute*": see CPR rules 19.6(5) and 19.7(1).

(1) A practice direction may set out circumstances in which a claim form may be issued under this Part without naming a defendant.

(2) The practice direction may set out those cases in which an application for permission must be made by application notice before the claim form is issued.

(3) The application notice for permission –

(a) need not be served on any other person; and

(b) must be accompanied by a copy of the claim form that the applicant proposes to issue.

(4) Where the court gives permission it will give directions about the future management of the claim.

In fact, neither of the two Practice Directions to CPR Part 8[58] deal with the circumstances in which a claim form may be issued without naming a defendant. However, paragraphs 7.15 and 7.16 of the Chancery Guide provide the following guidance:

Application to issue the claim form without naming defendants

7.15 CPR rule 8.2A permits the court to make an order in relation to a Part 8 claim (not a Part 7 claim) entitling the claimant to issue the claim without naming defendants. An order might be appropriate, for example, where the court is asked to make an order to assist executors who are unable to locate beneficiaries named in a will.

7.16 The application is made by application notice issued at Chancery Chambers. It will then be placed before the assigned Master. Alternatively in a simple case the Master may be willing to deal with it at 10.30 or 2.00 as an Application without Notice ("AWN").

58 viz. Practice Directions 8A and 8B.

CPR rule 19.7(2) provides:

> *The court may make an order appointing a person to represent any other person or persons in the claim where the person or persons to be represented –*
>
> *(a) are unborn;*
>
> *(b) cannot be found;*
>
> *(c) cannot easily be ascertained; or*
>
> *(d) are a class of persons who have the same interest in a claim and –*
>
> > *(i) one or more members of that class are within sub-paragraphs (a), (b) or (c); or*
> >
> > *(ii) to appoint a representative would further the overriding objective.*

This caters for several different scenarios:

(a) is self-explanatory;

(b) covers situations in which it is clear who the affected beneficiary is, but (reasonable) attempts to find him have proved unsuccessful;

(c) covers situations in which it is not clear who the affected beneficiary is, nor can this be easily clarified;

(d) covers two alternative situations where a class of persons has the same interest in the claim:

- (i) is self-explanatory;
- (ii) is potentially wide and flexible. It can be used, for example, where there is a large class of affected beneficiaries scattered around the world, all of whom have the same interest, and it would further the overriding objective to appoint one of

them to represent the whole class (e.g. by reducing procedural delay and costs) – ideally one who can be served within the jurisdiction.[59]

CPR rule 19.7(3) provides that an application for a representation order under CPR rule 19.7(2) may be made "*by any person who seeks to be appointed under the order or any party to the claim*", and may be made "*at any time before or after the claim has started*". CPR rule 19.7(4) provides that the application notice for such an order must be served on:

(a) all parties to the claim, if the claim has started;

(b) the person sought to be appointed, if that person is not the applicant or a party to the claim; and

(c) any other person as directed by the court.

It is important to note that where the court has made a representation order under CPR rule 19.7, the court's approval is required to settle the claim.[60] This is to safeguard the position of the represented parties and to ensure their representative does not enter into a compromise which is disadvantageous to them: CPR rule 19.7(6) gives the court jurisdiction to approve a settlement "*where it is satisfied that the settlement is for the benefit of all represented persons*".

Finally, CPR rule 19.8A provides:

Power to make judgements binding on non-parties

(1) This rule applies to any claim relating to –

(a) the estate of a deceased person;

(b) property subject to a trust; or

---

59 For an example, see *Public Trustee v Harrison* [2018] EWHC 166 (Ch) at [8].

60 CPR rule 19.7(5).

(c) the sale of any property.

(2) The court may at any time direct that notice of–

(a) the claim; or

(b) any judgment or order given in the claim,

be served on any person who is not a party but who is or may be affected by it.

(3) An application under this rule –

(a) may be made without notice; and

(b) must be supported by written evidence which includes the reasons why the person to be served should be bound by the judgment in the claim.

(4) Unless the court orders otherwise –

(a) a notice of a claim or of a judgment or order under this rule must be –

(i) in the form required by the practice direction;

(ii) issued by the court; and

(iii) accompanied by a form of acknowledgment of service with any necessary modifications;

(b) a notice of a claim must also be accompanied by –

(i) a copy of the claim form; and

(ii) such other statements of case, witness statements or affidavits as the court may direct; and

(c) a notice of a judgment or order must also be accompanied by a copy of the judgment or order.

(5) If a person served with notice of a claim files an acknowledgment of service of the notice within 14 days he will become a party to the claim.

(6) If a person served with notice of a claim does not acknowledge service of the notice he will be bound by any judgment given in the claim as if he were a party.

(7) If, after service of a notice of a claim on a person, the claim form is amended so as substantially to alter the relief claimed, the court may direct that a judgment shall not bind that person unless a further notice, together with a copy of the amended claim form, is served on him.

(8) Any person served with a notice of a judgment or order under this rule –

(a) shall be bound by the judgment or order as if he had been a party to the claim; but

(b) may, provided he acknowledges service –

> *(i) within 28 days after the notice is served on him, apply to the court to set aside or vary the judgment or order; and*
>
> *(ii) take part in any proceedings relating to the judgment or order.*

(9) The following rules of Part 10 (acknowledgment of service) apply –

(a) rule 10.4; and

(b) rule 10.5, subject to the modification that references to the defendant are to be read as references to the person served with the notice.

(10) A notice under this rule is issued on the date entered on the notice by the court.

The procedure in CPR rule 19.8A can be useful to bind interested beneficiaries who do not want to take an active role in the proceedings, such as the adult children of an 'active' interested beneficiary who are content to simply support their parent's position. However, it suggests that it is unlikely to be a good idea to press on with the proceedings and to then try to rely on CPR rule 19.8A to serve a judgment or order on an interested beneficiary who it is thought will want to actively have a say. In such cases there is a risk that such a beneficiary will then apply to set aside the judgment or order (pursuant to CPR rule 19.8A(8)(b)) to, in effect, re-open the case to advance his argument, and this could significantly increase the overall costs. In this sort of situation it is likely to be preferable to ensure that such a beneficiary is able to actively participate from the outset.

It should be borne in mind that the issue of representation is likely to be considered by the court at the first directions hearing, at which creative and pragmatic solutions can be considered with the Master, particularly in complex cases.[61]

Service

The usual rules for service contained in the CPR – mostly in CPR Part 6 – apply to claims for the rectification of a will. If it is necessary to seek the court's permission to serve the claim form out of the jurisdiction pursuant to CPR rule 6.36, the relevant ground of those listed in paragraph 3.1 of CPR Practice Direction 6B is ground (14), which expressly refers to claims "*for the rectification of a will*".

Responding to the claim

CPR Part 8 claims: defendant's acknowledgment of service and evidence

61 See e.g. *Re Harte* [2015] EWHC 2351 (Ch), in which the PRs were initially given permission to issue the construction and rectification claims without naming a defendant (pursuant to CPR rule 8.2A), and were then given directions as to the steps they should take to ascertain the intestacy beneficiaries (including by advertisement) and as to the parties to whom they should give notice of the proceedings pursuant to CPR rule 19.8A (see [3]-[4]).

A defendant who wishes to respond to the claim must file an acknowledgment of service in the relevant practice form (viz. form N210)[62] not more than 14 days after service of the claim form on him.[63] At the same time he must also serve his acknowledgment of service on the claimant and on any other party.[64] If he fails to do so, the defendant may attend the hearing of the claim but may not take part in the hearing unless the court gives permission.[65] The defendant must indicate in his acknowledgment of service whether he contests the claim, and if he seeks a different remedy from that set out in the claim form, what that remedy is.[66] If he wishes to object to the use of the CPR Part 8 procedure, he should also say so in his acknowledgment of service;[67] this might be the case, for example, where the defendant opposes the rectification sought by the claim and argues that there is a substantial dispute of fact. There is no need to file a defence, as CPR Part 15 does not apply to claims brought pursuant to CPR Part 8.[68]

A defendant who wishes to rely on written evidence must file it when he files his acknowledgment of service,[69] and must at the same time serve a copy of his evidence on the other parties.[70] As the time limit for the defendant to do this is quite short (viz. 14 days from service of the claim on him), paragraph 7.5 of CPR Practice Direction 8A allows the parties to agree in writing to extend that time limit by up to "*14 days*

---

62 Paragraph 5.2 of CPR Practice Direction 8A.

63 CPR rule 8.3(1); see also paragraph 9.5 of the Chancery Guide. Note that different (longer) periods apply if the proceedings have been served on the defendant out of the jurisdiction: see CPR rules 8.3(3) and 10.3(2).

64 CPR rule 8.3(1).

65 CPR rule 8.4(2).

66 CPR rule 8.3(2).

67 CPR rule 8.8(1); see also paragraph 9.5 of the Chancery Guide.

68 CPR rule 8.9(a) and paragraph 5.1 of CPR Practice Direction 8A; see also paragraph 9.6 of the Chancery Guide.

69 CPR rule 8.5(3) and paragraph 7.3 of CPR Practice Direction 8A; see also paragraph 9.6 of the Chancery Guide.

70 CPR rule 8.5(4).

after the defendant files his acknowledgment of service".[71] Such an agreement must be filed at court by the defendant at the same time as he files his acknowledgment of service.[72] Because of the somewhat awkward wording of paragraph 7.5(2)(b), it seems that in order to obtain the maximum time of 28 days from service of the claim form to file his evidence, a defendant must:

(a) first, agree in writing with the other parties that he may file his evidence 14 days after he files his acknowledgment of service; and then

(b) wait until the 14th day after he was served with the claim form, and on that day file both his acknowledgment of service and the written agreement.

This is because the 14-day extension runs from the date on which the defendant files his acknowledgment of service, as opposed to extending the period for filing of the defendant's evidence to 28 days from the date of service of the claim form on him.[73] The defendant may not rely on any written evidence which has not been served in accordance with the rules described above at the hearing of the claim unless the court gives permission.[74]

If a defendant requires more time to file his evidence, he should apply to the court for an extension of time by way of an application pursuant to CPR Part 23.[75] The Chancery Guide recognises that in substantial

---

71 Paragraph 7.5(2)(b) of CPR Practice Direction 8A; see also paragraph 9.6 of the Chancery Guide.

72 Paragraph 7.5(2)(a) of CPR Practice Direction 8A; see also paragraph 9.6 of the Chancery Guide.

73 Contrast the effect of filing an acknowledgment of service in CPR Part 7 claims, which is to extend the period within which the defendant must file his defence to 28 days from the date of service on him of the particulars of claim: CPR rule 15.4(1)(b).

74 CPR rule 8.6(1).

75 Paragraph 7.4 of CPR Practice Direction 8A; and see paragraph 9.7 of the Chancery Guide of the Chancery Guide.

matters the time limits for evidence imposed by CPR Part 8 "*may be burdensome upon defendants*" and indicates that in such matters the court will normally be willing to grant a reasonable extension.[76] If the parties are in agreement that such an extension should be granted, the application should be made by filing a consent order.[77] If there is no agreement an application notice must be issued and listed for hearing unless the Master considers that the application may be dealt with without a hearing.[78] The Chancery Guide requires parties to "*at all times act co-operatively and agree reasonable requests for additional time*" and indicates that the court is "*likely to order the opposing party to pay the costs of a contested application for additional time where the opposition is unreasonable*".[79]

As for the claimant's evidence, the contents of any witness statement(s) adduced by a defendant will of course depend on the circumstances of the particular case. In general terms, the topics one should consider covering are likely to be the same as those to be covered by the claimant in his evidence (discussed above). An aspect which can give rise to conflicting factual evidence is the extrinsic evidence of the testator's intention. This might be the case for example where that evidence consists of conversations the testator had with different people at different times about his will, which are inconsistent with one another.[80]

If a defendant has the probate or letters of administration in his possession or under his control, he must, unless the court orders otherwise, lodge it in the relevant office within 14 days after the service of the claim form on him.[81]

---

76 Paragraph 9.7 of the Chancery Guide of the Chancery Guide.

77 *Ibid.*

78 *Ibid.*

79 *Ibid.*

80 See for example the construction case of *Hives v Machin* [2017] EWHC 1414 (Ch), in which the judge heard and analysed conflicting oral evidence as to the testatrix's intentions, but ultimately concluded that section 21 AJA was not engaged and such evidence was therefore inadmissible (see in particular [39] to [59]).

CPR Part 7 claims: defendant's acknowledgement of service and defence

In most cases,[82] a defendant who wishes to defend a CPR Part 7 claim must either file a defence within 14 days of service of the particulars of claim on him,[83] or file an acknowledgment of service within in the same period[84] and then file a defence within 28 days of service of the particulars of claim.[85] A copy of the defence must also be served on the other parties.[86] The parties can agree to extend these time limits by up to 28 days;[87] if they do, the defendant must notify the court of the agreement in writing.[88]

At the same time as filing a defence, the defendant should consider whether he wishes or needs to bring a counterclaim. This is because the defendant can bring a counterclaim against the claimant by filing particulars of the counterclaim[89] without the court's permission if the counterclaim is filed at the same time as the defence;[90] however, the defendant will need the court's permission if the counterclaim is filed at any other time.[91] Whether it is necessary to bring a counterclaim will depend on the particular circumstances of the litigation and on the relief the defendant is seeking from the court. For example, if a defendant who is resisting a rectification claim is a beneficiary of a will which has already been admitted to probate and which does not cause any construction problems, it may be sufficient for him to simply file a

81 Paragraph 10.2 of CPR Practice Direction 57.

82 Special time limits apply, for example, where the proceedings are served on the defendant out of the jurisdiction: see e.g. CPR rules 10.3(2) and 15.4(2).

83 CPR rule 15.4(1)(a).

84 CPR rule 10.3(1).

85 CPR rule 15.4(1)(b).

86 CPR rule 15.6.

87 CPR rule 15.5(1).

88 CPR rule 15.5(2).

89 CPR rule 20.4(1).

90 CPR rule 20.4(2)(a).

91 CPR rule 20.4(2)(b).

defence denying that the claimant is entitled to the rectification he seeks (and thus impliedly asking the court to dismiss the claimant's rectification claim). On the other hand, if for example the defendant wishes to ask the court to rectify the will in a different way from that which the claimant is arguing for, and/or wishes to ask the court to determine the meaning of a particular provision of the will, then it may be necessary for him to both defend the claimant's rectification claim and bring a counterclaim.

As well as the rules in CPR rule 16.5 and CPR Practice Direction 16, the drafting guidelines contained in paragraphs 10.5 to 10.17 of the Chancery Guide apply to defences.

If a defendant has the probate or letters of administration in his possession or under his control, he must, unless the court orders otherwise, lodge it in the relevant office within 14 days after the service of the claim form on him.[92]

Default and summary judgment

It is generally not possible to obtain judgment in default in a rectification claim. The Chancery Guide explains that: "*If the claimant seeks discretionary relief such as a declaration, rectification, an injunction or other similar relief the Master will usually require to be satisfied that such relief is necessary, and if so ought to be granted, and a full witness statement will usually be required. In cases of complexity the application notice may need to be listed. Declaratory relief and relief by way of rectification will not be granted without evidence and will not ordinarily be appropriate for resolution by way of judgment in default.*"[93] Furthermore, if the claim is uncontested and is brought by CPR Part 8 proceedings, judgment in default is not available.[94]

92 Paragraph 10.2 of CPR Practice Direction 57.

93 Paragraph 12.3 of the Chancery Guide; see also paragraph 29.69 of the Chancery Guide.

94 CPR rules 8.1(5) and 12.2(b); see also paragraph 9.4 of the Chancery Guide.

On the other hand, it is generally possible to obtain summary judgment in a rectification claim in an appropriate case. This will usually be where the claim is opposed and is brought by CPR Part 7 proceedings, and the applicant is able to demonstrate that the claim or defence (as the case may be) has no real prospect of success and that there is no other compelling reason why the claim should be disposed of at a trial. However, if the claim is unopposed and is brought by way of CPR Part 8 proceedings, it will generally be unnecessary to apply for summary judgment, and the claimant can instead ask the court to list the claim for a disposal hearing, as Chief Master Marsh explained in *Sovereign Trustees Ltd v Lewis*:[95]

"*Part 8 claims are markedly different to Part 7 claims. Although there is no bar to issuing a Part 24 application [i.e. an application for summary judgment] in a Part 8 claim, it will rarely be necessary for the claimant to do so where it is seeking judgment on the whole of the claim. In part this is because the second limb of CPR 24.2 will normally have no application because there will be no 'trial' as such. Part 8 claims are normally resolved at a 'disposal hearing'. This is made clear by paragraph 8.1 of Practice Direction 8A which states:*

> *'8.1 The court may on the hearing date –*
>
> *(i) proceed to hear the case and dispose of the claim;*
>
> *(ii) give case management directions.'*
>
> *It follows that in most Part 8 claims, where the relief sought is unopposed, or cannot realistically be opposed, it will suffice for the claimant to ask the court to fix a disposal hearing at which the court may determine whether or not the relief sought by the claimant should be granted.*"

95 [2016] EWHC 2593 (Ch) at [3]. See also paragraph 29.91 of the Chancery Guide in relation to uncontentious claims for the rectification of pension schemes. However, it should be noted that in *The Girls' Day School Trust v GDST Pension Trustees Ltd* [2016] EWHC 1254 (Ch) summary judgment was granted without a hearing in an unopposed claim for the rectification of a pension scheme.

Claimant's reply

CPR Part 8 claims: claimant's evidence in reply

If the claimant wishes to rely on further written evidence in reply to the defendant's evidence, he must file it within 14 days of service of the defendant's evidence on him,[96] and he must also serve a copy of it on the other parties "*within the same time limit*".[97] As that time limit is also quite short, paragraph 7.5 of CPR Practice Direction 8A also allows the parties to agree in writing to extend it by up to 14 days; i.e. the maximum period which the parties can agree is that the claimant shall file his evidence in reply 28 days after service of the defendant's evidence on him.[98] Any such agreement should similarly be filed at court.[99] In the same way as a defendant, a claimant may not rely on any written evidence which has not been served in accordance with the rules described above at the hearing of the claim unless the court gives permission.[100]

If a claimant requires more time to file his evidence in reply to the defendant's, he too should apply to the court for an extension of time by way of an application pursuant to CPR Part 23.[101] The guidance contained in paragraph 9.7 of the Chancery Guide – which is considered above in the context of the defendant's evidence – applies equally to applications for extensions of time by claimants. In particular, parties should bear in mind that the court is likely to grant reasonable requests for extensions of time and expects parties to "*at all times act co-operatively and agree reasonable requests for additional time*"

96 CPR rule 8.5(5); and see paragraph 9.6 of the Chancery Guide.

97 CPR rule 8.5(6).

98 Paragraph 7.5(2)(b) of CPR Practice Direction 8A; and see paragraph 9.6 of the Chancery Guide.

99 Although the CPR does not appear to require this, paragraph 9.7 of the Chancery Guide does.

100 CPR rule 8.6(1).

101 Paragraph 7.4 of CPR Practice Direction 8A.

and may punish in costs a party who unreasonably opposes an application.[102]

CPR Part 7 claims: claimant's reply

If the claimant wishes to file a reply, he must file it with his directions questionnaire.[103] The CPR requires the claimant to serve a reply on the other parties "*at the same time it is filed*".[104] However, the Chancery Guide encourages claimants to serve replies before filing directions questionnaires if possible to give the other parties an opportunity to consider the reply before they file their own directions questionnaires.[105]

As well as the rules in CPR rule 16.7 and CPR Practice Direction 16, the drafting guidelines contained in paragraphs 10.5 to 10.17 of the Chancery Guide apply to replies.

Directions and case management

CPR Part 8 claims

In some CPR Part 8 cases the court may give directions immediately after the claim has been issued, either on the application of a party or of its own initiative, which may include fixing a hearing date.[106] This is likely to happen particularly in cases which have been issued without naming a defendant pursuant to CPR rule 8.2A.[107] However, it is more usual for the claim to be referred to the Master[108] only after an acknow-

102 Paragraph 9.7 of the Chancery Guide.

103 CPR rule 15.8(a).

104 CPR rule 15.8(b).

105 Paragraph 10.3 of the Chancery Guide.

106 Paragraph 6.1 of CPR Practice Direction 8A.

107 Paragraph 29.14 of the Chancery Guide.

108 Or to a District Judge of the High Court if the claim is in one of the District Registries.

ledgment of service has been filed or after the period for doing so has expired.[109]

At that stage the Master will consider whether the claim may be capable of being dealt with 'on the file', i.e. on the papers without a hearing.[110] This might be appropriate if the rectification claim is unopposed,[111] but even then the court may want to hear argument from the claimant at a hearing as to why rectification should in fact be granted.

If no acknowledgment of service has been filed, the Master may "*sometimes override the provisions of Part 8 by directing that the defendant must file and serve an acknowledgment and evidence by a specified date failing which the defendant will not be entitled to play any part in the disposal hearing*".[112] Doing so is "*intended to make explicit for a [litigant in person] what is already set out in the CPR*".[113] If this route is taken, directions may be given to lead straight to disposal hearing (without a directions hearing being held first).

On the other hand, if an acknowledgment of service has been filed, the claim is likely to be listed for a directions hearing in the first instance,[114] and some directions may be given as to how the parties should prepare for it.

At a directions hearing, the issues which the court is likely to consider are:[115]

---

109 Paragraph 6.2 of CPR Practice Direction 8A; see also paragraphs 9.10, 15.9 and 17.65 of the Chancery Guide.

110 Paragraph 17.65 of the Chancery Guide.

111 Paragraph 15.11 of the Chancery Guide. See e.g. the trust case of *Millar v Millar* [2018] EWHC 1926 (Ch).

112 Paragraph 15.09 of the Chancery Guide.

113 *Ibid.*

114 Paragraphs 15.10 and 17.66 of the Chancery Guide.

115 See paragraph 17.74 of the Chancery Guide.

(a) Evidence, including whether directions should be given for the filing of any further evidence (in addition to the evidence which will already have been filed by that point) and whether any witnesses should be required to attend to give oral evidence and be cross-examined at the disposal hearing.[116] If a rectification claim is proceeding pursuant to CPR Part 8 because it is unopposed (at least by the affected beneficiaries who are capacitous adults), it is likely to be decided on written evidence only.[117] However, if it is opposed but is proceeding pursuant to CPR Part 8 because it has been brought as an alternative to a construction claim, thought should be given as to whether to seek directions for witnesses (such as the draftsman, if the will was professionally prepared) to be required to attend to give oral evidence and be cross-examined at the disposal hearing.

(b) Representation of the parties, such as whether any litigation friend needs to be appointed and/or whether any representation order should be made and/or notice given pursuant to CPR rule 19.8A (as to which, see <u>Parties</u> above).

(c) Directions in relation to the disposal hearing, such as directions about when and how the disposal hearing should be listed,[118] its time estimate, and the level of judge required. As regards time estimate, this is likely to depend in particular on the number and complexity of the rectification arguments which are being advanced, and on whether there is going to be live oral evidence from witnesses who will be cross-examined. As regards level of judge, CPR rule 2.4 provides that in proceedings in the High

---

116 CPR rule 8.6(2) provides "*The court may require or permit a party to give oral evidence at the hearing*" and CPR rule 8.6(3) provides "*The court may give directions requiring the attendance for cross-examination of a witness who has given written evidence*".

117 See paragraph 9.3 of the Chancery Guide: "*Part 8 claims will generally be disposed of on written evidence without cross-examination. The witness statements with the claim form should be sufficient in most cases to define the issues*".

118 Unless oral evidence is envisaged, CPR Part 8 proceedings are usually entered in the General List: see paragraphs 21.5 and 21.6 of the Chancery Guide.

Court, any act which may be performed by the court may be performed "*by any judge, Master, Registrar in Bankruptcy or District Judge*".[119] Paragraph 7B.1 of CPR Practice Direction 2B does not impose any restriction on the jurisdiction of Masters in London to decide claims for the rectification of wills.[120] On the contrary, sub-paragraph 3 of paragraph 14.2 of the Chancery Guide lists "*Rectification*" as one of the "*non-excluded matters*" which paragraph 14.3 indicates "*should normally be listed before a Master*", "*whether for case management, interim relief or disposal*". Paragraph 14.3 goes on to provide: "*If it is considered that exceptionally the application should be heard by a High Court Judge the Master should be requested to release it.*" This is confirmed by paragraph 29.71 of the Chancery Guide, which provides: "*Since 6th April 2015 the Masters have jurisdiction to deal with all rectification claims. The Master will only refer an application which is consented to the judge if it raises issues of particular difficulty.*" Thus, rectification claims proceeding in London are likely to be decided by a Master. However, for claims proceeding in the District Registries it should be noted that paragraph 7B.2(e) provides that a District Judge in a District Registry may not make an order for rectification without the consent of the Supervising Judge for the region in which the District Judge is sitting, or without the consent of their nominee.

(d) 'Housekeeping' directions to prepare the case for the disposal hearing, such as directions relating to the hearing bundle,[121] skeleton arguments,[122] and other documents such as dramatis per-

---

119 Note the reference to 'District Judge' here is to a District Judge of the High Court (who is broadly the equivalent in the District Registries of a Master in London), not to a District Judge of the County Court.

120 This is confirmed by paragraph 29.71 of the Chancery Guide: "*Since 6th April 2015 the Masters have jurisdiction to deal with all rectification claims. The Master will only refer an application which is consented to the judge if it raises issues of particular difficulty.*"

121 Detailed rules in relation to hearing bundles are contained in paragraph 3 of CPR Practice Direction 39A and are supplemented by the guidance contained in paragraphs 21.34 to 21.72 of the Chancery Guide.

122 In relation to which see paragraphs 21.73 to 21.81 of the Chancery Guide.

sonae, chronologies, case summaries, lists of issues,[123] reading lists[124] and bundles of authorities.[125]

CPR Part 7 claims: costs and case management conference

If the rectification claim is proceeding by way of a CPR Part 7 claim, it will generally be referred to the Master for review following the filing of a defence.[126] The court will generally send the parties a Notice of Provisional Allocation (form N149C) with a letter explaining what the parties are required to do.[127] If the parties do not wish there to be a stay for alternative dispute resolution, they must serve and file with the court by the date specified in the letter the directions questionnaire, disclosure report, list of issues (agreed or not agreed), draft directions and costs budgets (if applicable).[128] The claimant must then lodge a bundle with the statements of case and all the additional documents served following the provisional notice of allocation which will be reviewed by the Master.[129] The Chancery Guide explains that it is "*incumbent on the parties to ensure that the court is provided with helpful and complete information because a number of important issues will be made on the file review*".[130] These include considering any request for a stay or for the continuation of an existing stay; whether the claim should remain in the Court in which it has been issued or be transferred (e.g. to one of the District Registries);[131] reviewing draft directions, including the appropriate case management track; and considering costs management.[132]

---

123 In relation to which see paragraphs 21.75, 21.76 and 21.83 of the Chancery Guide.

124 In relation to which see paragraph 21.82 of the Chancery Guide.

125 In relation to which see paragraphs 21.85 to 21.87 of the Chancery Guide.

126 Paragraph 15.7 of the Chancery Guide.

127 *Ibid.*

128 *Ibid.*

129 *Ibid.* and see also paragraph 17.7 of the Chancery Guide.

130 *Ibid.*

131 In relation to which see paragraphs 14.15 to 14.20 of the Chancery Guide.

132 See also paragraph 17.7 of the Chancery Guide.

In most cases, the claim will be listed for a costs and case management conference ("CCMC").[133] At such a hearing, the issues which the court is likely to consider are the same as those which would be considered at a directions hearing if the claim were proceeding as a CPR Part 8 claim (discussed above). However, the sequence of events is likely to be different: in CPR Part 8 claims, by the time the case reaches a directions hearing, witness statements will have already been filed and exchanged, and the relevant documents which the parties wish to rely on will usually have already been disclosed (generally as exhibits to the witness statements). On the other hand, in CPR Part 7 claims, directions for disclosure and witness statements are generally given at the CCMC.

Disclosure – CPR Part 7 claims

This section considers disclosure in claims which are brought pursuant to CPR Part 7. Disclosure in CPR Part 8 claims is considered above.

In general terms, in contested will rectification claims which involve a professionally prepared will, the key documentary evidence – and often the only documentary evidence – is usually the will file. Will files are rarely particularly extensive, usually running into the dozens of pages (sometimes into the hundreds, but very rarely into the thousands). As a result, there is normally little difficulty or cost in the file being disclosed in its entirety, usually when the rectification problem is being investigated (and thus before any proceedings are issued).

Where a will file relates to more than one client – which is not uncommon for example where both members of a couple have made wills at the same time using the same solicitor – it may be necessary to redact privileged information relating to the other client (unless that client waives privilege).

In addition to the will file, it may be useful to consider whether there could be any other documentary evidence of the testator's intentions,

---

133 Paragraph 17.3 of the Chancery Guide states: "*The majority of claims do not permit case management "on the file" and the court will rarely be able to approve agreed directions*".

for example in any diary or other notes he may have kept (including electronic notes such as draft emails or notes made on a computer or a mobile phone or a tablet). Often testators do not discuss what they might consider to be their private personal affairs with friends or even family, but another source of documentary evidence of the testator's intentions could be any correspondence in which these were discussed, including both formal correspondence, such as letters and emails, and more informal communications, such as text messages, WhatsApp messages or other forms of electronic communication.

CPR Practice Direction 51U contains a new 'disclosure pilot' which is intended to replace, and significantly change, the traditional approach to standard disclosure which has previously applied in most CPR Part 7 claims.[134] The Pilot came into force on 1st January 2019 and applies to both existing CPR Part 7 claims and to new CPR Part 7 claims issued after that date in the Business and Property Courts of England and Wales.[135] It will remain in force for two years.[136]

The provisions of the pilot are detailed. In summary, it is suggested that the following points are likely to be particularly relevant in rectification claims.

1. The pilot creates a new concept of 'Initial Disclosure'.[137] This is the requirement that each party provides the other parties at the same time as its statement of case – and thus before any directions for disclosure are given by the court – an 'Initial Disclosure List of Documents' that "*lists and is accompanied by copies of: (1) the key documents on which it has relied (expressly or otherwise) in support of the claims or defences advanced in its statement of case (and including the documents referred to in that statement of case); and (2) the key documents that are necessary to enable the other*

134 In relation to the application of the pilot in CPR Part 8 claims, see "Disclosure – Part 8 Claims" above.

135 Paragraph 1.2 of CPR Practice Direction 51U.

136 Paragraph 1.2 of CPR Practice Direction 51U.

137 Paragraph 5 of CPR Practice Direction 51U.

parties to understand the claim or defence they have to meet."[138] Initial Disclosure does not apply if it would require a party to disclose more than the larger of 1,000 pages or 200 documents.[139] It is suggested that this threshold is unlikely to be met in most rectification claims, and Initial Disclosure is therefore likely to apply. The parties can also agree in writing prior to the commencement of proceedings that Initial Disclosure should not apply; however, they should only do so with good reason, as the court may review the parties' reasons for disapplying Initial Disclosure at the first case management conference and may set aside such an agreement aside if it considers that Initial Disclosure "*is likely to provide significant benefits and the costs of providing Initial Disclosure are unlikely to be disproportionate to such benefits*".[140]

2. Once proceedings have commenced, the parties are under a duty "*to disclose, regardless of any order for disclosure made, known adverse documents, unless they are privileged*"[141] in accordance with the provisions of the pilot. 'Known adverse documents' are "*documents (other than privileged documents) that a party is actually aware (without undertaking any further search for documents than it has already undertaken or caused to be undertaken) both (a) are or were previously within its control and (b) are adverse.*"[142] A document is 'adverse' if "*it or any information it contains contradicts or materially damages the disclosing party's contention or version of events on an issue in dispute, or supports the contention or version of events of an opposing party on an issue in dispute*".[143] The duty to disclose adverse documents applies throughout the proceedings[144] and irrespective of any order for Extended Disclosure: "*if adverse*

138 Paragraph 5.1 of CPR Practice Direction 51U.

139 Paragraph 5.3(3) of CPR Practice Direction 51U.

140 Paragraph 5.8 of CPR Practice Direction 51U.

141 Paragraph 3.1(2) of CPR Practice Direction 51U.

142 Paragraph 2.8 of CPR Practice Direction 51U.

143 Paragraph 2.7 of CPR Practice Direction 51U.

144 Paragraph 3.3 of CPR Practice Direction 51U.

documents in the control of a party come to its knowledge at a later date they must (unless privileged) be disclosed without delay".[145]

3. A party wishing to seek disclosure of documents in addition to, or as an alternative to, Initial Disclosure must request 'Extended Disclosure'.[146] This is done by completing a 'Disclosure Review Document' in advance of the first case management conference in accordance with paragraph 7 of CPR Practice Direction 51U (no application notice is required).[147] An order for Extended Disclosure will only be made where the court "*is persuaded that it is appropriate to do so in order fairly to resolve one or more of the Issues for Disclosure*".[148] The order "*must be reasonable and proportionate having regard to the overriding objective*"[149] and to the seven factors listed in paragraph 6.4 of CPR Practice Direction 51U.[150] The 'Issues for Disclosure' are "*those key issues in dispute, which the parties consider will need to be determined by the court with some reference to contemporaneous documents in order for there to be a fair resolution of the proceedings*";[151] however, this does not extend

---

145 Paragraph 9.3 of CPR Practice Direction 51U.

146 Paragraph 6.1 of CPR Practice Direction 51U.

147 *Ibid.*

148 Paragraph 6.3 of CPR Practice Direction 51U.

149 Paragraph 6.4 of CPR Practice Direction 51U.

150 These are:

(1) the nature and complexity of the issues in the proceedings;

(2) the importance of the case, including any non-monetary relief sought;

(3) the likelihood of documents existing that will have probative value in supporting or undermining a party's claim or defence;

(4) the number of documents involved;

(5) the ease and expense of searching for and retrieval of any particular document (taking into account any limitations on the information available and on the likely accuracy of any costs estimates);

(6) the financial position of each party; and

(7) the need to ensure the case is dealt with expeditiously, fairly and at a proportionate cost.

151 Paragraph 7.3 of CPR Practice Direction 51U.

"*to every issue which is disputed in the statements of case by denial or non-admission.*"[152] The parties are required to identify and to try to agree the List of Issues for Disclosure in section 1A of the Disclosure Review Document.[153] In relation to each Issue for Disclosure, the parties must also consider which of the five 'Disclosure Models' identified in paragraph 8 of CPR Practice Direction 51U should apply.[154] Although the parties may agree that a particular Model should apply to a particular Issue for Disclosure, no Model will in fact apply without the approval of the court,[155] who will usually consider whether to make an order for Extended Disclosure and, if so, on what terms at the first case management conference.

4. The pilot also imposes a duty to "*to take reasonable steps to preserve documents […] that may be relevant to any issue in the proceedings*".[156] This duty applies to:

   (a) "*[a] person who knows that it is or may become a party to proceedings that have been commenced or who knows that it may become a party to proceedings that may be commenced*";[157] and

   (b) "*[l]egal representatives who have the conduct of litigation on behalf of a party to proceedings that have been commenced, or who are instructed with a view to the conduct of litigation where their client knows it may become a party to proceedings that have been or may be commenced*".[158]

   The duty to preserve documents applies to "*documents which might otherwise be deleted or destroyed in accordance with a doc-*

152 *Ibid.*

153 Paragraph 7 of CPR Practice Direction 51U.

154 See also paragraph 9 of CPR Practice Direction 51U.

155 Paragraph 8.2 of CPR Practice Direction 51U.

156 Paragraph 3.1(1) and 3.2(1) of CPR Practice Direction 51U.

157 Paragraph 3.1 of CPR Practice Direction 51U.

158 Paragraph 3.2 of CPR Practice Direction 51U.

ument retention policy or in the ordinary course of business"[159] and "*[p]reservation includes, in suitable cases, making copies of sources and documents and storing them.*"[160] Legal representatives are also under a duty to notify their client of the duty to preserve documents "*within a reasonable period of being instructed*"[161] and to obtain written confirmation from the client that any document deletion or destruction processes have been suspended for the duration of the proceedings in accordance with paragraphs 4.2 and 4.3 of CPR Practice Direction 51U.

As indicated above, in most rectification claims the key – and possibly the only – documentary evidence is likely to be the will file. In practice, this will usually be disclosed during pre-action correspondence. It also seems likely that in most cases all other relevant documentary evidence will be disclosed either pre-action or during Initial Disclosure, and that it will therefore rarely be necessary to seek an order for Extended Disclosure.

Depending on the circumstances, it may also be worth considering whether disclosure should be sought from a non-party pursuant to CPR rule 31.17.

Witness statements

In CPR Part 8 claims, witness statements will have already been filed and served at the early stages of the proceedings (as discussed above).

In CPR Part 7 claims, directions for the exchange of witness statements are normally given at the CCMC. Who should be asked to give evidence and what that topics that evidence should cover will depend on the particular circumstances of the case. In general terms, the topics which the evidence is likely to have to cover are the same which the particulars of claim should cover, viz.:

---

159 Paragraph 4.1 of CPR Practice Direction 51U; see also paragraph 4.2 and 4.3.

160 Paragraph 3.2 of CPR Practice Direction 51U.

161 Paragraph 4.4 of CPR Practice Direction 51U.

(a) the claimant's role and the capacity in which he brings the claim;

(b) the factual background;

(c) the current drafting of the will and its construction;

(d) what the testator's intentions are alleged to have been;

(e) how the current drafting of the will fails to give effect to the testator's intentions, and whether this is due to a clerical error and/or a failure to understand the testator's instructions;

(f) how the court is being asked to rectify the will;

(g) the position of the other interested parties.

In cases involving a professionally prepared will, the key witness evidence is generally likely to be that of the individual or individuals who were involved in taking instructions for will, drafting it and arranging its execution. Indeed, in some cases the draftsman may be the only witness.[162] Depending on how involved they were, the attesting witnesses may also be able to shed light on the testator's intentions and on the will making process.

If the testator discussed his intentions with family and/or friends (who may or may not be beneficiaries or intended beneficiaries of his will), these individuals may also be able to give evidence on the issue.

162 See e.g. *Re Bimson* [2010] EWHC 3679 (Ch) at [6].

Disposal hearing/trial

At the disposal hearing (in CPR Part 8 claims) or trial (in CPR Part 7 claims), the court will hear the argument in favour and against rectification. In CPR Part 8 claims, directions will have previously been given as to whether there should be oral evidence and cross-examination of any of the witnesses (e.g. the draftsman).

Disposal hearings/trials in rectification claims are generally listed in public, i.e. in a court which is open to members of the public.[163] Whilst it may be possible in some cases to persuade a court to list the claim in private pursuant to CPR rule 39.2(3),[164] or to impose some other less extensive reporting restriction,[165] a party seeking such an order is likely to have to show compelling reasons why the court should depart from the principle of open justice.[166]

Judgment

The Master or judge will decide how, when and where to deliver judgment. Judgment may be delivered orally immediately at the con-

---

163 Under the general rule in CPR rule 39.2(1).

164 The sub-rules of CPR rule 39.2(3) which may be engaged in construction claims are (c), (d) and (g), viz.:

(c) [the hearing] involves confidential information (including information relating to personal financial matters) and publicity would damage that confidentiality;

(d) a private hearing is necessary to protect the interests of any child or protected party;

[...]

(g) the court considers [a hearing in private] to be necessary, in the interests of justice."

On the other hand, sub-rule (f) is unlikely to be engaged in rectification cases, as that sub-rule is engaged in relation to hearings involving "*uncontentious matters arising in the administration of trusts or in the administration of a deceased person's estate*" (emphasis added).

165 See e.g. *ABC v JKL* [2019] EWHC 2416 (Ch), which involved the rectification of a deed of appointment.

166 See in this regard the Court of Appeal's guidance in *MN v OP* [2019] EWCA Civ 679 regarding privacy and reporting restrictions in the context of applications pursuant to the Variation of Trusts Act 1958.

clusion of the hearing (a so-called '*ex tempore*' judgment),[167] or may be reserved. A reserved judgment may be delivered orally at a later date or, more commonly, may be circulated in written draft to the parties and then formally handed down at a subsequent date. Sometimes – particularly in urgent cases – the court may announce its decision and make any necessary order at the conclusion of the hearing and provide its reasoned judgment at a later date.[168]

Costs

As indicated at 3.2.3 above, if the will was professionally prepared and the circumstances indicate that a professional negligence claim against the draftsman is likely, his insurers may have agreed in advance to fund the costs of the rectification claim. Where the claim is unopposed, the court will often be asked to make no order as to costs, on the basis that the parties will recover their costs from the draftsman's insurer as agreed.[169]

On the other hand, if the rectification claim is contested, the general rule (which applies in all civil litigation) is that the unsuccessful party will be ordered to pay the costs of the successful party.[170] However, costs are ultimately in the discretion of the court,[171] and the court may therefore decide to depart from that starting point and make a different costs order. In general terms, in deciding costs the court will try to ensure that the costs are in fact borne by the negligent draftsman and/or (in a contested case) by the party who has lost, and not by the successful party. In deciding precisely how this should be achieved, the court will have to take into account all of the circumstances, including the parties'

167 See e.g. *Slattery v Jagger* [2015] EWHC 3976 (Ch).

168 See e.g. *ABC v JKL* [2019] EWHC 2416 (Ch) at [4].

169 See e.g. the will rectification cases of *Re Bimson* [2010] EWHC 3679 (Ch) at [23] and *Gerling v Gerling* [2010] EWHC 3661 (Ch) at [50].

170 CPR rule 44.2.(2)(a).

171 Section 51(1) of the Senior Courts Act 1981.

respective interests under the will and who would in fact bear the costs if the costs are ordered to be paid out of the estate.[172]

Order

If the rectification claim succeeds, the order will need to make it clear precisely how the will is being rectified. It will usually be sensible for one of the recitals to record that the court was satisfied that the will is so expressed that it fails to carry out the testator's intentions in consequence of a clerical error or of a failure to understand the testator's instructions (as the case may be).

How the rectification is best recorded in the order is will depend on precisely what the rectification consists of. In general terms, it is suggested that:

(a) if the rectification is straightforward and can be clearly described in few words, this can be done in the body of the order (e.g. "pursuant to section 20(1)(b) of the Administration of Justice Act 1982, the Will is rectified by the replacement in clause 3 of the word "patricians" with the word "people"");[173]

(b) however, if the rectification is less straightforward, it is likely to be sensible for the body of the order to refer to a schedule (e.g. by providing: "pursuant to section 20(1)(b) of the Administration of Justice Act 1982, the Will is rectified in the manner set out in the Schedule hereto"), and for the schedule to then set out the rectified version of the relevant provisions of the will.

A copy of every order made for the rectification of a will must be sent to the Principal Registry of the Family Division for filing, and a memorandum of the order must be endorsed on, or permanently annexed to, the grant under which the estate is administered.[174] The order should contain a provision to that effect.

172 See e.g. and *Marley v Rawlings (costs)* [2014] UKSC 51 and *Slattery v Jagger* [2015] EWHC 3976 (Ch) at [103]-[112].

173 See Example 6.

174 Paragraph 11 of CPR Practice Direction 57.

Chapter 22 of the Chancery Guide contains guidance in relation to the drafting, filing and sealing of orders.

Appeals

A party who is dissatisfied with the court's decision must obtain the court's permission in order to appeal it.[175] The court will only grant permission to appeal if it considers that the appeal would have a real prospect of success, or that there is some other compelling reason for the appeal to be heard.[176]

Although this is not strictly required, it is generally sensible for a party who wishes to appeal to first seek permission from the lower court.[177] This is usually done when judgment is delivered or handed down and consequential issues, such as the terms of the order giving effect to the judgment and costs, are decided.

If the lower court refuses permission, or if permission was not sought from it, permission must be sought from the appeal court by filing an Appellant's Notice.[178] Unless the court orders otherwise, the time limit for doing so is "*21 days after the date of the decision of the lower court*".[179] That is a relatively short time limit, which cannot be extended by agreement between the parties,[180] and it must be borne in mind that the period starts to run from the date of the decision of the lower court and not, if later, the date on which consequential matters are decided or the date on which the order giving effect to the decision is approved and sealed.[181] If – as is quite common – the lower court's judgment is circu-

175 CPR rule 52.3(1).

176 CPR rule 52.6(1).

177 Pursuant to CPR rule 52.3(2)(a); see e.g. *In re T (A Child)* [2002] EWCA Civ 1736 at [12]-[13].

178 CPR rules 52.3(2)(b) and 52.12(1).

179 CPR rule 52.12(2)(b).

180 CPR rule 52.15(2).

181 See e.g. *Sayers v Clarke Walker (A Firm)* [2002] EWCA Civ 645 at [8]-[9] and *Owusu v Jackson* [2002] EWCA Civ 877 at [24]-[27].

lated to the parties in draft and then formally handed down in the absence of the parties, and a hearing to decide consequential matter is arranged at a later date, the lower court should be asked to direct[182] that the 21-day period will only start to run from the date of the later hearing, rather than from the date on which judgment was handed down.[183]

Compromise

In some cases it may be possible to compromise a rectification claim after proceedings have been issued.[184] The mechanism by which the compromise should be implemented will inevitably depend on its terms and on the particular circumstances of the case. In most cases, the following will have to be considered:

(a) Whether the compromise has any tax implications and, if so, whether it is desirable to implement it by way of a deed of variation which can be 'read back' for IHT and/or CGT purposes.[185]

(b) Whether a court order rectifying the will is required, and if so whether the court can be asked to make the order by consent without hearing full argument. In *Burford (Fareham) Ltd v Christian Vision*[186] (which involved the rectification of a deed of assignment of warranties) the court held that there is no "*blanket rule that rectification should not be ordered by consent*"[187] and that the question is one of the court's discretion. However, it should be borne in mind that this jurisdiction is exercised sparingly. In this regard, paragraph 29.69 of the Chancery Guide provides: "*It*

---

182 Pursuant to CPR 52.12(2)(a).

183 See e.g. *Jackson v Marina Homes Ltd* [2007] EWCA Civ 1404 at [8].

184 The circumstances in which it may be possible to resolve a rectification issue without the need for court proceedings are considered at 3.2.2 above.

185 See section 142 of the Inheritance Tax Act 1984 and section 62 of the Taxation of Chargeable Gains Act 1992.

186 [2005] EWHC 2533 (Ch).

187 [2005] EWHC 2533 (Ch) at [7].

is not the practice of the court to make an order for rectification by default or by consent. The court is sometimes asked to make an order for rectification to which all relevant parties consent, but the court will not, even in such a case, make an order without being satisfied that it is justified by the evidence. The court will therefore wish to scrutinise carefully the changes that are proposed, the reasons for them and the evidence in support".

(c) Whether the court's approval of the compromise is required, which will be the case where one or more of the parties is a minor,[188] an adult who lacks capacity to conduct litigation[189] and/or a party who has been appointed to represent others pursuant to CPR rule 19.7.[190]

Paragraphs 22.9 to 22.13 of the Chancery Guide contain guidance in relation to consent orders.

---

188 CPR rule 21.10.

189 *Ibid.*

190 CPR rule 19.7(5).

CHAPTER FOUR
CONSTRUCTION OF OTHER TRUST INSTRUMENTS

4.1 The law

In *Rafferty v Philp*[1] Norris J cited with approval the following passage from *Lewin on Trusts*:[2]

> *Lifetime settlements are no different from other documents in that the subjective intentions of their authors are irrelevant. What counts is the objective meaning that the words of the document convey to the court when considered as a whole in the light of the surrounding circumstances.*

In *Marley v Rawlings*[3] (which concerned a will) the Supreme Court provided the following general guidance in relation to the modern approach to the construction of different types of documents:[4]

> *19. When interpreting a contract, the court is concerned to find the intention of the party or parties, and it does this by identifying the meaning of the relevant words, (a) in the light of (i) the natural and ordinary meaning of those words, (ii) the overall purpose of the document, (iii) any other provisions of the document, (iv) the facts known or assumed by the parties at the time that the document was executed, and (v) common sense, but (b) ignoring subjective evidence of any party's intentions. [...]*

---

1 [2011] EWHC 709 (Ch).

2 [2011] EWHC 709 (Ch) at [23].

3 [2014] UKSC 2.

4 Other leading authorities on the modern approach to construction generally include *Chartbrook Ltd v Persimmon Homes Ltd* [2009] UKHL 38, *Rainy Sky SA v Kookmin Bank* [2011] UKSC 50 and *Arnold v Britton* [2015] UKSC 36.

> *20. When it comes to interpreting wills, it seems to me that the approach should be the same. Whether the document in question is a commercial contract or a will, the aim is to identify the intention of the party or parties to the document by interpreting the words used in their documentary, factual and commercial context. As Lord Hoffmann said in Kirin-Amgen Inc v Hoechst Marion Roussel Ltd [2005] 1 All ER 667, para 64, "No one has ever made an acontextual statement. There is always some context to any utterance, however meagre." To the same effect, Sir Thomas Bingham MR said in Arbuthnott v Fagan [1995] CLC 1396, 1400 that "courts will never construe words in a vacuum".*
>
> *21. Of course, a contract is agreed between a number of parties, whereas a will is made by a single party. However, that distinction is an unconvincing reason for adopting a different approach in principle to interpretation of wills: it is merely one of the contextual circumstances which has to be borne in mind when interpreting the document concerned. Thus, the court takes the same approach to interpretation of unilateral notices as it takes to interpretation of contracts: see Mannai Investment Co Ltd v Eagle Star Life Assurance Co Ltd [1997] AC 749, […]*
>
> *22. Another example of a unilateral document which is interpreted in the same way as a contract is a patent—see the approach adopted by Lord Diplock in Catnic Components Ltd v Hill & Smith Ltd [1982] RPC 183, 243, cited with approval, expanded, and applied in Kirin-Amgen at paras 27–32 by Lord Hoffmann. A notice and a patent are both documents intended by its originator to convey information, and so, too, is a will.*
>
> *23. In my view, at least subject to any statutory provision to the contrary, the approach to the interpretation of contracts as set out in the cases discussed in para 19 above is therefore just as appropriate for wills as it is for other unilateral documents.*

Several cases since *Marley v Rawlings* have confirmed that the approach identified by the Supreme Court in that case applies to the construction of unilateral trust instruments such as declarations of trust in a family context.[5]

Section 21 of the Administration of Justice Act 1982 only applies to wills.[6] As a result, when construing trust instruments other than wills, the distinction between evidence of the settlor's subjective intention (which is not admissible) and other evidence of the so-called 'factual matrix' surrounding the making of the instrument (which is) can be significant. Moreover, it may not always be easy to determine what evidence is in fact relevant to the 'factual matrix'.[7]

In *Re Hand*[8] the court accepted that human rights considerations can be relevant to the construction of a will. The reference in a 1946 will to "*children*" *prima facie* had to be construed as excluding adopted children as a result of the Adoption of Children Act 1926, which treated adopted children as children of their natural, rather than their adoptive, parents for succession purposes. Although that position had been reversed in 1950, it had been preserved in relation to existing dispositions. However, the court concluded that it was required by the Human Rights Act 1998 to read down the relevant preserving legislation,[9] and to construe "*children*" as including two adopted children so as not to breach their human rights.[10] The full impact of this decision is yet to be

---

5 *Millar v Millar* [2018] EWHC 1926 (Ch) at [17]-[23], and in particular at [23]; *Public Trustee v Harrison-Mills* [2018] EWHC 166 (Ch) at [18] (the Court of Appeal overturned the decision on costs, but not on construction: [2019] EWCA Civ 966); *Armstrong v Armstrong* [2019] EWHC 2259 (Ch) at [21]-[22].

6 This is discussed at 2.1.

7 See e.g. *Public Trustee v Harrison-Mills* [2018] EWHC 166 (Ch), in which the court concluded that there was no admissible evidence of the 'factual matrix' surrounding the making of the two documents the court was being asked to construe, and decided that the documents had to be construed by considering their wording only (at [18]-[21]). (The Court of Appeal overturned the decision on costs, but not on construction: [2019] EWCA Civ 966.)

8 [2017] EWHC 533 (Ch).

9 Paragraph 6(1) of Schedule 2 to the Adoption Act 1976.

10 The relevant human rights were the right to respect for private and family life, protected by article 8 of the European Convention on Human Rights, and the

explored.[11] The earlier decision in *Re Erskine 1948 Trust*[12] indicates that human rights considerations can be equally relevant to the construction of other trust instruments.

4.2 Practice and procedure

4.2.1 Who is affected?

The first question trustees should ask themselves when faced with a construction problem is: who is affected by it?

The reason for this is that construction problems have a right answer – and one, or possibly several, wrong ones. Therefore trustees should not try to decide themselves what they think the answer is and then act on that basis. If they do and if they proceed on the basis of an answer which later turns out to be the wrong one, they can be personally liable for breach of trust (i.e. for having administered or distributed the trust fund incorrectly).

It follows that the main concern for trustees faced with a construction problem is to ensure that before they take any step based on a particular construction they protect themselves from potential personal liability for breach of trust, which they can do by obtaining either the binding consent of all affected beneficiaries or authorisation from the court. To get to that position, the trustees will first have to establish who the affected beneficiaries are.

Needless to say, the answer to this will depend on the particular circumstances, and can vary widely. In simple terms, the way to go about ascertaining the affected beneficiaries is to consider the different possible constructions (which may be two or more) and then consider who

---

right not to be discriminated against on the on the ground of "*birth or other status*", protected by article 14.

11 See e.g. *PQ v RS* [2019] EWHC 1643 (Ch), in which Chief Master Marsh expressed no view as to whether *Re Hand* had been correctly decided (at [24]).

12 [2012] EWHC 732 (Ch).

would benefit under each possible construction, as illustrated by the following examples.

Example 7

In 1968 Dr Bartolo settled a valuable investment portfolio to be held on trust for Marcellina for life, and following her death "*for such child or children of mine as shall then be living, if more than one in equal shares absolutely*", and in default for Count Almaviva absolutely.

Dr Bartolo had only one child, Figaro, who was born out of wedlock.

Following Marcellina's death, there are two possible constructions:

(a) Figaro qualifies as a "*child*" of Dr Bartolo and is therefore entitled to the trust fund; or

(b) Figaro does not qualify as a "*child*" of Dr Bartolo because he is illegitimate, and the trust fund therefore passes to Count Almaviva.

The affected beneficiaries are therefore:

(a) Figaro; and

(b) Count Almaviva.

Example 8[13]

Rigoletto and his late wife owned their home as tenants in common in equal shares. By her will, she left her 50% share in the property to her daughter, Gilda. After receiving tax advice, in 2005 Gilda settled the 50% share in the property she had inherited from her mother on trust for Rigoletto for life, and in remainder for herself, subject to an overriding discretionary power of appointment in favour of a class including herself, her spouse and her children and remoter issue.

---

13 This example is loosely based on the facts of *Millar v Millar* [2018] EWHC 1926 (Ch).

Rigoletto and Gilda have recently changed advisors and their new solicitors, Marullo & Co, have discovered that the 2005 trust deed contains a settlor exclusion clause.

There are two possible constructions:

(a) the settlor exclusion clause applies and takes precedence over Gilda's interests; or

(b) the settlor exclusion clause does not apply.

The affected beneficiaries are therefore:

(a) Rigoletto;

(b) Gilda; and

(c) the discretionary class of Gilda's spouse and her children and remoter issue.

<u>Example 9</u>

Shortly before his death, Sarastro executed a deed of trust by which he settled a temple he owned on trust for Pamina for life and thereafter to "*those members of the Enlightened Brotherhood to whom I was particularly close*". A few weeks later he died intestate.

The issue is whether the gift in remainder:

(a) is valid and takes effect; or

(b) is void for uncertainty, and thus gives rise to a resulting trust and in turn a partial intestacy.

The affected beneficiaries are therefore:

(a) the members of the intended class; and

(b) Sarastro's intestacy beneficiaries.

If the construction problem affects the amount of tax payable, some thought should be given to whether it is also necessary to involve HMRC.

The corollary to the above is that trustees should bear in mind that they have no personal interest in how the construction problem is resolved between the affected beneficiaries. It is generally not for the trustees to try to second guess what the settlor might have intended, nor to form a view as to which of the affected beneficiaries is more 'worthy' or 'deserving'. The trustees should remain neutral and impartial, and simply do what they are told, either by a unanimous binding agreement reached by all of the affected beneficiaries, or by the court.

4.2.2. Can the problem be resolved by agreement?

In principle, a construction problem can be resolved by the unanimous agreement of all of the beneficiaries affected by it. Therefore, once the trustees have identified all of the affected beneficiaries, the next question they should ask themselves is: can the problem be resolved by agreement?

Suppose that in Example 7 above Figaro and Count Almaviva reach an agreement as to how to share the trust fund between them. They are the only two parties affected by the uncertainty. If they are able to agree what should happen to the trust fund, then provided they are both capacitous adults, they can resolve the construction problem between themselves without having to go to court. The trustees' only concern will be to ensure that the agreement is properly documented so that they cannot later be criticised by Figaro or Count Almaviva for acting in accordance with it.

Resolving the problem by agreement is usually significantly cheaper and quicker than asking the court to do so. As indicated above, if the construction problem affects the amount of tax payable, some thought should be given to whether it is also necessary to obtain the agreement of HMRC.

In practice, construction problems are generally only resolved by agreement in the most straightforward cases. Two reasons can be identified for this. First, beneficiaries often have different views about what the settlor did or did not intend, and are therefore simply unable to reach an agreement. Secondly, to avoid exposing themselves to potential personal liability to disappointed beneficiaries, trustees must obtain the binding consent of all of the beneficiaries who are affected by the construction problem. This will not be possible if the construction problem affects beneficiaries who are minors, unborn, lack capacity and/or cannot be found. As those types of beneficiaries are unable to give the trustees their binding consent, in cases in which they are affected, the court's intervention is likely to be necessary.

A useful way to explore whether the construction problem can be resolved by agreement is for the trustees, who are often the first to spot the problem, to obtain advice from counsel on the construction problem and then share that advice with all affected beneficiaries and canvass their views. If the trust incorporates clause 12.3 of the STEP Standard Provisions (2nd edition), the trustees should consider obtaining the advice of counsel of "*at least five years' standing*" if they want to rely on the protection from liability afforded by that clause.[14]

---

14 Clause 12.3 and the following two clauses provide:

12.3 A Trustee shall not be liable for acting in accordance with the advice of counsel, of at least five years' standing, with respect to the Trust. The Trustees may in particular conduct legal proceedings in accordance with such advice without obtaining a court order. A Trustee may recover from the Trust Fund any expenses where he has acted in accordance with such advice.

12.4 Clause 12.3 does not apply:

12.4.1 in relation to a Trustee who knows or has reasonable cause to suspect that the advice was given in ignorance of material facts;

12.4.2 if proceedings are pending to obtain the decision of the court on the matter;

12.4.3 in relation to a Trustee who has a personal interest in the subject matter of the advice; or

12.4.4 in relation to a Trustee who has committed a breach of trust relating to the subject matter of the advice.

12.5 Clause 12.3 does not prejudice any right of any Person to follow property or income into the hands of any Person, other than a purchaser, who may have received it.

This process should help both the trustees and all the affected beneficiaries to understand their respective positions, which in turn should inform all involved whether there is any hope of the construction problem being resolved by agreement and, if so, how this might be achieved. Depending on the circumstances, the affected beneficiaries may wish to try to reach an agreement by, for example, negotiating in correspondence, at a round-table meeting or at a mediation.

As indicated above, trustees should bear in mind that they have no personal interest in how the construction problem is resolved between the affected beneficiaries. Their focus should be to ensure:

(a) that they obtain the binding consent of all affected beneficiaries so they are protected from potential personal liability for breach of trust (i.e. for having distributed to the wrong person); and

(b) that the agreement is one which the trustees can in fact implement. For example, the trustees should consider whether the agreement has tax consequences and, if so, how these should be addressed.

However, if all affected beneficiaries manage to reach a binding agreement which the trustees can implement, it is not for the trustees to 'approve' or 'disapprove' of it in any moral or ethical sense, e.g. on the basis that they think the settlor would or would not have liked it. It also follows from this that trustees are generally not required to actively participate in any negotiations between the affected beneficiaries; indeed, trustees should ensure they do not incur unnecessary costs by doing so.

In cases in which professional negligence proceedings against the draftsman have also been threatened or are on foot, it may be sensible to try to compromise the professional negligence at the same time.

There are two further tools which can help achieve a pragmatic solution without the court's intervention in a suitable case. The first is the possibility of the trustees agreeing to distribute on a particular basis provided the recipient beneficiaries in return provide the trustees with suitable indemnities, possibly backed by security. Such indemnities would be designed to protect the trustees against the risk that they may be personally liable to disappointed beneficiaries if the basis on which they have distributed subsequently turns out to be wrong. The second is the possibility of obtaining insurance to provide the trustees with that same protection.

Whether either of these tools is a useful one will depend on all of the particular surrounding circumstances. As a rather crude rule of thumb, it is suggested that the greater the financial value of the construction problem, the less likely these tools are to provide a practical solution. This is because the greater the amount of money that turns on the construction problem, the greater the potential liability of the trustees, and thus the more nervous both the beneficiaries and any insurance company will be in providing trustees with adequate protection. Further, in high value cases there is less of a risk of the trust fund being significantly depleted by the costs involved in making a court application, which might also point towards a court application being the better option.

4.2.3. Professional negligence

If the trust instrument was professionally prepared, it may be possible to argue that the construction problem amounts to professional negligence by the draftsman. If so, a professional negligence claim against the draftsman is usually threatened, and sometimes issued, before a construction claim is brought.

Depending on the circumstances, if both the professional negligence claim and the construction claim have merit, the draftsman's insurers might agree to fund the construction claim, particularly if the costs involved in doing so are likely to be lower than their potential exposure in the event the professional negligence claim is successful.[15]

15 See e.g. the will rectification case of *Re Bimson* [2010] EWHC 3679 (Ch) at [23].

4.2.4. Court intervention: section 48 of the Administration of Justice Act 1985

A construction problem will usually be incapable of resolution by agreement without the court's intervention for one of two reasons (and sometimes both):

(a) all affected beneficiaries cannot reach an agreement; or

(b) all adult capacitous affected beneficiaries have reached an agreement, but the problem also affects beneficiaries who are minors, unborn, lack capacity and/or cannot be found.

Section 48 of the Administration of Justice Act 1985 ("AJA") contains a mechanism which can be useful in the latter situation (but not the former). The section provides:

> ***48.— Power of High Court to authorise action to be taken in reliance on counsel's opinion.***
>
> *(1) Where—*
>
> *(a) any question of construction has arisen out of the terms of a will or a trust; and*
>
> *(b) an opinion in writing given by a person who has a 10 year High Court qualification, within the meaning of section 71 of the Courts and Legal Services Act 1990, has been obtained on that question by the personal representatives or trustees under the will or trust,*
>
> *the High Court may, on the application of the personal representatives or trustees and without hearing argument, make an order authorising those persons to take such steps in reliance on the said opinion as are specified in the order.*
>
> *(2) The High Court shall not make an order under subsection (1) if it appears to the court that a dispute exists which would make it inappropriate for the court to make the order without hearing argument.*

There are two important points to note in relation to this mechanism. First, the procedure cannot be used where "*a dispute exists which would make it inappropriate for the court to make the order without hearing argument*" (section 48(2) AJA). That will be generally be the case where two or more affected beneficiaries are actively advancing two or more competing constructions, both of which are "*reasonably tenable*"[16]. However, it may also be the case where two conflicting opinions have been obtained from two different counsel as to the correct construction and the court feels it cannot resolve the conflict without hearing argument, as in *Greenwold v Pike.*[17]

Secondly, it is important to understand the nature of an order made under section 48 AJA and distinguish it from an order made at the conclusion of a contested construction claim (which is considered in the next section). An order made under section 48 AJA permits the trustees to proceed in accordance with counsel's opinion, and protects them from personal liability for breach of trust if counsel's opinion later turns out to be wrong. However, it does not require the court to determine the construction problem itself, nor therefore to decide whether counsel's opinion is correct. It is therefore an order which is akin to a *Re Benjamin*[18] order (which authorises PRs to proceed on the footing that certain facts which cannot be established with certainty are correct).[19]

The significance of this is that an order made under section 48 AJA therefore leaves open the possibility that an affected beneficiary may subsequently[20] bring a contested construction claim and the court may

16 Paragraph 29.35 of the Chancery Guide. The paragraph, which is set out in full below, provides that the court may order a party who disagreed with the opinion when having "*no reasonably tenable argument [to the] contrary*" to pay "*all or part of any costs thrown away*".

17 [2007] EWHC 2202 (Ch).

18 [1902] 1 Ch. 723.

19 The classic example is an order authorising PRs to distribute the estate on the footing that a beneficiary who cannot be found predeceased the testator (which were the circumstances in *Re Benjamin* itself).

20 E.g. after he has attained majority.

at that stage determine that the opinion from counsel (in accordance with which the trustees have proceeded) is wrong. If this were to happen, the trustees will be protected from personal liability for breach of trust because they have acted as authorised by the court's order (viz. in accordance with counsel's opinion). However, it would be open to the disappointed beneficiary to try to recover from the recipient beneficiaries any property which was distributed to them in accordance with the construction which the court has subsequently determined is wrong (subject to any applicable defences, such as laches and limitation).[21]

The question whether the mechanism provided by section 48 AJA should be used despite the fact that it carries this risk is generally answered by weighing up that risk against the costs saving in not having a fully contested construction claim. The mechanism provided by section 48 AJA is likely to be attractive if the trust fund is small and the capacitous adult beneficiaries are therefore keen to ensure that it is not depleted by a fully contested construction claim and/or the circumstances suggest that the risk of any beneficiary subsequently bringing a challenge is small or negligible. On the other hand, if the trust fund is large and/or it is thought that there is a serious risk that a beneficiary may subsequently bring a challenge, it may be worth incurring the extra cost of having a fully contested construction claim so as to have the construction problem resolved once and for all. For a rare example of a reported judgment which led to the making of an order under section 48 AJA, see *Re Duffy*.[22]

The CPR contain some procedural rules which apply to a claim for an order under section 48 AJA. Such a claim must be made in the High Court[23] and must be brought in the Chancery Division,[24] i.e. what has

21 The leading authority on this difficult topic remains the House of Lords decision in *Ministry of Health v Simpson* [1951] AC 251. In relation to the limitation period applicable to this sort of claim, see *Davies v Sharples* [2006] EWHC 362 (Ch).

22 [2013] EWHC 2395 (Ch).

23 This is required by section 48(1) AJA itself, which confers jurisdiction to make the relevant order on the High Court.

24 CPR rule 64.1(3).

now become the Property, Trusts and Probate List (ChD) of the Business and Property Courts of England and Wales. It must be brought by the trustees[25] and can be brought either in the Rolls Building in London or in one of the District Registries (Birmingham, Bristol, Cardiff, Leeds, Liverpool, Manchester, Newcastle-upon-Tyne, Preston, Mold and Caernarfon).[26]

Rule 64.3 CPR requires such a claim to be made by way of a CPR Part 8 claim form.[27] Paragraph 5 of CPR Practice Direction 64A provides:[28]

> *A Part 8 claim form for an application by trustees under section 48 of the Administration of Justice Act 1985 (power of High Court to authorise action to be taken in reliance on legal opinion) may be issued without naming a defendant, under rule 8.2A. No separate application for permission under rule 8.2A need be made.*

Chapter 29 of the Chancery Guide provides the following detailed procedural guidance, which helpfully lists the topics which need to be addressed in the witness statement filed in support of the claim:[29]

> ***Applications under section 48 of the Administration of Justice Act 1985***
>
> *29.29 Applications under section 48 of the Administration of Justice Act 1985 should be made by Part 8 claim form without naming a*

25 This is required by section 48(1) AJA itself, which refers to "*the application of the personal representatives or trustees*".

26 Paragraph 30.1 of the Chancery Guide. Chapter 30 of the Chancery Guide contains helpful information regarding Chancery business outside London, including contact details of the various District Registries.

27 CPR rule 64.3 applies to claims under section 48 AJA as a result of CPR rule 64.2(a).

28 Consistently with this, CPR rule 64.4 expressly states that its provisions (which govern who should be a party to a claim) do not apply to a claim under section 48 AJA.

29 This derives (with necessary modifications) from *Practice Direction (Chancery: Construction Summons)* [1987] 1 WLR 251.

defendant, under rule 8.2A. No separate application for permission under rule 8.2A need be made.

29.30 The claim should be supported by a witness statement or affidavit to which are exhibited: (a) copies of all relevant documents;

(b) instructions to a person with a 10-year High Court qualification within the meaning of the Courts and Legal Services Act 1990 ("the qualified person");

(c) the qualified person's opinion; and

(d) draft terms of the desired order.

The application is for an order to authorise the trustees to act on the basis of a legal opinion, which may deal with construction issues; it should not seek a decision of the court itself on the construction of any instrument.

29.31 The witness statement or affidavit (or exhibits thereto) should state:

(a) the reason for the application;

(b) the names of all persons who are, or may be, affected by the order sought;

(c) all surrounding circumstances admissible and relevant in construing the document;

(d) the date of qualification of the qualified person and his or her experience in the construction of trust documents;

(e) the approximate value of the fund or property in question;

(f) whether it is known to the applicant that a dispute exists and, if so, details of such dispute; and

(g) what steps are proposed to be taken in reliance on the opinion.

> *29.32 When the file is placed before the Master he or she will consider whether the evidence is complete and, if it is, whether it is appropriate for the Master to deal with the matter, or to send the file to the Judge.*
>
> *29.33 The Master or Judge will consider the papers and, if necessary, direct service of notices under CPR rule 19.8A or request further information. If the court is satisfied that the order sought is appropriate, it will be made and sent to the claimant.*
>
> *29.34 If following service of notices under rule 19.8A any acknowledgment of service is received, the claimant must apply to the Master (on notice to the parties who have so acknowledged service) for directions. If the claimant desires to pursue the application to the court, the Master will ordinarily direct that the case proceeds as a Part 8 claim.*
>
> *29.35 If on the hearing of the claim the court is of the opinion that any party who entered an acknowledgment of service has no reasonably tenable argument contrary to the qualified person's opinion, in the exercise of the court's discretion it may order such party to pay all or part of any costs thrown away.*

Because applications pursuant to section 48 AJA are only suitable in non-contentious cases (as explained above), the incidence of the costs of the proceedings is also likely to be agreed in advance between the trustees and the adult capacitous affected beneficiaries. The usual agreement is likely to be that the costs of the proceedings will be borne by the trust as an administration expense. As the only active parties will be the trustees and the application must be uncontested (because the procedure is otherwise unsuitable), the costs should be relatively modest.

4.2.5. Court intervention: construction claim in the Chancery Division

If the affected beneficiaries cannot reach an agreement and the mechanism provided by section 48 AJA cannot be used or is considered undesirable,[30] the solution will be to ask the court to resolve the construction problem by way of a contested construction claim.

Starting the claim

A claim asking the court to resolve a construction problem is a claim "*for the court to determine [a] question arising in (i) the administration of the estate of a deceased person; or (ii) the execution of a trust*" within CPR rule 64.2(a). Indeed, it is highly likely to be one of the types of claims which are listed in paragraph 1(1) of CPR Practice Direction 64A as examples of claims which may be made under CPR rule 64.2(a), viz.:

(1) a claim for the determination of any of the following questions –

(a) any question as to who is included in any class of persons having –

(i) a claim against the estate of a deceased person;

(ii) a beneficial interest in the estate of such a person; or

(iii) a beneficial interest in any property subject to a trust;

(b) any question as to the rights or interests of any person claiming –

(i) to be a creditor of the estate of a deceased person;

(ii) to be entitled under a will or on the intestacy of a deceased person; or

(iii) to be beneficially entitled under a trust;

30 E.g. because it is desirable to see the construction problem resolved once and for all.

As a result, Section I of CPR Part 64 applies to such a claim, which in turn means the claim must be made by issuing a CPR Part 8 claim form.[31]

The claim is started by filing a CPR Part 8 claim form and accompanying evidence (considered below). No particulars of claim are required.[32] Claims brought by CPR Part 8 are automatically allocated to the multi-track.[33]

Claim form N208 should be used.[34] CPR rule 8.2 provides that the claim form must state:

(a) that CPR Part 8 applies;

(b) the question which the claimant wants the court to decide, or the remedy which the claimant is seeking and the legal basis for the claim to that remedy;

(c) if the claim is being made under an enactment, what that enactment is;

(d) if the claimant is claiming in a representative capacity, what that capacity is; and

(e) if the defendant is sued in a representative capacity, what that capacity is.

Although in some cases rectification will not be relevant, claims for construction and rectification are often brought in the alternative.[35] A construction problem may also arise in the context of another dispute,

31 CPR rule 64.3.

32 CPR rule 8.9(a), which disapplies CPR Part 16; see also paragraph 9.4 of the Chancery Guide.

33 CPR rule 8.9(c); see also paragraph 9.4 of the Chancery Guide.

34 Paragraph 4.2 of CPR Practice Direction 8A; see also paragraph 9.5 of the Chancery Guide.

35 See e.g. *Millar v Millar* [2018] EWHC 1926 (Ch) and *Armstrong v Armstrong* [2019] EWHC 2259 (Ch).

such as a professional negligence claim. In these sorts of circumstances, the procedural rules governing any other claim must also be borne in mind. Where the construction problem is one of several aspects in dispute, it may be worth considering whether the court should be asked to deal with any aspect as a preliminary issue.[36]

Limitation

No limitation period applies to construction claims. However, a time limit or limitation period may be relevant if the dispute involves one or more other claims to which a time limit or limitation period does apply, such as a professional negligence claim.

Which court

The County Court appears to have jurisdiction to determine a construction problem if the value of the trust fund does not exceed £350,000.[37] However, in practice most construction claims are issued in the High Court, where they must be brought in the Chancery Division,[38] i.e. what has now become the Property, Trusts and Probate List (ChD) of the Business and Property Courts of England and Wales. If it is to be issued in the High Court, a construction claim can be issued either in the Rolls Building in London or in one of the District Registries (Birmingham, Bristol, Cardiff, Leeds, Liverpool, Manchester, Newcastle-upon-Tyne, Preston, Mold and Caernarfon).[39]

---

36 As was done in the context of wills in *Burnard v Burnard* [2014] EWHC 340 (Ch) (see [7]) and *Tish v Olley* [2018] EWHC 1069 (Ch) (see [1]).

37 Section 23 of the County Courts Act 1984 and article 3 of the County Court Jurisdiction Order 2014 (SI 2014/503). This assumes that the relevant construction claim is a type of "*proceedings for the execution of any trust*" within section 23(b).

38 CPR rule 64.1(3). See also Section 61 and paragraphs 1(c) and 1(d) of Schedule 1 to the Senior Courts Act 1981 and paragraphs 29.2(c) and 29.2(d) of the Chancery Guide.

39 Paragraph 30.1 of the Chancery Guide. Chapter 30 of the Chancery Guide contains helpful information regarding Chancery business outside London, including contact details of the various District Registries.

Evidence

The claimant must file the evidence on which he intends to rely when his claim form is issued[40] (unless the claimant only intends to rely on the evidence contained in the claim form itself, which it is suggested is unlikely to be the case in construction claims). This will generally be in the form of one or more witness statements.[41] The claimant's evidence must be served on the defendant with the claim form.[42]

The contents of the witness statement(s) will of course depend on the circumstances of the particular case, and on whether the claimant is a neutral trustee who is simply explaining the construction problem to the court, or an interested beneficiary who is advancing a particular construction. In general terms, the topics which one should consider covering in the evidence filed in support of the claim are likely to be:

(a) the claimant's role and the capacity in which he brings the claim;

(b) the factual background (or 'factual matrix');

(c) the construction problem;

(d) how the trust document was prepared;

(e) the position of the other interested parties.

If the trust document was professionally prepared, some thought should be given as to whether evidence should be obtained from the draftsman responsible for preparing it (if available). As indicated above, it must be borne in mind that evidence of the settlor's subjective intention is not admissible to help resolve construction problems.

---

40 CPR rule 8.5(1) and paragraph 7.1 of CPR Practice Direction 8A; see also paragraph 9.6 of the Chancery Guide.

41 Paragraph 7.2 of CPR Practice Direction 8A.

42 CPR rule 8.5(2).

It should also be borne in mind that the CPR requires witness statements to be in the witness's own words[43] and that construction problems are usually issues of law rather than fact. The temptation to include in a witness statement extensive legal submissions and references to case law should generally be resisted, particularly in witness statements of lay witnesses; these are properly a matter for skeleton arguments and submissions.[44]

Disclosure

CPR Practice Direction 51U contains a new 'disclosure pilot' which sets out detailed rules concerning disclosure that apply to claims in the Business and Property Courts of England and Wales. The pilot came into force on 1st January 2019 and applies to both existing claims and to new claims issued after that date.[45] It will remain in force for two years.[46]

A Practice Note by Chief Master Marsh dated 27th March 2019[47] clarifies that the pilot "*does not directly apply to Part 8 claims because Part 8 contains its own regime for the disclosure of documents that are relied on by the parties*".[48] In particular, the pilot's new concept of 'Initial Disclosure' does not apply to CPR Part 8 claims.[49] However, paragraph 5 of the Practice Note explains:

> "*The court has power to make an order for extended disclosure under the pilot in a case proceeding under Part 8. It will adopt such ele-*

---

43 Paragraph 18.1 of CPR Practice Direction 32; see also paragraph 19.2 of the Chancery Guide.

44 See paragraph 19.3 of the Chancery Guide.

45 Paragraph 1.2 of CPR Practice Direction 51U.

46 Paragraph 1.2 of CPR Practice Direction 51U.

47 Available here: https://www.judiciary.uk/wp-content/uploads/2019/03/Practice-Note-27_03_19.pdf

48 Paragraph 3 of the Practice Note.

49 Paragraph 5.1 of CPR Practice Direction 51U; see also paragraph 4 of the Practice Note.

> *ments of the Practice Direction as are appropriate to the case and the scope of disclosure that is sought. The party requesting disclosure will need to identify the issues for disclosure and the Model or Models that apply. It is not expected that the full procedure for extended disclosure, including completion of all elements of the Disclosure Review Document, will normally be required.*"

Given the disclosure obligations already imposed by CPR Part 8, it is suggested that orders for extended disclosure pursuant to the pilot are likely to be rare in construction claims. Some support of this can be found in paragraph 17.74 of the Chancery Guide: "*It is rare for orders for disclosure to be made in a Part 8 claim because for most types of Part 8 claim it should suffice for the parties to rely upon the documents they exhibit*".

Prospective (or pre-emptive) costs orders

In some construction cases it may be appropriate to consider at an early stage of the proceedings whether a mechanism should be put in place for the costs of one or more of the parties to be paid out of the estate or trust fund in any event irrespective of the outcome.[50] This can be either by way of a contractual agreement by the trustees or by a so-called prospective (or pre-emptive) costs order by the court. This issue tends to arise primarily in pension cases, where an individual pension scheme member may be made a party to complex litigation as representative of other scheme members, and it may be unfair for him to have to bear his costs personally at least until the conclusion of the litigation, which can create a cash flow problem.[51] However, the issue is unlikely to arise in claims concerning the correct construction of a family trust.

Where the issue does arise, the eight sub-paragraphs of paragraph 6 of CPR Practice Direction 64A contain some detailed guidance about pro-

50 The costs orders which are likely to be made at the conclusion of the proceedings are considered at "*Costs*" below.

51 The principles governing the making of a prospective costs order have been considered in a line of pensions cases which includes *McDonald v Horn* [1995] 1 All ER 961 and *IBM United Kingdom Pensions Trust Ltd v Metcalfe* [2012] EWHC 125 (Ch).

spective costs orders, as do paragraphs 29.19 and 29.20 of the Chancery Guide, and a model form of prospective costs order is appended to CPR Practice Direction 64A.

Costs management

CPR rule 3.12 now makes it clear that costs management does not apply to CPR Part 8 claims unless the court orders that it should pursuant to CPR rule 3.12(1A).[52] Paragraph 5(e) of CPR Practice Direction 3E provides that an order for costs management may be "*particularly appropriate*" in "*any Part 8 or other claims or applications involving a substantial dispute of fact and/or likely to require oral evidence and/or extensive disclosure*". A party seeking an order that costs management should apply to the proceedings should "*give notice to the other parties and the court well in advance of the directions hearing and explain, preferably in a witness statement, why such an order is sought*".[53]

In trust construction claims an obligation to file and serve a costs budget may nonetheless be imposed by paragraph 5 of CPR Practice Direction 3F. Significantly, the obligation applies early on in the proceedings when the party files his evidence (as explained below).

Section II of Practice Direction 3F is entitled '*Costs Capping in Relation to Trust Funds*'; paragraph 5 is the Section's only paragraph. It supplements CPR rules 3.19 to 3.21 and paragraphs 1 to 4 of Practice Direction 3F,[54] which govern costs capping orders generally. The provisions of the paragraph are designed to "*enable the parties to consider whether to apply for, and the court to consider whether to make of its own initiative, a costs capping order in relation to proceedings relating to trust funds*".[55]

The obligation to file and serve a costs budget is imposed by paragraphs 5.4 and 5.5, which provide:

52 In relation to which see also and paragraph 2 of CPR Practice Direction 3E.

53 Paragraph 17.71 of the Chancery Guide.

54 Paragraph 5.3 of CPR Practice Direction 3F.

55 Paragraph 5.2 of CPR Practice Direction 3F.

5.4 Any party to such proceedings who intends to apply for an order for the payment of costs out of the trust fund must file and serve on all other parties written notice of that intention together with a budget of the costs likely to be incurred by that party.

5.5 The documents mentioned in paragraph 5.4 must be filed and served –

[…]

(b) in a Part 8 claim, with the evidence (or, if a defendant does not intend to serve and file evidence, with the acknowledgement of service).

Finally, paragraph 5.6 provides that when the proceedings first come before the court for directions, the court may make a costs capping order of its own initiative, whether or not any party has applied for such an order.

In most construction claims, all parties will seek an order that their costs of the proceedings be paid out of the trust fund[56] – or at least will "*intend*" to apply for such an order when the proceedings are started and/or when the relevant party files his evidence. This appears to trigger the obligation (imposed by paragraph 5.4) to file and serve on all other parties both "*written notice of that intention*" and a budget "*of the costs likely to be incurred by that party*".

On the other hand, costs capping orders are rare in construction claims (other than in pension cases), and anecdotal evidence suggests that this provision is rarely (if ever) complied with or enforced in practice in such claims. It is also unclear what the sanction for non-compliance is (if any). However, the provision is there, and practitioners ought to be aware of it, at least unless and until it is amended by the Civil Procedure Rule Committee.

56 See further under "Costs" below.

Parties

Determining who should be made a party to a construction claim often requires some careful thought. In general, it is useful to bear in mind that:

(a) the court will expect someone to argue in favour of each of the various possible constructions (which may be two or more);

(b) it is generally desirable to take steps to ensure that everyone affected by the construction problem will be bound by the court's order;[57]

(c) the trustees should generally remain neutral in their capacity as trustees and not argue in favour of one of the possible constructions;

(d) however, where the claim is unopposed and/or no beneficiary with a contrary interest wishes to take an active role, it may be incumbent on the trustees as "*watchdog*"[58] for unrepresented or unborn beneficiaries to assist the court by "*bringing to the court's attention any relevant legal propositions or argument affecting the position of unrepresented beneficiaries or parties*"[59] to ensure the court is able to reach the right result; and

(e) if the construction problem affects the amount of tax payable, it may be necessary to notify, and perhaps even join, HMRC.

As a starting point, CPR rule 64.4(1) provides the following rules in relation to who the parties should be:

---

57 See e.g. *Millar v Millar* [2018] EWHC 1926 (Ch), in which the court noted that the claimants had not joined or sought a representation order in respect of a class of spouses who had a contingent interest, who would therefore not be bound by the court's order (at [9]).

58 *Re Druce's Settlement Trusts* [1962] 1 WLR 363 at 370.

59 *State Street Bank & Trust Co v Sompo Japan Insurance Inc* [2010] EWHC 1461 (Ch) at [30]. See also e.g. *Re Hemming* [2008] EWHC 8565 (Ch) at [40].

(1) In a claim to which this Section applies, other than an application under section 48 of the Administration of Justice Act 1985 –

(a) all the trustees must be parties;

(b) if the claim is made by trustees, any of them who does not consent to being a claimant must be made a defendant; and

(c) the claimant may make parties to the claim any persons with an interest in or claim against the estate, or an interest under the trust, who it is appropriate to make parties having regard to the nature of the order sought.

The claim can generally be brought either by the trustees, or by one or more of the beneficiaries.

All trustees must be parties (CPR rule 64.4(1)(a) and (b) above), which is unsurprising given that they need to be bound by the order. What may be less clear is how to ensure that all affected beneficiaries are joined or are otherwise bound by the court's order.

In cases involving a limited number of affected beneficiaries, the answer may be fairly straightforward. The simplest example is where there are two possible constructions and the only affected beneficiaries are capacitous adults, as in Example 7 above (assuming Figaro and Count Almaviva are capacitous adults). In such cases, either the trustees bring the claim and join the affected beneficiaries as defendants,[60] or one of the affected beneficiaries can bring the claim and join the trustees and the other affected beneficiaries as defendants. In either case, the trustees should generally adopt a neutral position and let the affected beneficiaries advance the two alternative construction arguments. Exceptionally, the particular circumstances may mean that it is convenient for the trustees to advance one of the construction arguments; if so, they should ensure that they do so without jeopardising their neutrality.[61]

---

60 See e.g. *Re Erskine 1948 Trust* [2012] EWHC 732 (Ch) at [5].

61 See e.g. the will case of *Re Wippell* [2018] EWHC 730 (Ch) at [8].

Where one or more of the affected beneficiaries is a minor or lacks capacity and is to be a party to the claim, that beneficiary will need a litigation friend.[62] CPR Part 21 contains detailed guidance on the procedure for the appointment of a litigation friend.

On the other hand, the position may be more complicated where the construction problem affects a large number of beneficiaries (e.g. large classes) and/or where some of the affected beneficiaries are minors, unborn, lack capacity and/or cannot be found. In Example 9 above, the class of intestacy beneficiaries may be large and/or its members difficult to trace, and it may be difficult to ascertain all members of the other class. In these sorts of cases, there is likely to be a tension between ensuring on the one hand that everyone who has an interest is properly represented and has an opportunity to be heard, and trying on the other to avoid depleting the estate or trust by incurring significant costs tracing and communicating with large classes of beneficiaries.

How the balance should be struck will inevitably depend on the circumstances of the particular case. In complicated cases, the provisions of CPR rule 8.2A, rule 19.7 and/or 19.8A can be of considerable assistance.[63] These govern respectively the circumstances in which a CPR Part 8 claim may be issued without naming a defendant, the appointment of a party to represent the interests of others, and the service of proceedings and/or orders on non-parties so as to bind them.

CPR rule 8.2A provides:

> *Issue of claim form without naming defendants*
>
> *(1) A practice direction may set out circumstances in which a claim form may be issued under this Part without naming a defendant.*

---

62 CPR rule 21.2(1).

63 The relevance of these rules to claims concerning trusts is highlighted by paragraphs 29.12, 29.15 and 29.16 of the Chancery Guide, considered below. Note that CPR rule 19.6, which is entitled "*Representative parties with same interest*", does not apply to claims "*about [...] (b) property subject to a trust, or (c) the meaning of a document, including a statute*": see CPR rules 19.6(5) and 19.7(1).

> *(2) The practice direction may set out those cases in which an application for permission must be made by application notice before the claim form is issued.*
>
> *(3) The application notice for permission –*
>
> *(a) need not be served on any other person; and*
>
> *(b) must be accompanied by a copy of the claim form that the applicant proposes to issue.*
>
> *(4) Where the court gives permission it will give directions about the future management of the claim.*

In fact, neither of the two Practice Directions to CPR Part 8[64] deal with the circumstances in which a claim form may be issued without naming a defendant. However, paragraphs 7.15 and 7.16 of the Chancery Guide provide the following guidance:

> *Application to issue the claim form without naming defendants*
>
> *7.15 CPR rule 8.2A permits the court to make an order in relation to a Part 8 claim (not a Part 7 claim) entitling the claimant to issue the claim without naming defendants. An order might be appropriate, for example, where the court is asked to make an order to assist executors who are unable to locate beneficiaries named in a will.*
>
> *7.16 The application is made by application notice issued at Chancery Chambers. It will then be placed before the assigned Master. Alternatively in a simple case the Master may be willing to deal with it at 10.30 or 2.00 as an Application without Notice ("AWN").*

Similarly, paragraph 29.12 of the Chancery Guide provides:

64 viz. Practice Directions 8A and 8B.

> *29.12 Rule 8.2A (issue of claim form without naming a defendant) can also be relevant [to applications by trustees for directions in relation to the administration of a trust]. Normally, permission to issue the claim form under rule 8.2A is required (see Chapter 7 paragraphs 15-16 above). In urgent cases this can be obtained on an application without notice. But in some cases the claim form may be issued under rule 8.2A without first seeking permission.*

Paragraph 29.13 of the Chancery Guide explains that it may be appropriate to adopt this procedure where, for example, "*the only possible defendant(s) cannot be located (eg no address can be given, or it is unknown if they survive), or there are too many possible defendants*".[65] Paragraph 15.8 of the Chancery Guide indicates that such applications are generally considered by the Master as part of file work and that the application should "*explain carefully why the order is appropriate*".

CPR rule 19.7(2) provides:

> *The court may make an order appointing a person to represent any other person or persons in the claim where the person or persons to be represented –*
>
> *(a) are unborn;*
>
> *(b) cannot be found;*
>
> *(c) cannot easily be ascertained; or*
>
> *(d) are a class of persons who have the same interest in a claim and –*
>
> *(i) one or more members of that class are within sub-paragraphs (a), (b) or (c); or*

---

65 In so far as relevant, the paragraph provides: "*One example [of cases in which the claim form may be issued under rule 8.2A without first seeking permission] is where the only possible defendant(s) cannot be located (eg no address can be given, or it is unknown if they survive), or there are too many possible defendants. The Master will then give any directions required. Applications for Benjamin orders may also fall into this category, as well as applications for permission to distribute the estates of deceased Lloyds' names (see below). [...]*"

> *(ii) to appoint a representative would further the overriding objective.*

This caters for several different scenarios:

(a) is self-explanatory;

(b) covers situations in which it is clear who the affected beneficiary is, but (reasonable) attempts to find him have proved unsuccessful;

(c) covers situations in which it is not clear who the affected beneficiary is, nor can this be easily clarified;

(d) covers two alternative situations where a class of persons has the same interest in the claim:

 (i) is self-explanatory;

 (ii) is potentially wide and flexible. It can be used, for example, where there is a large class of affected beneficiaries scattered around the world, all of whom have the same interest, and it would further the overriding objective to appoint one of them to represent the whole class (e.g. by reducing procedural delay and costs) – ideally one who can be served within the jurisdiction.[66]

CPR rule 19.7(3) provides that an application for a representation order under CPR rule 19.7(2) may be made "*by any person who seeks to be appointed under the order or any party to the claim*", and may be made "*at any time before or after the claim has started*". CPR rule 19.7(4) provides that the application notice for such an order must be served on:

> *(a) all parties to the claim, if the claim has started;*

66 For an example, see *Public Trustee v Harrison* [2018] EWHC 166 (Ch) at [8].

(b) the person sought to be appointed, if that person is not the applicant or a party to the claim; and

(c) any other person as directed by the court.

It is important to note that where the court has made a representation order under CPR rule 19.7, the court's approval is required to settle the claim.[67] This is to safeguard the position of the represented parties and to ensure their representative does not enter into a compromise which is disadvantageous to them: CPR rule 19.7(6) gives the court jurisdiction to approve a settlement "*where it is satisfied that the settlement is for the benefit of all represented persons*".

Finally, CPR rule 19.8A provides:

Power to make judgements binding on non-parties

(1) This rule applies to any claim relating to –

[…]

(b) property subject to a trust; or

(c) the sale of any property.

(2) The court may at any time direct that notice of –

(a) the claim; or

(b) any judgment or order given in the claim,

be served on any person who is not a party but who is or may be affected by it.

(3) An application under this rule –

(a) may be made without notice; and

67 CPR rule 19.7(5).

(b) must be supported by written evidence which includes the reasons why the person to be served should be bound by the judgment in the claim.

(4) Unless the court orders otherwise –

(a) a notice of a claim or of a judgment or order under this rule must be –

(i) in the form required by the practice direction;

(ii) issued by the court; and

(iii) accompanied by a form of acknowledgment of service with any necessary modifications;

(b) a notice of a claim must also be accompanied by –

(i) a copy of the claim form; and

(ii) such other statements of case, witness statements or affidavits as the court may direct; and

(c) a notice of a judgment or order must also be accompanied by a copy of the judgment or order.

(5) If a person served with notice of a claim files an acknowledgment of service of the notice within 14 days he will become a party to the claim.

(6) If a person served with notice of a claim does not acknowledge service of the notice he will be bound by any judgment given in the claim as if he were a party.

(7) If, after service of a notice of a claim on a person, the claim form is amended so as substantially to alter the relief claimed, the court may direct that a judgment shall not bind that person unless a further notice, together with a copy of the amended claim form, is served on him.

(8) Any person served with a notice of a judgment or order under this rule –

(a) shall be bound by the judgment or order as if he had been a party to the claim; but

(b) may, provided he acknowledges service –

(i) within 28 days after the notice is served on him, apply to the court to set aside or vary the judgment or order; and

(ii) take part in any proceedings relating to the judgment or order.

(9) The following rules of Part 10 (acknowledgment of service) apply –

(a) rule 10.4; and

(b) rule 10.5, subject to the modification that references to the defendant are to be read as references to the person served with the notice.

(10) A notice under this rule is issued on the date entered on the notice by the court.

The procedure in CPR rule 19.8A can be useful to bind interested beneficiaries who do not want to take an active role in the proceedings, such as the adult children of an 'active' interested beneficiary who are content to simply support their parent's position. However, it suggests that it is unlikely to be a good idea to press on with the proceedings and to then try to rely on CPR rule 19.8A to serve a judgment or order on an interested beneficiary who it is thought will want to actively have a say. In such cases there is a risk that such a beneficiary will then apply to set aside the judgment or order (pursuant to CPR rule 19.8A(8)(b)) to, in effect, re-open the case to advance his argument, and this could significantly increase the overall costs. In this sort of situation it is likely to be preferable to ensure that such a beneficiary is able to actively participate from the outset.

It should be borne in mind that the issue of representation is likely to be considered by the court at the first directions hearing, at which creative and pragmatic solutions can be considered with the Master, particularly in complex cases.[68]

Service

The usual rules for service contained in the CPR – mostly in CPR Part 6 – apply to claims for the construction of a trust instrument. If it is necessary to seek the court's permission to serve the claim form out of the jurisdiction pursuant to CPR rule 6.36, the grounds listed in paragraph 3.1 of CPR Practice Direction 6B which are likely to be relevant are grounds (11) to (12A):

> *Claims about property within the jurisdiction*
>
> *(11) The subject matter of the claim relates wholly or principally to property within the jurisdiction, provided that nothing under this paragraph shall render justiciable the title to or the right to possession of immovable property outside England and Wales.*
>
> *Claims about trusts etc.*
>
> *(12) A claim is made in respect of a trust which is created [...] by a written instrument, or created orally and evidenced in writing, and which is governed by the law of England and Wales.*
>
> *(12A) A claim is made in respect of a trust which is created [...] by a written instrument, or created orally and evidenced in writing, and which provides that jurisdiction in respect of such a claim shall be conferred upon the courts of England and Wales.*

68 See e.g. the will case of *Re Harte* [2015] EWHC 2351 (Ch), in which the PRs were initially given permission to issue the construction and rectification claims without naming a defendant (pursuant to CPR rule 8.2A), and were then given directions as to the steps they should take to ascertain the intestacy beneficiaries (including by advertisement) and as to the parties to whom they should give notice of the proceedings pursuant to CPR rule 19.8A (see [3]-[4]).

Responding to the claim

A defendant who wishes to respond to the claim must file an acknowledgment of service in the relevant practice form (viz. form N210)[69] not more than 14 days after service of the claim form on him.[70] At the same time he must also serve his acknowledgment of service on the claimant and on any other party.[71] If he fails to do so, the defendant may attend the hearing of the claim but may not take part in the hearing unless the court gives permission.[72] The defendant must indicate in his acknowledgment of service whether he contests the claim, and if he seeks a different remedy from that set out in the claim form, what that remedy is.[73] If he wishes to object to the use of the CPR Part 8 procedure, he should also say so in his acknowledgment of service[74] – although this is likely to be rare in construction claims, as such claims must be started by issuing a Part 8 claim form[75] and tend not to involve substantial disputes of fact. There is no need to file a defence, as CPR Part 15 does not apply to claims brought pursuant to CPR Part 8.[76]

A defendant who wishes to rely on written evidence must file it when he files his acknowledgment of service,[77] and must at the same time serve a copy of his evidence on the other parties.[78] As the time limit for the defendant to do this is quite short (viz. 14 days from service of the

69 Paragraph 5.2 of CPR Practice Direction 8A.

70 CPR rule 8.3(1); see also paragraph 9.5 of the Chancery Guide. Note that different (longer) periods apply if the proceedings have been served on the defendant out of the jurisdiction: see CPR rules 8.3(3) and 10.3(2).

71 CPR rule 8.3(1).

72 CPR rule 8.4(2).

73 CPR rule 8.3(2).

74 CPR rule 8.8(1); see also paragraph 9.5 of the Chancery Guide.

75 CPR rule 64.3.

76 CPR rule 8.9(a) and paragraph 5.1 of CPR Practice Direction 8A; see also paragraph 9.6 of the Chancery Guide.

77 CPR rule 8.5(3) and paragraph 7.3 of CPR Practice Direction 8A; see also paragraph 9.6 of the Chancery Guide.

78 CPR rule 8.5(4).

claim on him), paragraph 7.5 of CPR Practice Direction 8A allows the parties to agree in writing to extend that time limit by up to "*14 days after the defendant files his acknowledgment of service*".[79] Such an agreement must be filed at court by the defendant at the same time as he files his acknowledgment of service.[80] Because of the somewhat awkward wording of paragraph 7.5(2)(b), it seems that in order to obtain the maximum time of 28 days from service of the claim form to file his evidence, a defendant must:

(a) first, agree in writing with the other parties that he may file his evidence 14 days after he files his acknowledgment of service; and then

(b) wait until the 14th day after he was served with the claim form, and on that day file both his acknowledgment of service and the written agreement.

This is because the 14-day extension runs from the date on which the defendant files his acknowledgment of service, as opposed to extending the period for filing of the defendant's evidence to 28 days from the date of service of the claim form on him.[81] The defendant may not rely on any written evidence which has not been served in accordance with the rules described above at the hearing of the claim unless the court gives permission.[82]

If a defendant requires more time to file his evidence, he should apply to the court for an extension of time by way of an application pursuant

---

79 Paragraph 7.5(2)(b) of CPR Practice Direction 8A; see also paragraph 9.6 of the Chancery Guide.

80 Paragraph 7.5(2)(a) of CPR Practice Direction 8A; see also paragraph 9.6 of the Chancery Guide.

81 Contrast the effect of filing an acknowledgment of service in CPR Part 7 claims, which is to extend the period within which the defendant must file his defence to 28 days from the date of service on him of the particulars of claim: CPR rule 15.4(1)(b).

82 CPR rule 8.6(1).

to CPR Part 23.[83] The Chancery Guide recognises that in substantial matters the time limits for evidence imposed by CPR Part 8 "*may be burdensome upon defendants*" and indicates that in such matters the court will normally be willing to grant a reasonable extension.[84] If the parties are in agreement that such an extension should be granted, the application should be made by filing a consent order.[85] If there is no agreement an application notice must be issued and listed for hearing unless the Master considers that the application may be dealt with without a hearing.[86] The Chancery Guide requires parties to "*at all times act co-operatively and agree reasonable requests for additional time*" and indicates that the court is "*likely to order the opposing party to pay the costs of a contested application for additional time where the opposition is unreasonable*".[87]

As for the claimant's evidence, the contents of any witness statement(s) adduced by a defendant will of course depend on the circumstances of the particular case. In general terms, the topics one should consider covering are likely to be the same as those to be covered by the claimant in his evidence (discussed above).

It is generally not possible to obtain judgment in default in a claim commenced by pursuant to CPR Part 8[88] or a claim which seeks declaratory relief,[89] and construction claims are usually both.

---

83 Paragraph 7.4 of CPR Practice Direction 8A; and see paragraph 9.7 of the Chancery Guide of the Chancery Guide.

84 Paragraph 9.7 of the Chancery Guide of the Chancery Guide.

85 *Ibid.*

86 *Ibid.*

87 *Ibid.*

88 CPR rules 8.1(5) and 12.2(b); see also paragraph 9.4 of the Chancery Guide.

89 Paragraph 12.3 of the Chancery Guide provides "*If the claimant seeks discretionary relief such as a declaration, rectification, an injunction or other similar relief the Master will usually require to be satisfied that such relief is necessary, and if so ought to be granted, and a full witness statement will usually be required. In cases of complexity the application notice may need to be listed. Declaratory relief and relief by way of rectification will not be granted without evidence and will not ordinarily be appropriate for resolution by way of judgment in default*"; see also paragraph 29.69

If the claim is unopposed and is brought by way of CPR Part 8 proceedings, it will generally be unnecessary to apply for summary judgment, and the claimant can instead ask the court to list the claim for a disposal hearing, as Chief Master Marsh explained in *Sovereign Trustees Ltd v Lewis*:[90]

> "*Part 8 claims are markedly different to Part 7 claims. Although there is no bar to issuing a Part 24 application [i.e. an application for summary judgment] in a Part 8 claim, it will rarely be necessary for the claimant to do so where it is seeking judgment on the whole of the claim. In part this is because the second limb of CPR 24.2 will normally have no application because there will be no 'trial' as such. Part 8 claims are normally resolved at a 'disposal hearing'. This is made clear by paragraph 8.1 of Practice Direction 8A which states:*
>
> *'8.1 The court may on the hearing date –*
>
> *(i) proceed to hear the case and dispose of the claim;*
>
> *(ii) give case management directions.'*
>
> *It follows that in most Part 8 claims, where the relief sought is unopposed, or cannot realistically be opposed, it will suffice for the claimant to ask the court to fix a disposal hearing at which the court may determine whether or not the relief sought by the claimant should be granted.*"

Claimant's evidence in reply

If the claimant wishes to rely on further written evidence in reply to the defendant's evidence, he must file it within 14 days of service of the defendant's evidence on him,[91] and he must also serve a copy of it on

of the Chancery Guide.

90 [2016] EWHC 2593 (Ch) at [3]. However, see also *Guthrie v Morel* [2015] EWHC 3172 (Ch), where summary judgment was granted in a contested will construction claim.

91 CPR rule 8.5(5); and see paragraph 9.6 of the Chancery Guide.

the other parties "*within the same time limit*".[92] As that time limit is also quite short, paragraph 7.5 of CPR Practice Direction 8A also allows the parties to agree in writing to extend it by up to 14 days; i.e. the maximum period which the parties can agree is that the claimant shall file his evidence in reply 28 days after service of the defendant's evidence on him.[93] Any such agreement should similarly be filed at court.[94] In the same way as a defendant, a claimant may not rely on any written evidence which has not been served in accordance with the rules described above at the hearing of the claim unless the court gives permission.[95]

If a claimant requires more time to file his evidence in reply to the defendant's, he too should apply to the court for an extension of time by way of an application pursuant to CPR Part 23.[96] The guidance contained in paragraph 9.7 of the Chancery Guide – which is considered above in the context of the defendant's evidence – applies equally to applications for extensions of time by claimants. In particular, parties should bear in mind that the court is likely to grant reasonable requests for extensions of time and expects parties to "*at all times act co-operatively and agree reasonable requests for additional time*" and may punish in costs a party who unreasonably opposes an application.[97]

Directions hearing

In some cases the court may give directions immediately after the claim has been issued, either on the application of a party or of its own initiative, which may include fixing a hearing date.[98] This is likely to happen

92 CPR rule 8.5(6).

93 Paragraph 7.5(2)(b) of CPR Practice Direction 8A; and see paragraph 9.6 of the Chancery Guide.

94 Although the CPR does not appear to require this, paragraph 9.7 of the Chancery Guide does.

95 CPR rule 8.6(1).

96 Paragraph 7.4 of CPR Practice Direction 8A.

97 Paragraph 9.7 of the Chancery Guide.

98 Paragraph 6.1 of CPR Practice Direction 8A.

particularly in cases which have been issued without naming a defendant pursuant to CPR rule 8.2A.[99] However, it is more usual for the claim to be referred to the Master[100] only after an acknowledgment of service has been filed or after the period for doing so has expired.[101]

At that stage the Master will consider whether the claim may be capable of being dealt with 'on the file', i.e. on the papers without a hearing.[102] This might be appropriate if the claim is undefended,[103] but in practice it is rare for contested construction claims to be dealt with in this way.

Instead, if no acknowledgment of service has been filed, the Master may "*sometimes override the provisions of Part 8 by directing that the defendant must file and serve an acknowledgment and evidence by a specified date failing which the defendant will not be entitled to play any part in the disposal hearing*".[104] Doing so is "*intended to make explicit for a [litigant in person] what is already set out in the CPR*".[105] If this route is taken, directions may be given to lead straight to disposal hearing (without a directions hearing being held first).

On the other hand, if an acknowledgment of service has been filed, the claim is likely to be listed for a directions hearing in the first instance,[106] and some directions may be given as to how the parties should prepare for it.

---

99 Paragraph 29.14 of the Chancery Guide.

100 Or to a District Judge of the High Court if the claim is in one of the District Registries.

101 Paragraph 6.2 of CPR Practice Direction 8A; see also paragraphs 9.10, 15.9 and 17.65 of the Chancery Guide.

102 Paragraph 17.65 of the Chancery Guide.

103 Paragraph 15.11 of the Chancery Guide. See e.g. *Millar v Millar* [2018] EWHC 1926 (Ch).

104 Paragraph 15.09 of the Chancery Guide.

105 *Ibid.*

106 Paragraphs 15.10 and 17.66 of the Chancery Guide.

At a directions hearing, the issues which the court is likely to consider are:[107]

(a) Evidence, including whether directions should be given for the filing of any further evidence (in addition to the evidence which will already have been filed by that point) and whether any witnesses should be required to attend to give oral evidence and be cross-examined at the disposal hearing.[108] In general, the CPR Part 8 procedure is designed for claims which do not involve substantial disputes of fact, and the starting point in CPR Part 8 claims seems to be that there should be no oral evidence at the disposal hearing unless the court orders otherwise.[109] Furthermore, claims concerning the construction of a trust instrument rarely turn on conflicting factual evidence, particularly given that extrinsic evidence of the settlor's subjective intention is inadmissible.[110] It is therefore rare for directions to be given for oral evidence and cross-examination in claims concerning the construction of trust instruments.

(b) Representation of the parties, such as whether any litigation friend needs to be appointed and/or whether any representation order should be made and/or notice given pursuant to CPR rule 19.8A (as to which, see <u>Parties</u> above).

---

107 See paragraph 17.74 of the Chancery Guide.

108 CPR rule 8.6(2) provides "*The court may require or permit a party to give oral evidence at the hearing*" and CPR rule 8.6(3) provides "*The court may give directions requiring the attendance for cross-examination of a witness who has given written evidence*".

109 See paragraph 9.3 of the Chancery Guide: "*Part 8 claims will generally be disposed of on written evidence without cross-examination. The witness statements with the claim form should be sufficient in most cases to define the issues*".

110 This can be contrasted with claims for the construction of wills, where such evidence may be admissible if section 21 of the Administration of Justice Act 1982 is engaged. See for example *Hives v Machin* [2017] EWHC 1414 (Ch), in which the judge heard and considered conflicting oral evidence as to the testatrix's intentions, but ultimately concluded that section 21 AJA was not engaged and that such evidence was therefore inadmissible (see in particular [39] to [59]).

(c) Directions in relation to the disposal hearing, such as directions about when and how the disposal hearing should be listed,[111] its time estimate, and the level of judge required. As regards time estimate, this is likely to depend in particular on the number and complexity of the construction arguments which are being advanced, and on whether extrinsic evidence is admissible pursuant to section 21 AJA and, if so, whether that evidence consists of live oral evidence from witnesses who will be cross-examined. As regards level of judge, CPR rule 2.4 provides that in proceedings in the High Court, any act which may be performed by the court may be performed "*by any judge, Master, Registrar in Bankruptcy or District Judge*".[112] Section II of CPR Practice Direction 2B does not impose any restriction on the jurisdiction of Masters or District Judges in relation to construction claims. On the contrary, sub-paragraph 3 of paragraph 14.2 of the Chancery Guide lists "*Declarations*" as one of the "*non-excluded matters*" which paragraph 14.3 indicates "*should normally be listed before a Master*", "*whether for case management, interim relief or disposal*". Paragraph 14.3 goes on to provide: "*If it is considered that exceptionally the application should be heard by a High Court Judge the Master should be requested to release it.*"[113] Construction claims can therefore be heard either by a Master (or a District Judge in a District Registry), or by a High Court Judge. In practice, the factors which are likely to determine whether the claim will be released to a High Court Judge are likely to include the complexity and significance of the construction issue, and the amount at stake.

---

111 Unless oral evidence is envisaged, CPR Part 8 proceedings are usually entered in the General List: see paragraphs 21.5 and 21.6 of the Chancery Guide.

112 Note the reference to 'District Judge' here is to a District Judge of the High Court (who is broadly the equivalent in the District Registries of a Master in London), not to a District Judge of the County Court.

113 Paragraph 29.10 of the Chancery Guide echoes this: "*Most applications relating to trusts will be dealt with by a Master and should therefore be listed before a Master. They will only be heard by a High Court Judge if, exceptionally, the application is released to the Judge.*"

(d) 'Housekeeping' directions to prepare the case for the disposal hearing, such as directions relating to the hearing bundle,[114] skeleton arguments,[115] and other documents such as dramatis personae, chronologies, case summaries, lists of issues,[116] reading lists[117] and bundles of authorities.[118] As regards the latter, it is important to bear in mind that the court is being asked to construe the particular trust instrument in question (or one of its provisions) in the circumstances in which it was made, and is therefore unlikely to be assisted by the citation of numerous authorities which have construed similar provisions in different wills made in different circumstances. The Privy Council made this clear in the will case of *Sammut v Manzi*:[119]

> *There were placed before their Lordships no less than 17 decided cases, some of which involved decisions on wording that bore some similarity with that used in the present case. Little assistance in construing a will is likely to be gained by consideration of how other judges have interpreted similar wording in other cases. Counsel rightly recognised that the starting point must be to look at the natural meaning of the wording of the will to be construed without reference to other decisions or to prima facie principles of construction.*

(e) Whether the court should make a costs capping order of its own initiative pursuant to CPR rules 3.19 to 3.21. These are rare in practice in construction claims.

---

114 Detailed rules in relation to hearing bundles are contained in paragraph 3 of CPR Practice Direction 39A and are supplemented by the guidance contained in paragraphs 21.34 to 21.72 of the Chancery Guide.

115 In relation to which see paragraphs 21.73 to 21.81 of the Chancery Guide.

116 In relation to which see paragraphs 21.75, 21.76 and 21.83 of the Chancery Guide.

117 In relation to which see paragraph 21.82 of the Chancery Guide.

118 In relation to which see paragraph 21.85 to 21.87 of the Chancery Guide.

119 [2009] 1 WLR 1834 at [3]-[4].

Disposal hearing

At the disposal hearing, the court will hear the competing construction arguments, which may be two or, sometimes, more.

Disposal hearings in construction claims are generally listed in public, i.e. in a court which is open to members of the public.[120] Whilst it may be possible in some cases to persuade a court to list the claim in private pursuant to CPR rule 39.2(3),[121] or to impose some other less extensive reporting restriction, a party seeking such an order is likely to have to show compelling reasons why the court should depart from the principle of open justice.[122]

Judgment

The Master or judge will decide how, when and where to deliver judgment. Judgment may be delivered orally immediately at the conclusion of the hearing (a so-called '*ex tempore*' judgment) or may be reserved. A reserved judgment may be delivered orally at a later date or, more commonly, may be circulated in written draft to the parties and then formally handed down at a subsequent date.

---

120 Under the general rule in CPR rule 39.2(1).

121 The sub-rules of CPR rule 39.2(3) which may be engaged in construction claims are (c), (d) and (g), viz.:

(c) [the hearing] involves confidential information (including information relating to personal financial matters) and publicity would damage that confidentiality;

(d) a private hearing is necessary to protect the interests of any child or protected party;
[...]

(g) the court considers [a hearing in private] to be necessary, in the interests of justice."

On the other hand, sub-rule (f) is unlikely to be engaged where the correct construction is in dispute, as that sub-rule is engaged in relation to hearings involving "*uncontentious matters arising in the administration of trusts or in the administration of a deceased person's estate*" (emphasis added).

122 See in this regard the Court of Appeal's guidance in *MN v OP* [2019] EWCA Civ 679 regarding privacy and reporting restrictions in the context of applications pursuant to the Variation of Trusts Act 1958.

Costs

In *Re Buckton*,[123] Kekewich J identified the following two classes of cases in which he considered it appropriate to order that all parties' costs be paid out of the estate or trust (instead of following the general rule, now contained in CPR rule 44.2.(2)(a), that the unsuccessful party will be ordered to pay the costs of the successful party):

> *In a large proportion of the summonses adjourned into Court for argument the applicants are trustees of a will or settlement who ask the Court to construe the instrument of trust for their guidance, and in order to ascertain the interests of the beneficiaries, or else ask to have some question determined which has arisen in the administration of the trusts. In cases of this character I regard the costs of all parties as necessarily incurred for the benefit of the estate, and direct them to be taxed as between solicitor and client and paid out of the estate. It is, of course, possible that trustees may come to the Court without due cause. A question of construction or of administration may be too clear for argument, or it may be the duty of trustees to inform a claimant that they must administer their trust on the footing that his claim is unfounded, and leave him to take whatever course he thinks fit. But, although I have thought it necessary sometimes to caution timid trustees against making applications which might with propriety be avoided, I act on the principle that trustees are entitled to the fullest possible protection which the Court can give them, and that I must give them credit for not applying to the Court except under advice which, though it may appear to me unsound, must not be readily treated as unwise. I cannot remember any case in which I have refused to deal with the costs of an application by trustees in the manner above mentioned.*
>
> *There is a second class of cases differing in form, but not in substance, from the first. In these cases it is admitted on all hands, or it is apparent from the proceedings, that although the application is made, not by trustees (who are respondents), but by some of the beneficiaries, yet it is made by reason of some difficulty of construction, or adminis-*

123 [1907] 2 Ch 406.

> *tration, which would have justified an application by the trustees, and it is not made by them only because, for some reason or other, a different course has been deemed more convenient. To cases of this class I extend the operation of the same rule as is observed in cases of the first class. The application is necessary for the administration of the trust, and the costs of all parties are necessarily incurred for the benefit of the estate regarded as a whole.*

Construction claims generally fall in either the first or the second class of cases identified in *Re Buckton* (depending on whether the claim is brought by the trustees or a beneficiary). As a result, the general starting point is that the costs of all of the parties will be payable out of the trust.

Costs are however ultimately in the discretion of the court,[124] and the court may therefore decide to depart from that starting point and make a different costs order. It may decide to do so, for example, if it considers that the unreasonable conduct of one of the parties has materially increased costs unnecessarily,[125] or that the construction problem was not in fact a problem at all because one of the possible constructions was unarguable.[126] As indicated at 4.2.3 above, in cases involving professional negligence, the draftsman's insurers may have agreed in advance to pay the costs of the rectification claim.[127]

---

124 Section 51(1) of the Senior Courts Act 1981.

125 See *Harrison-Mills v Public Trustee* [2019] EWCA Civ 966 at [66].

126 In *Re Buckton* [1907] 2 Ch 406 Kekewich J acknowledged the possibility that trustees "*may come to the Court without due cause*". However, his subsequent comments suggest that cases in which PRs or trustees will be deprived of their costs as a result will be rare: "*although I have thought it necessary sometimes to caution timid trustees against making applications which might with propriety be avoided, I act on the principle that trustees are entitled to the fullest possible protection which the Court can give them, and that I must give them credit for not applying to the Court except under advice which, though it may appear to me unsound, must not be readily treated as unwise.*" See also *Harrison-Mills v Public Trustee* [2019] EWCA Civ 966 at [59].

127 See e.g. the will case of *Slattery v Jagger* [2015] EWHC 3976 (Ch) at [103]-[112] (which involved both a construction and a rectification claim).

In general terms, in deciding costs the court will try to ensure that the costs are in fact borne by the negligent draftsman and/or (in a contested case) by the party who has lost, and not by the successful party. In deciding precisely how this should be achieved, the court will have to take into account all of the circumstances, including the parties' respective interests under the will and who would in fact bear the costs if the costs are ordered to be paid out of the trust.[128]

Order

In construction claims the order which gives effect to the judgment will generally consist of two parts:

(a) a declaration by which the court formally declares the correct meaning of the trust instrument, or of one or more of its provisions; and

(b) an order directing the trustees to administer the trust in question in accordance with the declaration.

Chapter 22 of the Chancery Guide contains guidance in relation to the drafting, filing and sealing of orders.

Appeals

A party who is dissatisfied with the court's decision must obtain the court's permission in order to appeal it.[129] The court will only grant permission to appeal if it considers that the appeal would have a real prospect of success, or that there is some other compelling reason for the appeal to be heard.[130]

Although this is not strictly required, it is generally sensible for a party who wishes to appeal to first seek permission from the lower court.[131] This is usually done when judgment is delivered or handed down and

128 See e.g. the wills cases of *Marley v Rawlings (costs)* [2014] UKSC 51 and *Slattery v Jagger* [2015] EWHC 3976 (Ch) at [103]-[112].

129 CPR rule 52.3(1).

130 CPR rule 52.6(1).

consequential issues, such as the terms of the order giving effect to the judgment and costs, are decided.

If the lower court refuses permission, or if permission was not sought from it, permission must be sought from the appeal court by filing an Appellant's Notice.[132] Unless the court orders otherwise, the time limit for doing so is "*21 days after the date of the decision of the lower court*".[133] That is a relatively short time limit, which cannot be extended by agreement between the parties,[134] and it must be borne in mind that the period starts to run from the date of the decision of the lower court and not, if later, the date on which consequential matters are decided or the date on which the order giving effect to the decision is approved and sealed.[135] If – as is quite common – the lower court's judgment is circulated to the parties in draft and then formally handed down in the absence of the parties, and a hearing to decide consequential matter is arranged at a later date, the lower court should be asked to direct[136] that the 21-day period will only start to run from the date of the later hearing, rather than from the date on which judgment was handed down.[137]

Compromise

In some cases it may be possible to compromise a construction claim after proceedings have been issued.[138] The mechanism by which the compromise should be implemented will inevitably depend on its terms

---

131 Pursuant to CPR rule 52.3(2)(a); see e.g. *In re T (A Child)* [2002] EWCA Civ 1736 at [12]-[13].

132 CPR rules 52.3(2)(b) and 52.12(1).

133 CPR rule 52.12(2)(b).

134 CPR rule 52.15(2).

135 See e.g. *Sayers v Clarke Walker (A Firm)* [2002] EWCA Civ 645 at [8]-[9] and *Owusu v Jackson* [2002] EWCA Civ 877 at [24]-[27].

136 Pursuant to CPR 52.12(2)(a).

137 See e.g. *Jackson v Marina Homes Ltd* [2007] EWCA Civ 1404 at [8].

138 The circumstances in which it may be possible to resolve a construction issue without the need for court proceedings are considered at 4.2.2 above.

and on the particular circumstances of the case. In most cases, the following will have to be considered:

(a) Whether the compromise has any tax implications and, if so, how these should be addressed.

(b) Whether a declaration by the court as to the correct construction of the trust instrument, or of one or more of its provisions, is required or desirable, and if so whether the court can be asked to make it by consent without hearing full argument in accordance with the principles in *Hayim v Couch*,[139] *Pavilion Property Trustees Ltd v Permira Advisers LLP*[140] and *Singh v Singh*.[141] It should be borne in mind that this jurisdiction tends to be exercised sparingly.

(c) Whether the court's approval of the compromise is required, which will be the case where one or more of the parties is a minor,[142] an adult who lacks capacity to conduct litigation[143] and/or a party who has been appointed to represent others pursuant to CPR rule 19.7.[144]

Paragraphs 22.9 to 22.13 of the Chancery Guide contain guidance in relation to consent orders.

---

139 [2009] EWHC 1040 (Ch) at [12]-[18].

140 [2014] EWHC 145 (Ch) at [9]-[10].

141 [2014] EWHC 2762 (Ch) at [5]-[9].

142 CPR rule 21.10.

143 *Ibid.*

144 CPR rule 19.7(5).

CHAPTER FIVE
RECTIFICATION OF OTHER TRUST INSTRUMENTS

5.1 The law

The equitable jurisdiction to rectify other trust instruments such as trust deeds[1] is well established.[2] In *Allnutt v Wilding*[3] the Court of Appeal explained the nature of the jurisdiction as follows: "*rectification is about putting the record straight. In the case of a voluntary settlement, rectification involves bringing the trust document into line with the true intentions of the settlor as held by him at the date when he executed the document. This can be done by the court when, owing to a mistake in the drafting of the document, it fails to record the settlor's true intentions. The mistake may, for example, consist of leaving out words that were intended to be put into the document, or putting in words that were not intended to be in the document; or through a misunderstanding by those involved about the meanings of the words or expressions that were used in the document. Mistakes of this kind have the effect that the document, as executed, is not a true record of the settlor's intentions.*"[4]

In *Giles v Royal National Institute for the Blind*,[5] Barling J summarised four key principles which the court must apply when deciding whether

1 The rectification of bilateral documents, such as contracts, is a large topic in itself which is outside the scope of this book.

2 An early example of the jurisdiction being referred to is *Walker v Armstrong* (1856) 8 DeGM&G 531. In *Re Butlin's Settlement* [1976] Ch 251 Brightman J (as he then was) held there was "*no doubt*" that the court has power to rectify a settlement "*notwithstanding that it is a voluntary settlement and not the result of a bargain, such as an ante-nuptial marriage settlement*" (at 260F).

3 [2007] EWCA Civ 412.

4 [2007] EWCA Civ 412 at [11]. This echoes the Court of Appeal's earlier decision in *Racal Group Services Ltd v Ashmore* [1995] STC 1151, where the following passage from *Snell's Principles of Equity* (29th ed., 1990) was cited with approval (at 1154h): "*What is rectified is not a mistake in the transaction itself, but a mistake in the way in which that transaction has been expressed in writing*".

to rectify a unilateral document (derived primarily from the Court of Appeal's decision in *Racal Group Services Ltd v Ashmore*):[6]

> *(1) While equity has power to rectify a written instrument so that it accords with the true intention of its maker, as a discretionary remedy rectification is to be treated with caution. One aspect of that caution is that the claimant's case should be established by clear evidence of the true intention to which effect has not been given in the instrument. Such proof is on the civil standard of balance of probability. But as the alleged true intention of necessity contradicts the written instrument, there must be convincing proof to counteract the evidence of a different intention represented by the document itself;*
>
> *(2) There must be a flaw in the written document such that it does not give effect to the parties'/donor's agreement/intention, as opposed to the parties/donor merely being mistaken as to the consequences of what they have agreed/intended; for example it is not sufficient merely that the document fails to achieve the desired fiscal objective;*
>
> *(3) The specific intention of the parties/donor must be shown; it is not sufficient to show that the parties did <u>not</u> intend what was recorded; they also have to show what they did intend, with some degree of precision;*
>
> *(4) There must be an issue capable of being contested between the parties notwithstanding that all relevant parties consent. This criterion has been much criticised: the purpose of it, and its actual content and scope, are by no means clear. In Racal Peter Gibson LJ expressly approved the following summary of the principle by Vinelott J in the same case. Vinelott J stated that the court must be satisfied:*
>
> *"that there is an issue capable of being contested, between the parties or between a covenantor or a grantor and the person he intended to*

---

5 [2014] EWHC 1373 (Ch). The case involved the rectification of a deed of variation of a will.

6 [1995] STC 1151.

> *benefit, it being irrelevant first that rectification of the document is sought or consented to by them all, and second that rectification is desired because it has beneficial fiscal consequences. On the other hand, the court will not order rectification of a document as between the parties or as between a grantor or covenantor and an intended beneficiary, if their rights will be unaffected and if the only effect of the order will be to secure a fiscal benefit."*

Whilst all four points are important, it is worth commenting further on (3) in particular. In order to succeed, the party seeking rectification has to establish with sufficient cogency and precision not just that something has gone wrong, but also what the settlor's actual intention in fact was. This is because the court will only rectify the document in a particular way if it is satisfied that once it has done so the rectified document will accurately reflect the settlor's actual intentions. Whilst establishing that something has gone wrong can be fairly straightforward, establishing the settlor's actual intention can prove a stumbling block. This is particularly the case where the settlor has a particular fiscal objective in mind, but may have delegated the precise mechanics of how to achieve that objective to his advisers. In those cases, it may be straightforward to establish that something has gone wrong where the fiscal objective has not been achieved, but it may be difficult (or even impossible) to establish with sufficient cogency and precision what the settlor actually intended the document to say. This is because the settlor may never in fact have given the precise mechanics particular thought and/or may have been content to follow the advice as to the precise mechanics given by his advisors. This sort of problem is illustrated by both *Racal Group Services Ltd v Ashmore*[7] and *Allnutt v Wilding*,[8] in both of which the rectification claim failed because although the court was satisfied that something had gone wrong, the party seeking rectification was unable to establish with sufficient cogency and precision what the settlor's actual intention had in fact been.[9]

---

7 [1995] STC 1151.

8 [2007] EWCA Civ 412.

9 See *Racal Group Services Ltd v Ashmore* [1995] STC 1151 at 1160b-e; *Allnutt v Wilding* [2007] EWCA Civ 412 at [20]-[21] and [26].

The Court of Appeal in *Day v Day*[10] made it clear that in cases involving voluntary instruments, what is relevant is "*the subjective intention of the settlor*"[11] and it is "*not a legal requirement for rectification of a voluntary settlement that there is any outward expression or objective communication of the settlor's intention equivalent to the need to show an outward expression of accord for rectification of a contract for mutual mistake*".[12] In order to ascertain the settlor's intention at the time the instrument was made, it is legitimate to have regard to conduct which post-dates the instrument.[13]

No limitation period applies to a claim for the rectification of a trust instrument other than a will.[14] However, as the remedy is equitable, it seems likely that the court could refuse to grant relief on the grounds of acquiescence and/or laches.[15] The interests of third parties will also be relevant.[16] In cases involving professionally prepared instruments in which professional negligence proceedings are likely to be relevant,

10 [2013] EWCA Civ 280.

11 [2013] EWCA Civ 280 at [22].

12 *Ibid.*

13 See e.g. *Gallaher v Gallaher Pensions Ltd* [2005] EWHC 42 (Ch) at [141], *Merchant Navy Officers Pension Fund Trustees v Watkins* [2013] EWHC 4741 (Ch) at [20], *Saga Group Ltd v Paul* [2016] EWHC 2344 (Ch) at [43], *Sovereign Trustees Ltd v Lewis* [2016] EWHC 2593 (Ch) at [15(iii)] and *A v D* [2017] EWHC 2222 (Ch) at [50].

14 See e.g. *Oatley v Oately* [2014] EWHC 1956 (Ch) where a trust deed was rectified 19 years after it was made notwithstanding that the problem at first been spotted, and rectification considered, over 4 years before the rectification claim was issued, and *Unipart Group Ltd v UGC Pension Trustees Ltd* [2018] EWHC 2124 (Ch) where a deed governing a pension scheme was rectified 16 years after it was made notwithstanding that the problem had arguably first been spotted over 10 years before the rectification claim was issued.

15 See e.g. *Snell's Equity*, 33rd ed., at 16-025. See also *Oatley v Oately* [2014] EWHC 1956 (Ch), where the court indicated that "*in the light of the fact that rectification is a discretionary equitable remedy, it is relevant to take into account when determining whether to exercise the discretion, any delay and the effect of that delay before the remedy has been sought*" (at [86]).

16 *Ibid.*

regard must be had to the limitation period which applies to those proceedings.

5.2 Practice and procedure

5.2.1 Who is affected?

The first question trustees should ask themselves when faced with a rectification problem is: who is affected by it?

The main concern for trustees faced with a possible rectification problem is to ensure that before they take any step based on a particular provision of the trust instrument, they protect themselves from potential personal liability for breach of trust, which they can do by obtaining either the binding consent of all affected beneficiaries or authorisation from the court. To get to that position, the trustees will first have to establish who the affected beneficiaries are.

Needless to say, the answer to this will depend on the particular circumstances, and can vary widely. In simple terms, the way to go about ascertaining the affected beneficiaries is to consider the different possible outcomes depending on whether the trust instrument is or is not rectified (which may be two or more) and then consider who would benefit in each situation, as illustrated by the following examples.

<u>Example 10</u>

Wotan decides to make provision for his ten daughters by settling the benefit of a life insurance policy on trust for them. At the meeting with his solicitor, Mr Mime of Fasolt & Fafner Solicitors, Wotan gives Mr Mime a piece of paper on which he has written the names of his ten daughters; nine names appear on the front, and the final name on the back.

After the meeting, Mr Mime drafts a trust deed using a precedent from his firm's database and posts it to Wotan with instructions on how to execute it, which Wotan does.

Following Wotan's death it transpires that clause 5 of the trust deed identifies the beneficiaries as "*my daughters Gerhilde, Ortlinde, Waltraute, Schwertleite, Helmwige, Siegrune, Grimgerde and Roßweiße*". However, Wotan's tenth daughter, Brünnhilde – whose name appeared on the back of the piece of paper – has been omitted.

The issue is whether clause 5 should be rectified by adding Brünnhilde.

The affected beneficiaries are therefore Wotan's ten daughters.

Example 11

Just over 10 years ago, Mimì unexpectedly inherited from a distant cousin two semi-detached houses on the same street: numbers 21 and 27 Cold Hand Lane. For the past 10 years, Mimì and her partner Rodolfo have been living at 21 Cold Hand Lane, which is the larger of the two properties (having been extended into the loft by Mimì late cousin). The other property has been let out to tenants, Marcello and Musetta, with whom Mimì and Rodolfo have become close friends.

Musetta has recently lost her job and she and Marcello, who is a stay at home dad, are struggling financially. To help them, Mimì instructs her solicitor, Mr Murger of Illica & Giacosa Solicitors, to settle 27 Cold Hand Lane on trust for Marcello and Musetta during their joint lives; thereafter the property is to pass to such of Mimì's children and remoter issue as are then living, if more than one in equal shares.

Some years after executing the deed, Mimì decides to make a will. As part of this process, it transpires that the trust deed identifies the trust property as 21 (rather than 27) Cold Hand Lane. The title number in the deed is also the title number of number 21 rather than that of number 27.

The issue is whether the trust deed should be rectified to correct the house number and title number.

The affected beneficiaries are Mimì, Rodolfo, their children and remoter issue, and Marcello and Musetta.

Example 12

Don Giovanni instructs his solicitor, Lorenzo Da Ponte, to create a discretionary trust for the benefit of all of his former girlfriends, explaining that his trusted servant, Leporello, has their details. Mr Da Ponte liaises with Leporello and prepares a trust deed, which lists the names of 2,065 beneficiaries in a 52-page schedule. A few days after executing the trust deed, Don Giovanni dies of food poisoning.

It subsequently transpires that the trust instrument does not contain any discretionary power, and instead requires the trustees to hold the trust fund on trust for 125 years, and only then to distribute it to such of the beneficiaries who are alive, if more than one in equal shares, or in default to the Red Cross.

The issue is whether the trust instrument should be rectified by the insertion of discretionary powers which the trustees can exercise in favour of the beneficiaries during the trust period. The affected beneficiaries are therefore the 2,065 listed beneficiaries and the Red Cross.

If the rectification problem affects the amount of tax payable, some thought should be given to whether it is also necessary to involve HMRC.[17]

The corollary to the above is that trustees should bear in mind that they have no personal interest in how the rectification problem is resolved between the affected beneficiaries. It is not for the trustees to try to second guess what the settlor might have intended, nor to form a view as to which of the affected beneficiaries is more 'worthy' or 'deserving'. The trustees should remain neutral and impartial, and simply do what they are told, either by a unanimous binding agreement reached by all of the affected beneficiaries, or by the court.

17 Paragraph 29.70 of the Chancery Guide.

5.2.2 Can the problem be resolved by agreement?

Some rectification problems can be resolved by the unanimous agreement of all of the beneficiaries affected by it. Therefore, once the trustees have identified all of the affected beneficiaries, the next question they should ask themselves is: can the problem be resolved by agreement?

Suppose that in Example 10 above, Wotan's ten daughters agree to split the trust fund between all of them equally (including Brünnhilde). They are the only two individuals affected by the uncertainty. If they are all capacitous adults and agree what should happen to the property, they can resolve the construction problem between themselves without having to go to court. The trustees' only concern will be to ensure that the agreement is properly documented so that they cannot later be criticised by any of the ten daughters for acting in accordance with it.

Resolving the problem by agreement is usually significantly cheaper and quicker than asking the court to do so. As indicated above, if the rectification problem affects the amount of tax payable, some thought should be given to whether it is also necessary to obtain the agreement of HMRC.

In practice, rectification problems are generally only resolved by agreement in the most straightforward cases. Two reasons can be identified for this. First, beneficiaries often have different views about what the settlor did or did not intend, and are therefore simply unable to reach an agreement. Secondly, to avoid exposing themselves to potential personal liability to disappointed beneficiaries, trustees must obtain the binding consent of all of the beneficiaries who are affected by the problem. This will not be possible if the problem affects beneficiaries who are minors, unborn, lack capacity and/or cannot be found. As those types of beneficiaries are unable to give the trustees their binding consent, in cases in which they are affected, the court's intervention will be necessary.

A useful way to explore whether the rectification problem can be resolved by agreement is for the trustees, who are often the first to spot the problem, to obtain advice from counsel on the rectification problem and then share that advice with all affected beneficiaries and canvass their views. If the will incorporates clause 12.3 of the STEP Standard Provisions (2nd edition), the trustees should consider obtaining the advice of counsel of "*at least five years' standing*" if they want to rely on the protection from liability afforded by that clause.[18]

This process should help both the trustees and all affected beneficiaries understand their respective positions, which in turn should inform all involved whether there is any hope of the rectification problem being resolved by agreement and, if so, how this might be achieved. Depending on the circumstances, the affected beneficiaries may wish to try to reach an agreement by, for example, negotiating in correspondence, at a round-table meeting or at a mediation.

As indicated above, trustees should bear in mind that they have no personal interest in how the rectification problem is resolved between the affected beneficiaries. The focus of the trustees should be to ensure:

---

18 Clause 12.3 and the following two clauses provide:

12.3 A Trustee shall not be liable for acting in accordance with the advice of counsel, of at least five years' standing, with respect to the Trust. The Trustees may in particular conduct legal proceedings in accordance with such advice without obtaining a court order. A Trustee may recover from the Trust Fund any expenses where he has acted in accordance with such advice.

12.4 Clause 12.3 does not apply:

12.4.1 in relation to a Trustee who knows or has reasonable cause to suspect that the advice was given in ignorance of material facts;

12.4.2 if proceedings are pending to obtain the decision of the court on the matter;

12.4.3 in relation to a Trustee who has a personal interest in the subject matter of the advice; or

12.4.4 in relation to a Trustee who has committed a breach of trust relating to the subject matter of the advice.

12.5 Clause 12.3 does not prejudice any right of any Person to follow property or income into the hands of any Person, other than a purchaser, who may have received it.

(a) that they obtain the binding consent of all affected beneficiaries so they are protected from potential personal liability for breach of trust (i.e. for having distributed to the wrong person); and

(b) that the agreement is one which the trustees can in fact implement. For example, the trustees should consider whether the agreement has tax consequences and, if so, how these should be addressed.

However, if all affected beneficiaries manage to reach a binding agreement which the trustees can implement, it is not for the trustees to 'approve' or 'disapprove' of it in any moral or ethical sense, e.g. on the basis that they think the settlor would or would not have liked it. It also follows from this that trustees are generally not required to actively participate in any negotiations between the affected beneficiaries; indeed, trustees should ensure they do not incur unnecessary costs by doing so.

In cases in which professional negligence proceedings against the draftsman have also been threatened or are on foot, it may be sensible to try to compromise the professional negligence at the same time.

There are two further tools which can help achieve a pragmatic solution without the court's intervention in a suitable case. The first is the possibility of the trustees agreeing to distribute on a particular basis provided the recipient beneficiaries in return provide the trustees with suitable indemnities, possibly backed by security. Such indemnities would be designed to protect the trustees against the risk that they may be personally liable to disappointed beneficiaries if the basis on which they have distributed subsequently turns out to be wrong. The second is the possibility of obtaining insurance to provide the trustees with that same protection.

Whether either of these tools is a useful one will depend on all of the particular surrounding circumstances. As a rather crude rule of thumb, it is suggested that the greater the financial value of the rectification problem, the less likely these tools are to provide a practical solution. This is because the greater the amount of money that turns on the rectification problem, the greater the potential liability of the trustees, and thus the more nervous both the beneficiaries and any insurance company will be in providing trustees with adequate protection. Further, in high value cases there is less of a risk of the trust fund being significantly depleted by the costs involved in making a court application, which might also point towards a court application being the better option.

5.2.3 Professional negligence

If the trust instrument was professionally prepared, it may be possible for a disappointed beneficiary to argue that the rectification problem amounts to professional negligence of the draftsman and seek damages on the basis of *White v Jones.*[19] In these sorts of circumstances, the disappointed beneficiary is usually under a duty to mitigate his loss by seeking to rectify the will before pursuing professional negligence proceedings against the draftsman[20] (although the professional negligence claim may have to be issued protectively and stayed, or a limitation standstill agreed, if limitation is a concern).

Depending on the circumstances, if both the professional negligence claim and the rectification claim have merit, the draftsman's insurers might agree to fund the rectification claim, particularly if the costs involved in doing so are likely to be lower than their potential exposure in the event the professional negligence claim is successful.[21]

---

19 [1995] 2 AC 207.

20 See e.g. *Walker v Geo H Medlicott & Son* [1999] 1 WLR 727 and *Horsfall v Haywards* [1999] 1 FLR 1182. See also *Grattan v McNaughton* [2001] WTLR 1305 in which the claimant was criticised for pursuing the professional negligence claim first up to and including trial, and only once that claim had been dismissed, pursuing a rectification claim based on the same evidence which she had issued only 14 days before the trial of the professional negligence claim. Although no application to strike out the rectification claim on the grounds that it was an abuse of process was pursued, the judge indicated that he would have been "*provisionally very attracted to it*" as it could not be "*in the public interest to permit virtually the same issues in relation to the drafting of the will to be litigated twice*".

21 See e.g. *Re Bimson* [2010] EWHC 3679 (Ch) at [23].

If the trust instrument was professionally prepared, it may be possible to argue that the rectification problem amounts to professional negligence of the draftsman, in the sense that it amounts to a breach by the draftsman of his duty to exercise reasonable care and skill in drafting a trust instrument which accurately recorded the settlor's instructions. If so, a professional negligence claim against the draftsman is usually threatened, and sometimes issued, before a rectification claim is brought.

Depending on the circumstances, if both the professional negligence claim and the rectification claim have merit, the draftsman's insurers might agree to fund the rectification claim, particularly if the costs involved in doing so are likely to be lower than their potential exposure in the event the professional negligence claim is successful.

5.2.4 Court intervention: rectification claims in the Chancery Division

Starting the claim

In many cases rectification claims are brought by way of CPR Part 8 proceedings. This may be because the claim is not opposed by the beneficiaries who are capacitous adults, but it also affects beneficiaries who are minors, unborn, lack capacity and/or cannot be found, and/or it is necessary to obtain a court order granting rectification because the drafting problem has tax consequences.[22] This may also be done because the rectification claim is being brought together with one or more other claims – typically a construction claim[23] – which must be brought by way of a CPR Part 8 claim (see 4.2.4.). In this sort of situation, the procedural rules governing the other claim(s) must also be borne in mind. Some thought should also be given as to whether the court should be asked to deal with any aspects in dispute as a preliminary issue.[24]

---

22 See e.g. *Racal Group Services Ltd v Ashmore* [1995] STC 1151 and *Allnutt v Wilding* [2007] EWCA Civ 412.

23 See e.g. *Millar v Millar* [2018] EWHC 1926 (Ch) and *Armstrong v Armstrong* [2019] EWHC 2259 (Ch).

On the other hand, if the rectification claim is brought on its own and is opposed, it is likely to involve a substantial dispute of fact, and it is therefore likely to be more appropriate for the claim to be brought as a CPR Part 7 claim rather than a CPR Part 8 claim.[25]

Limitation

As indicated above, it seems no limitation period applies to a claim for the rectification of a trust instrument. However, as the remedy is equitable, it seems likely that the court could refuse to grant relief on the grounds of acquiescence and/or laches.[26] The interests of third parties will also be relevant.[27]

Which court

The County Court appears to have jurisdiction to determine a claim for the rectification of a trust instrument if the value of the trust fund does not exceed £350,000.[28] However, in practice rectification claims are invariably issued in the Chancery Division of the High Court,[29] i.e. what has now become the Property, Trusts and Probate List (ChD) of the Business and Property Courts of England and Wales. A rectification claim can be issued either in the Rolls Building in London or in one of the District Registries (Birmingham, Bristol, Cardiff, Leeds, Liverpool, Manchester, Newcastle-upon-Tyne, Preston, Mold and Caernarfon).[30]

---

24 As in *Burnard v Burnard* [2014] EWHC 340 (Ch) (see [7]) and *Tish v Olley* [2018] EWHC 1069 (Ch) (see [1]).

25 CPR rule 8.1(2)(a).

26 See e.g. *Snell's Equity*, 33rd ed., at 16-025.

27 *Ibid.*

28 Section 23 of the County Courts Act 1984 and article 3 of the County Court Jurisdiction Order 2014 (SI 2014/503). This assumes that the rectification claim in question is a type of "*proceedings for relief against [...] mistake*" within section 23(g).

29 Section 61 and paragraph 1(g) of Schedule 1 to the Senior Courts Act 1981.

30 Paragraph 30.1 of the Chancery Guide. Chapter 30 of the Chancery Guide contains helpful information regarding Chancery business outside London, including contact details of the various District Registries.

Evidence/Pleadings

A distinction needs to be drawn between rectification claims brought by way of a CPR Part 8 claim and those brought by way of a CPR Part 7 claim.[31]

CPR Part 8 claims: evidence

If the rectification claim is brought by way of a CPR Part 8 claim, the claimant must file the evidence on which he intends to rely when his claim form is issued[32] (unless the claimant only intends to rely on the evidence contained in the claim form itself, which it is suggested is unlikely to be the case in rectification claims). This will generally be in the form of one or more witness statements.[33] The claimant's evidence must be served on the defendant with the claim form.[34]

The contents of the witness statement(s) will of course depend on the circumstances of the particular case. In general terms, the topics which one should consider covering in the evidence filed in support of the claim are likely to be:

(a) the claimant's role and the capacity in which he brings the claim;

(b) the factual background;

(c) the current drafting of the trust instrument and its construction;

(d) what the settlor's intention are alleged to have been;

(e) how the current drafting of the trust instrument fails to correctly record the settlor's intentions;

(f) how the court is being asked to rectify the trust instrument;

---

31 See "Starting the claim" above.

32 CPR rule 8.5(1) and paragraph 7.1 of CPR Practice Direction 8A; see also paragraph 9.6 of the Chancery Guide.

33 Paragraph 7.2 of CPR Practice Direction 8A.

34 CPR rule 8.5(2).

(g) the position of the other interested parties.

If the trust instrument was professionally prepared, some thought should be given as to whether evidence should be obtained from the draftsman responsible for preparing it (if available).

It should be borne in mind that the CPR requires witness statements to be in the witness's own words.[35] Furthermore, the temptation to include in a witness statement extensive legal submissions and references to case law should generally be resisted, particularly in witness statements of lay witnesses; these are properly a matter for skeleton arguments and submissions.[36]

CPR Part 7 claims: particulars of claim

If the rectification claim is brought by way of a CPR Part 7 claim,[37] the particulars of claim must either be contained in or served with the claim form, or be served on the defendant within 14 days after service of the claim form, subject to them being served no later than the latest time for serving the claim form.[38] The contents of the particulars of claim will of course depend on the circumstances of the particular case. In general terms, the topics which the party seeking rectification should consider covering in the particulars of claim are likely to be the same as those the claimant's evidence should over in CPR Part 8 claims, viz.:

(a) the claimant's role and the capacity in which he brings the claim;

(b) the factual background;

(c) the current drafting of the trust instrument and its construction;

(d) what the settlor's intentions are alleged to have been;

---

35 Paragraph 18.1 of CPR Practice Direction 32; see also paragraph 19.2 of the Chancery Guide.

36 See paragraph 19.3 of the Chancery Guide.

37 See "Starting the claim" above.

38 CPR rule 7.4.

(e) how the current drafting of the trust instrument fails to correctly record the settlor's intentions;

(f) how the court is being asked to rectify the trust instrument;

(g) the position of the other interested parties.

As well as the rules in CPR rule 16.4 and CPR Practice Direction 16, the drafting guidelines contained in paragraphs 10.5 to 10.17 of the Chancery Guide apply to particulars of claim.

Disclosure – CPR Part 8 claims

This section considers disclosure in claims which are brought pursuant to CPR Part 8. Disclosure in CPR Part 7 claims is considered below.

CPR Practice Direction 51U contains a new 'disclosure pilot' which sets out detailed rules concerning disclosure that apply to claims in the Business and Property Courts of England and Wales. The pilot came into force on 1st January 2019 and applies to both existing claims and to new claims issued after that date.[39] It will remain in force for two years.[40]

A Practice Note by Chief Master Marsh dated 27th March 2019[41] clarifies that the pilot "*does not directly apply to Part 8 claims because Part 8 contains its own regime for the disclosure of documents that are relied on by the parties*".[42] In particular, the pilot's new concept of 'Initial Disclosure' does not apply to CPR Part 8 claims.[43] However, paragraph 5 of the Practice Note explains:

---

39 Paragraph 1.2 of CPR Practice Direction 51U.

40 Paragraph 1.2 of CPR Practice Direction 51U.

41 Available here: https://www.judiciary.uk/wp-content/uploads/2019/03/Practice-Note-27_03_19.pdf

42 Paragraph 3 of the Practice Note.

43 Paragraph 5.1 of CPR Practice Direction 51U; see also paragraph 4 of the Practice Note.

> "*The court has power to make an order for extended disclosure under the pilot in a case proceeding under Part 8. It will adopt such elements of the Practice Direction as are appropriate to the case and the scope of disclosure that is sought. The party requesting disclosure will need to identify the issues for disclosure and the Model or Models that apply. It is not expected that the full procedure for extended disclosure, including completion of all elements of the Disclosure Review Document, will normally be required.*"

Given the disclosure obligations already imposed by CPR Part 8, it is suggested that orders for extended disclosure pursuant to the pilot are likely to be rare in construction claims. Some support of this can be found in paragraph 17.74 of the Chancery Guide: "*It is rare for orders for disclosure to be made in a Part 8 claim because for most types of Part 8 claim it should suffice for the parties to rely upon the documents they exhibit*".

<u>Costs management</u>

CPR Part 8 claims

CPR rule 3.12 now makes it clear that costs management does not apply to CPR Part 8 claims unless the court orders that it should pursuant to CPR rule 3.12(1A).[44] Paragraph 5(e) of CPR Practice Direction 3E provides that an order for costs management may be "*particularly appropriate*" in "*any Part 8 or other claims or applications involving a substantial dispute of fact and/or likely to require oral evidence and/or extensive disclosure*". A party seeking an order that costs management should apply to the proceedings should "*give notice to the other parties and the court well in advance of the directions hearing and explain, preferably in a witness statement, why such an order is sought*".[45]

CPR Part 7 claims

---

44 In relation to which see also and paragraph 2 of CPR Practice Direction 3E.

45 Paragraph 17.71 of the Chancery Guide.

If a rectification claim is brought by way of CPR Part 7 proceedings, it is likely to be a multi-track claim and costs management is likely to apply to it, unless the court dispenses with costs management pursuant to CPR rule 3.12(e). It seems likely that the court will only do so if it is satisfied that the litigation can be conducted justly and at proportionate cost in accordance with the overriding objective without costs management.[46] Costs budgets and budget discussion reports will have to be filed and exchanged in accordance with the procedure contained in Section II of CPR Part 3.

Parties

Determining who should be made a party to a rectification claim often requires some careful thought. In general, it is useful to bear in mind that:

(a) if the rectification problem is being resolved by way of a contested rectification claim, it should be clear that there are at least two opposing parties, and who they are; they will need to be joined;

(b) the court will want to ensure that everyone affected by the rectification problem has an opportunity to be heard;

(c) in a contentious situation, the trustees should generally remain neutral in their capacity as trustees and not advocate in favour or against rectification, and should instead let the opposing beneficiaries fight it out;

(d) however, where the claim is unopposed and/or no beneficiary with a contrary interest wishes to take an active role, it may be incumbent on the trustees as "*watchdog*"[47] for unrepresented or

---

46 This is the basis on which the court can decide (pursuant to CPR rule 3.15(2)) not to make a costs management order even where costs budgets have been filed. Paragraph 17.4 of the Chancery Guide makes it clear that "*[t]he fact that none of the parties wish the claim to be subject to costs management is a material factor but it is not determinative because the court must consider the broader test in CPR 3.15(2) in each case*".

47 *Re Druce's Settlement Trusts* [1962] 1 WLR 363 at 370.

unborn beneficiaries to assist the court by "*bringing to the court's attention any relevant legal propositions or argument affecting the position of unrepresented beneficiaries or parties*"[48] to ensure the court is able to reach the right result; and

(e) if the rectification problem affects the amount of tax payable, it may be necessary to notify, and perhaps even join, HMRC.[49]

All of the current trustees should be joined as a party to a rectification claim to ensure they are bound by the order. What may be less clear is how to ensure that all affected beneficiaries are joined and are able to have their say.

In cases involving a limited number of affected beneficiaries, the answer may be fairly straightforward. The simplest example is where there are two possible outcomes and the only affected beneficiaries are capacitous adults, as in Example 10 above (assuming the ten daughters are all capacitous adults). In such cases, it may be sensible for the trustees to leave it to the beneficiary who would benefit from the rectification to bring the claim, and to join both the trustees and the other affected beneficiaries as defendants. As the contest is in substance between the affected beneficiaries, the trustees should adopt a neutral position and let the affected beneficiaries advance the two alternative arguments.

Where one or more of the affected beneficiaries is a minor or lacks capacity and is to be a party to the claim, that beneficiary will need a litigation friend.[50] CPR Part 21 contains detailed guidance on the procedure for the appointment of a litigation friend.

On the other hand, the position may be more complicated where the rectification problem affects a large number of beneficiaries (e.g. large classes) – as in Example 12 above – and/or where some of the affected beneficiaries are minors, unborn, lack capacity and/or cannot be found

48 *State Street Bank & Trust Co v Sompo Japan Insurance Inc* [2010] EWHC 1461 (Ch) at [30]. See also e.g. *Re Hemming* [2008] EWHC 8565 (Ch) at [40].

49 See paragraph 29.70 of the Chancery Guide.

50 CPR rule 21.2(1).

(which could also be a problem in Example 12). In these sorts of cases, there is likely to be a tension between ensuring on the one hand that everyone who has an interest is properly represented and has an opportunity to be heard, and trying on the other to avoid depleting the estate or trust by incurring significant costs tracing and communicating with large classes of beneficiaries.

How the balance should be struck will inevitably depend on the circumstances of the particular case. In complicated cases, the provisions of CPR rule 8.2A, rule 19.7 and/or 19.8A can be of considerable assistance.[51] These govern respectively the circumstances in which a CPR Part 8 claim may be issued without naming a defendant, the appointment of a party to represent the interests of others, and the service of proceedings and/or orders on non-parties so as to bind them.

CPR rule 8.2A provides:

> *Issue of claim form without naming defendants*
>
> *(1) A practice direction may set out circumstances in which a claim form may be issued under this Part without naming a defendant.*
>
> *(2) The practice direction may set out those cases in which an application for permission must be made by application notice before the claim form is issued.*
>
> *(3) The application notice for permission –*
>
> *(a) need not be served on any other person; and*
>
> *(b) must be accompanied by a copy of the claim form that the applicant proposes to issue.*

---

51 The relevance of these rules to claims concerning estates and trusts is highlighted by paragraphs 29.12, 29.15 and 29.16 of the Chancery Guide, considered below. Note that CPR rule 19.6, which is entitled "*Representative parties with same interest*", does not apply to claims "*about (a) the estate of a deceased person, (b) property subject to a trust, or (c) the meaning of a document, including a statute*": see CPR rules 19.6(5) and 19.7(1).

(4) Where the court gives permission it will give directions about the future management of the claim.

In fact, neither of the two Practice Directions to CPR Part 8[52] deal with the circumstances in which a claim form may be issued without naming a defendant. However, paragraphs 7.15 and 7.16 of the Chancery Guide provide the following guidance:

Application to issue the claim form without naming defendants

7.15 CPR rule 8.2A permits the court to make an order in relation to a Part 8 claim (not a Part 7 claim) entitling the claimant to issue the claim without naming defendants. An order might be appropriate, for example, where the court is asked to make an order to assist executors who are unable to locate beneficiaries named in a will.

7.16 The application is made by application notice issued at Chancery Chambers. It will then be placed before the assigned Master. Alternatively in a simple case the Master may be willing to deal with it at 10.30 or 2.00 as an Application without Notice ("AWN").

CPR rule 19.7(2) provides:

The court may make an order appointing a person to represent any other person or persons in the claim where the person or persons to be represented –

(a) are unborn;

(b) cannot be found;

(c) cannot easily be ascertained; or

(d) are a class of persons who have the same interest in a claim and –

52 viz. Practice Directions 8A and 8B.

> *(i) one or more members of that class are within sub-paragraphs (a), (b) or (c); or*
>
> *(ii) to appoint a representative would further the overriding objective.*

This caters for several different scenarios:

(a) is self-explanatory;

(b) covers situations in which it is clear who the affected beneficiary is, but (reasonable) attempts to find him have proved unsuccessful;

(c) covers situations in which it is not clear who the affected beneficiary is, nor can this be easily clarified;

(d) covers two alternative situations where a class of persons has the same interest in the claim:

  (i) is self-explanatory;

  (ii) is potentially wide and flexible. It can be used, for example, where there is a large class of affected beneficiaries scattered around the world, all of whom have the same interest, and it would further the overriding objective to appoint one of them to represent the whole class (e.g. by reducing procedural delay and costs) – ideally one who can be served within the jurisdiction.[53]

CPR rule 19.7(3) provides that an application for a representation order under CPR rule 19.7(2) may be made "*by any person who seeks to be appointed under the order or any party to the claim*", and may be made "*at any time before or after the claim has started*". CPR rule 19.7(4) provides that the application notice for such an order must be served on:

---

53 For an example, see *Public Trustee v Harrison* [2018] EWHC 166 (Ch) at [8].

(a) all parties to the claim, if the claim has started;

(b) the person sought to be appointed, if that person is not the applicant or a party to the claim; and

(c) any other person as directed by the court.

It is important to note that where the court has made a representation order under CPR rule 19.7, the court's approval is required to settle the claim.[54] This is to safeguard the position of the represented parties and to ensure their representative does not enter into a compromise which is disadvantageous to them: CPR rule 19.7(6) gives the court jurisdiction to approve a settlement "*where it is satisfied that the settlement is for the benefit of all represented persons*".

Finally, CPR rule 19.8A provides:

Power to make judgements binding on non-parties

(1) This rule applies to any claim relating to –

[...];

(b) property subject to a trust; or

(c) the sale of any property.

(2) The court may at any time direct that notice of –

(a) the claim; or

(b) any judgment or order given in the claim,

be served on any person who is not a party but who is or may be affected by it.

(3) An application under this rule –

54 CPR rule 19.7(5).

(a) may be made without notice; and

(b) must be supported by written evidence which includes the reasons why the person to be served should be bound by the judgment in the claim.

(4) Unless the court orders otherwise –

(a) a notice of a claim or of a judgment or order under this rule must be –

(i) in the form required by the practice direction;

(ii) issued by the court; and

(iii) accompanied by a form of acknowledgment of service with any necessary modifications;

(b) a notice of a claim must also be accompanied by –

(i) a copy of the claim form; and

(ii) such other statements of case, witness statements or affidavits as the court may direct; and

(c) a notice of a judgment or order must also be accompanied by a copy of the judgment or order.

(5) If a person served with notice of a claim files an acknowledgment of service of the notice within 14 days he will become a party to the claim.

(6) If a person served with notice of a claim does not acknowledge service of the notice he will be bound by any judgment given in the claim as if he were a party.

(7) If, after service of a notice of a claim on a person, the claim form is amended so as substantially to alter the relief claimed, the court may direct that a judgment shall not bind that person unless a

further notice, together with a copy of the amended claim form, is served on him.

(8) Any person served with a notice of a judgment or order under this rule –

(a) shall be bound by the judgment or order as if he had been a party to the claim; but

(b) may, provided he acknowledges service –

(i) within 28 days after the notice is served on him, apply to the court to set aside or vary the judgment or order; and

(ii) take part in any proceedings relating to the judgment or order.

(9) The following rules of Part 10 (acknowledgment of service) apply –

(a) rule 10.4; and

(b) rule 10.5, subject to the modification that references to the defendant are to be read as references to the person served with the notice.

(10) A notice under this rule is issued on the date entered on the notice by the court.

The procedure in CPR rule 19.8A can be useful to bind interested beneficiaries who do not want to take an active role in the proceedings, such as the adult children of an 'active' interested beneficiary who are content to simply support their parent's position. However, it suggests that it is unlikely to be a good idea to press on with the proceedings and to then try to rely on CPR rule 19.8A to serve a judgment or order on an interested beneficiary who it is thought will want to actively have a say. In such cases there is a risk that such a beneficiary will then apply to set aside the judgment or order (pursuant to CPR rule 19.8A(8)(b)) to, in effect, re-open the case to advance his argument, and this could significantly increase the overall costs. In this sort of situation it is likely to be preferable to ensure that such a beneficiary is able to actively participate from the outset.

It should be borne in mind that the issue of representation is likely to be considered by the court at the first directions hearing, at which creative and pragmatic solutions can be considered with the Master, particularly in complex cases.[55]

Service

The usual rules for service contained in the CPR – mostly in CPR Part 6 – apply to claims for the rectification of a will. If it is necessary to seek the court's permission to serve the claim form out of the jurisdiction pursuant to CPR rule 6.36, the grounds listed in paragraph 3.1 of CPR Practice Direction 6B which are likely to be relevant are grounds (11) to (12A):

> *Claims about property within the jurisdiction*
>
> *(11) The subject matter of the claim relates wholly or principally to property within the jurisdiction, provided that nothing under this paragraph shall render justiciable the title to or the right to possession of immovable property outside England and Wales.*
>
> *Claims about trusts etc.*
>
> *(12) A claim is made in respect of a trust which is created [...] by a written instrument, or created orally and evidenced in writing, and which is governed by the law of England and Wales.*
>
> *(12A) A claim is made in respect of a trust which is created [...] by a written instrument, or created orally and evidenced in writing, and*

55 See e.g. the will case of *Re Harte* [2015] EWHC 2351 (Ch), in which the PRs were initially given permission to issue the construction and rectification claims without naming a defendant (pursuant to CPR rule 8.2A), and were then given directions as to the steps they should take to ascertain the intestacy beneficiaries (including by advertisement) and as to the parties to whom they should give notice of the proceedings pursuant to CPR rule 19.8A (see [3]-[4]).

which provides that jurisdiction in respect of such a claim shall be conferred upon the courts of England and Wales.

Responding to the claim

CPR Part 8 claims: defendant's acknowledgment of service and evidence

A defendant who wishes to respond to the claim must file an acknowledgment of service in the relevant practice form (viz. form N210)[56] not more than 14 days after service of the claim form on him.[57] At the same time he must also serve his acknowledgment of service on the claimant and on any other party.[58] If he fails to do so, the defendant may attend the hearing of the claim but may not take part in the hearing unless the court gives permission.[59] The defendant must indicate in his acknowledgment of service whether he contests the claim, and if he seeks a different remedy from that set out in the claim form, what that remedy is.[60] If he wishes to object to the use of the CPR Part 8 procedure, he should also say so in his acknowledgment of service;[61] this might be the case, for example, where the defendant opposes the rectification sought by the claim and argues that there is a substantial dispute of fact. There is no need to file a defence, as CPR Part 15 does not apply to claims brought pursuant to CPR Part 8.[62]

A defendant who wishes to rely on written evidence must file it when he files his acknowledgment of service,[63] and must at the same time serve a

56 Paragraph 5.2 of CPR Practice Direction 8A.

57 CPR rule 8.3(1); see also paragraph 9.5 of the Chancery Guide. Note that different (longer) periods apply if the proceedings have been served on the defendant out of the jurisdiction: see CPR rules 8.3(3) and 10.3(2).

58 CPR rule 8.3(1).

59 CPR rule 8.4(2).

60 CPR rule 8.3(2).

61 CPR rule 8.8(1); see also paragraph 9.5 of the Chancery Guide.

62 CPR rule 8.9(a) and paragraph 5.1 of CPR Practice Direction 8A; see also paragraph 9.6 of the Chancery Guide.

copy of his evidence on the other parties.[64] As the time limit for the defendant to do this is quite short (viz. 14 days from service of the claim on him), paragraph 7.5 of CPR Practice Direction 8A allows the parties to agree in writing to extend that time limit by up to "*14 days after the defendant files his acknowledgment of service*".[65] Such an agreement must be filed at court by the defendant at the same time as he files his acknowledgment of service.[66] Because of the somewhat awkward wording of paragraph 7.5(2)(b), it seems that in order to obtain the maximum time of 28 days from service of the claim form to file his evidence, a defendant must:

(a) first, agree in writing with the other parties that he may file his evidence 14 days after he files his acknowledgment of service; and then

(b) wait until the 14th day after he was served with the claim form, and on that day file both his acknowledgment of service and the written agreement.

This is because the 14-day extension runs from the date on which the defendant files his acknowledgment of service, as opposed to extending the period for filing of the defendant's evidence to 28 days from the date of service of the claim form on him.[67] The defendant may not rely on any written evidence which has not been served in accordance with

63 CPR rule 8.5(3) and paragraph 7.3 of CPR Practice Direction 8A; see also paragraph 9.6 of the Chancery Guide.

64 CPR rule 8.5(4).

65 Paragraph 7.5(2)(b) of CPR Practice Direction 8A; see also paragraph 9.6 of the Chancery Guide.

66 Paragraph 7.5(2)(a) of CPR Practice Direction 8A; see also paragraph 9.6 of the Chancery Guide.

67 Contrast the effect of filing an acknowledgment of service in CPR Part 7 claims, which is to extend the period within which the defendant must file his defence to 28 days from the date of service on him of the particulars of claim: CPR rule 15.4(1)(b).

the rules described above at the hearing of the claim unless the court gives permission.[68]

If a defendant requires more time to file his evidence, he should apply to the court for an extension of time by way of an application pursuant to CPR Part 23.[69] The Chancery Guide recognises that in substantial matters the time limits for evidence imposed by CPR Part 8 "*may be burdensome upon defendants*" and indicates that in such matters the court will normally be willing to grant a reasonable extension.[70] If the parties are in agreement that such an extension should be granted, the application should be made by filing a consent order.[71] If there is no agreement an application notice must be issued and listed for hearing unless the Master considers that the application may be dealt with without a hearing.[72] The Chancery Guide requires parties to "*at all times act co-operatively and agree reasonable requests for additional time*" and indicates that the court is "*likely to order the opposing party to pay the costs of a contested application for additional time where the opposition is unreasonable*".[73]

As for the claimant's evidence, the contents of any witness statement(s) adduced by a defendant will of course depend on the circumstances of the particular case. In general terms, the topics one should consider covering are likely to be the same as those to be covered by the claimant in his evidence (discussed above). An aspect which can give rise to conflicting factual evidence is the extrinsic evidence of the settlor's intention. This might be the case for example where that evidence consists of conversations the settlor had with different people at different times about the trust, which are inconsistent with one another.[74]

---

68 CPR rule 8.6(1).

69 Paragraph 7.4 of CPR Practice Direction 8A; and see paragraph 9.7 of the Chancery Guide of the Chancery Guide.

70 Paragraph 9.7 of the Chancery Guide of the Chancery Guide.

71 *Ibid.*

72 *Ibid.*

73 *Ibid.*

CPR Part 7 claims: defendant's acknowledgement of service and defence

In most cases,[75] a defendant who wishes to defend a CPR Part 7 claim must either file a defence within 14 days of service of the particulars of claim on him,[76] or file an acknowledgment of service within in the same period[77] and then file a defence within 28 days of service of the particulars of claim.[78] A copy of the defence must also be served on the other parties.[79] The parties can agree to extend these time limits by up to 28 days;[80] if they do, the defendant must notify the court of the agreement in writing.[81]

At the same time as filing a defence, the defendant should consider whether he wishes or needs to bring a counterclaim. This is because the defendant can bring a counterclaim against the claimant by filing particulars of the counterclaim[82] without the court's permission if the counterclaim is filed at the same time as the defence;[83] however, the defendant will need the court's permission if the counterclaim is filed at any other time.[84] Whether it is necessary to bring a counterclaim will depend on the particular circumstances of the litigation and on the

---

74 See for example the will construction case of *Hives v Machin* [2017] EWHC 1414 (Ch), in which the judge heard and analysed conflicting oral evidence as to the testatrix's intentions, but ultimately concluded that section 21 AJA was not engaged and such evidence was therefore inadmissible (see in particular [39] to [59]).

75 Special time limits apply, for example, where the proceedings are served on the defendant out of the jurisdiction: see e.g. CPR rules 10.3(2) and 15.4(2).

76 CPR rule 15.4(1)(a).

77 CPR rule 10.3(1).

78 CPR rule 15.4(1)(b).

79 CPR rule 15.6.

80 CPR rule 15.5(1).

81 CPR rule 15.5(2).

82 CPR rule 20.4(1).

83 CPR rule 20.4(2)(a).

84 CPR rule 20.4(2)(b).

relief the defendant is seeking from the court. For example, if a defendant who is resisting a rectification claim is a beneficiary of a trust created by a deed which does not cause any construction problems, it may be sufficient for him to simply file a defence denying that the claimant is entitled to the rectification he seeks (and thus impliedly asking the court to dismiss the claimant's rectification claim). On the other hand, if for example the defendant wishes to ask the court to rectify the trust instrument in a different way from that which the claimant is arguing for, and/or wishes to ask the court to determine the meaning of a particular provision of the trust instrument, then it may be necessary for him to both defend the claimant's rectification claim and bring a counterclaim.

As well as the rules in CPR rule 16.5 and CPR Practice Direction 16, the drafting guidelines contained in paragraphs 10.5 to 10.17 of the Chancery Guide apply to defences.

Default and summary judgment

It is generally not possible to obtain judgment in default in a rectification claim. The Chancery Guide explains that: "*If the claimant seeks discretionary relief such as a declaration, rectification, an injunction or other similar relief the Master will usually require to be satisfied that such relief is necessary, and if so ought to be granted, and a full witness statement will usually be required. In cases of complexity the application notice may need to be listed. Declaratory relief and relief by way of rectification will not be granted without evidence and will not ordinarily be appropriate for resolution by way of judgment in default.*"[85]

On the other hand, it is generally possible to obtain summary judgment in a rectification claim in an appropriate case. This will usually be where the claim is opposed and is brought by CPR Part 7 proceedings, and the applicant is able to demonstrate that the claim or defence (as the case may be) has no real prospect of success and that there is no other compelling reason why the claim should be disposed of at a trial.

85 Paragraph 12.3 of the Chancery Guide; see also paragraph 29.69 of the Chancery Guide.

However, if the claim is unopposed and is brought by way of CPR Part 8 proceedings, it will generally be unnecessary to apply for summary judgment, and the claimant can instead ask the court to list the claim for a disposal hearing, as Chief Master Marsh explained in *Sovereign Trustees Ltd v Lewis*:[86]

> "*Part 8 claims are markedly different to Part 7 claims. Although there is no bar to issuing a Part 24 application [i.e. an application for summary judgment] in a Part 8 claim, it will rarely be necessary for the claimant to do so where it is seeking judgment on the whole of the claim. In part this is because the second limb of CPR 24.2 will normally have no application because there will be no 'trial' as such. Part 8 claims are normally resolved at a 'disposal hearing'. This is made clear by paragraph 8.1 of Practice Direction 8A which states:*
>
> *'8.1 The court may on the hearing date –*
>
> *(i) proceed to hear the case and dispose of the claim;*
>
> *(ii) give case management directions.'*
>
> *It follows that in most Part 8 claims, where the relief sought is unopposed, or cannot realistically be opposed, it will suffice for the claimant to ask the court to fix a disposal hearing at which the court may determine whether or not the relief sought by the claimant should be granted.*"

Claimant's reply

CPR Part 8 claims: claimant's evidence in reply

If the claimant wishes to rely on further written evidence in reply to the defendant's evidence, he must file it within 14 days of service of the

86 [2016] EWHC 2593 (Ch) at [3]. See also paragraph 29.91 of the Chancery Guide in relation to uncontentious claims for the rectification of pension schemes. However, it should be noted that in *The Girls' Day School Trust v GDST Pension Trustees Ltd* [2016] EWHC 1254 (Ch) summary judgment was granted without a hearing in an unopposed claim for the rectification of a pension scheme.

defendant's evidence on him,[87] and he must also serve a copy of it on the other parties "*within the same time limit*".[88] As that time limit is also quite short, paragraph 7.5 of CPR Practice Direction 8A also allows the parties to agree in writing to extend it by up to 14 days; i.e. the maximum period which the parties can agree is that the claimant shall file his evidence in reply 28 days after service of the defendant's evidence on him.[89] Any such agreement should similarly be filed at court.[90] In the same way as a defendant, a claimant may not rely on any written evidence which has not been served in accordance with the rules described above at the hearing of the claim unless the court gives permission.[91]

If a claimant requires more time to file his evidence in reply to the defendant's, he too should apply to the court for an extension of time by way of an application pursuant to CPR Part 23.[92] The guidance contained in paragraph 9.7 of the Chancery Guide – which is considered above in the context of the defendant's evidence – applies equally to applications for extensions of time by claimants. In particular, parties should bear in mind that the court is likely to grant reasonable requests for extensions of time and expects parties to "*at all times act co-operatively and agree reasonable requests for additional time*" and may punish in costs a party who unreasonably opposes an application.[93]

---

87 CPR rule 8.5(5); and see paragraph 9.6 of the Chancery Guide.

88 CPR rule 8.5(6).

89 Paragraph 7.5(2)(b) of CPR Practice Direction 8A; and see paragraph 9.6 of the Chancery Guide.

90 Although the CPR does not appear to require this, paragraph 9.7 of the Chancery Guide does.

91 CPR rule 8.6(1).

92 Paragraph 7.4 of CPR Practice Direction 8A.

93 Paragraph 9.7 of the Chancery Guide.

CPR Part 7 claims: claimant's reply

If the claimant wishes to file a reply, he must file it with his directions questionnaire.[94] The CPR requires the claimant to serve a reply on the other parties "*at the same time it is filed*".[95] However, the Chancery Guide encourages claimants to serve replies before filing directions questionnaires if possible to give the other parties an opportunity to consider the reply before they file their own directions questionnaires.[96]

As well as the rules in CPR rule 16.7 and CPR Practice Direction 16, the drafting guidelines contained in paragraphs 10.5 to 10.17 of the Chancery Guide apply to replies.

Directions and case management

CPR Part 8 claims

In some CPR Part 8 cases the court may give directions immediately after the claim has been issued, either on the application of a party or of its own initiative, which may include fixing a hearing date.[97] This is likely to happen particularly in cases which have been issued without naming a defendant pursuant to CPR rule 8.2A.[98] However, it is more usual for the claim to be referred to the Master[99] only after an acknowledgment of service has been filed or after the period for doing so has expired.[100]

---

94 CPR rule 15.8(a).

95 CPR rule 15.8(b).

96 Paragraph 10.3 of the Chancery Guide.

97 Paragraph 6.1 of CPR Practice Direction 8A.

98 Paragraph 29.14 of the Chancery Guide.

99 Or to a District Judge of the High Court if the claim is in one of the District Registries.

100 Paragraph 6.2 of CPR Practice Direction 8A; see also paragraphs 9.10, 15.9 and 17.65 of the Chancery Guide.

At that stage the Master will consider whether the claim may be capable of being dealt with 'on the file', i.e. on the papers without a hearing.[101] This might be appropriate if the claim is unopposed,[102] but even then the court may want to hear argument from the claimant at a hearing as to why rectification should in fact be granted.[103]

If no acknowledgment of service has been filed, the Master may "*sometimes override the provisions of Part 8 by directing that the defendant must file and serve an acknowledgment and evidence by a specified date failing which the defendant will not be entitled to play any part in the disposal hearing*".[104] Doing so is "*intended to make explicit for a [litigant in person] what is already set out in the CPR*".[105] If this route is taken, directions may be given to lead straight to disposal hearing (without a directions hearing being held first).

On the other hand, if an acknowledgment of service has been filed, the claim is likely to be listed for a directions hearing in the first instance,[106] and some directions may be given as to how the parties should prepare for it.

At a directions hearing, the issues which the court is likely to consider are:[107]

(a) Evidence, including whether directions should be given for the filing of any further evidence (in addition to the evidence which will already have been filed by that point) and whether any witnesses should be required to attend to give oral evidence and be

101 Paragraph 17.65 of the Chancery Guide.

102 Paragraph 15.11 of the Chancery Guide. See e.g. *Millar v Millar* [2018] EWHC 1926 (Ch).

103 See e.g. *Andrews v Andrews* [2014] EWHC 1725 (Ch) and *Armstrong v Armstrong* [2019] EWHC 2259 (Ch).

104 Paragraph 15.09 of the Chancery Guide.

105 *Ibid.*

106 Paragraphs 15.10 and 17.66 of the Chancery Guide.

107 See paragraph 17.74 of the Chancery Guide.

cross-examined at the disposal hearing.[108] If a rectification claim is proceeding pursuant to CPR Part 8 because it is unopposed (at least by the affected beneficiaries who are capacitous adults), it is likely to be decided on written evidence only.[109] However, if it is opposed but is proceeding pursuant to CPR Part 8 because it has been brought as an alternative to a construction claim, thought should be given as to whether to seek directions for witnesses (such as the draftsman, if the trust instrument was professionally prepared) to be required to attend to give oral evidence and be cross-examined at the disposal hearing.

(b) Representation of the parties, such as whether any litigation friend needs to be appointed and/or whether any representation order should be made and/or notice given pursuant to CPR rule 19.8A (as to which, see Parties above).

(c) Directions in relation to the disposal hearing, such as directions about when and how the disposal hearing should be listed,[110] its time estimate, and the level of judge required. As regards time estimate, this is likely to depend in particular on the number and complexity of the rectification arguments which are being advanced, and on whether there is going to be live oral evidence from witnesses who will be cross-examined. As regards level of judge, CPR rule 2.4 provides that in proceedings in the High Court, any act which may be performed by the court may be performed "*by any judge, Master, Registrar in Bankruptcy or District Judge*".[111] Paragraph 7B.1 of CPR Practice Direction 2B does not impose any restriction on the jurisdiction of Masters in London

108 CPR rule 8.6(2) provides "*The court may require or permit a party to give oral evidence at the hearing*" and CPR rule 8.6(3) provides "*The court may give directions requiring the attendance for cross-examination of a witness who has given written evidence*".

109 See paragraph 9.3 of the Chancery Guide: "*Part 8 claims will generally be disposed of on written evidence without cross-examination. The witness statements with the claim form should be sufficient in most cases to define the issues*".

110 Unless oral evidence is envisaged, CPR Part 8 proceedings are usually entered in the General List: see paragraphs 21.5 and 21.6 of the Chancery Guide.

to decide claims for the rectification of trust instruments.[112] On the contrary, sub-paragraph 3 of paragraph 14.2 of the Chancery Guide lists "*Rectification*" as one of the "*non-excluded matters*" which paragraph 14.3 indicates "*should normally be listed before a Master*", "*whether for case management, interim relief or disposal*". Paragraph 14.3 goes on to provide: "*If it is considered that exceptionally the application should be heard by a High Court Judge the Master should be requested to release it.*" This is confirmed by paragraph 29.71 of the Chancery Guide, which provides: "*Since 6th April 2015 the Masters have jurisdiction to deal with all rectification claims. The Master will only refer an application which is consented to the judge if it raises issues of particular difficulty.*" Thus, rectification claims proceeding in London are likely to be decided by a Master. However, for claims proceeding in the District Registries it should be noted that paragraph 7B.2(e) provides that a District Judge in a District Registry may not make an order for rectification without the consent of the Supervising Judge for the region in which the District Judge is sitting, or without the consent of their nominee.

(d) 'Housekeeping' directions to prepare the case for the disposal hearing, such as directions relating to the hearing bundle,[113] skeleton arguments,[114] and other documents such as dramatis per-

---

111 Note the reference to 'District Judge' here is to a District Judge of the High Court (who is broadly the equivalent in the District Registries of a Master in London), not to a District Judge of the County Court.

112 This is confirmed by paragraph 29.71 of the Chancery Guide: "*Since 6th April 2015 the Masters have jurisdiction to deal with all rectification claims. The Master will only refer an application which is consented to the judge if it raises issues of particular difficulty.*"

113 Detailed rules in relation to hearing bundles are contained in paragraph 3 of CPR Practice Direction 39A and are supplemented by the guidance contained in paragraphs 21.34 to 21.72 of the Chancery Guide.

114 In relation to which see paragraphs 21.73 to 21.81 of the Chancery Guide.

sonae, chronologies, case summaries, lists of issues,[115] reading lists[116] and bundles of authorities.[117]

CPR Part 7 claims: costs and case management conference

If the rectification claim is proceeding by way of a CPR Part 7 claim, it will generally be referred to the Master for review following the filing of a defence.[118] The court will generally send the parties a Notice of Provisional Allocation (form N149C) with a letter explaining what the parties are required to do.[119] If the parties do not wish there to be a stay for alternative dispute resolution, they must serve and file with the court by the date specified in the letter the directions questionnaire, disclosure report, list of issues (agreed or not agreed), draft directions and costs budgets (if applicable).[120] The claimant must then lodge a bundle with the statements of case and all the additional documents served following the provisional notice of allocation which will be reviewed by the Master.[121] The Chancery Guide explains that it is "*incumbent on the parties to ensure that the court is provided with helpful and complete information because a number of important issues will be made on the file review*".[122] These include considering any request for a stay or for the continuation of an existing stay; whether the claim should remain in the Court in which it has been issued or be transferred (e.g. to one of the District Registries);[123] reviewing draft directions, including the appropriate case management track; and considering costs management.[124]

---

115 In relation to which see paragraphs 21.75, 21.76 and 21.83 of the Chancery Guide.

116 In relation to which see paragraph 21.82 of the Chancery Guide.

117 In relation to which see paragraphs 21.85 to 21.87 of the Chancery Guide.

118 Paragraph 15.7 of the Chancery Guide.

119 *Ibid.*

120 *Ibid.*

121 *Ibid.* and see also paragraph 17.7 of the Chancery Guide.

122 *Ibid.*

123 In relation to which see paragraphs 14.15 to 14.20 of the Chancery Guide.

124 See also paragraph 17.7 of the Chancery Guide.

In most cases, the claim will be listed for a costs and case management conference ("CCMC").[125] At such a hearing, the issues which the court is likely to consider are the same as those which would be considered at a directions hearing if the claim were proceeding as a CPR Part 8 claim (discussed above). However, the sequence of events is likely to be different: in CPR Part 8 claims, by the time the case reaches a directions hearing, witness statements will have already been filed and exchanged, and the relevant documents which the parties wish to rely on will usually have already been disclosed (generally as exhibits to the witness statements). On the other hand, in CPR Part 7 claims, directions for disclosure and witness statements are generally given at the CCMC.

Disclosure – CPR Part 7 claims

This section considers disclosure in claims which are brought pursuant to CPR Part 7. Disclosure in CPR Part 8 claims is considered above.

In general terms, in contested rectification claims which involve a professionally prepared trust instrument, the key documentary evidence – and often the only documentary evidence – is usually the file relating to the instrument. Such files are rarely particularly extensive, usually running into the dozens of pages (sometimes into the hundreds, but very rarely into the thousands). As a result, there is normally little difficulty or cost in the file being disclosed in its entirety, usually when the rectification problem is being investigated (and thus before any proceedings are issued).

Where a file relates to more than one client – which is not uncommon for example where both members of a couple have undertaken a tax planning exercise at the same time using the same solicitor – it may be necessary to redact privileged information relating to the other client (unless that client waives privilege).

In addition to the file, it may be useful to consider whether there could be any other documentary evidence of the settlor's intentions, for

125 Paragraph 17.3 of the Chancery Guide states: "*The majority of claims do not permit case management "on the file" and the court will rarely be able to approve agreed directions*".

example in any diary or other notes he may have kept (including electronic notes such as draft emails or notes made on a computer or a mobile phone or a tablet). Often settlors do not discuss what they might consider to be their private personal affairs with friends or even family, but another source of documentary evidence of the settlor's intentions could be any correspondence in which these were discussed, including both formal correspondence, such as letters and emails, and more informal communications, such as text messages, WhatsApp messages or other forms of electronic communication.

CPR Practice Direction 51U contains a new 'disclosure pilot' which is intended to replace, and significantly change, the traditional approach to standard disclosure which has previously applied in most CPR Part 7 claims.[126] The Pilot came into force on 1st January 2019 and applies to both existing CPR Part 7 claims and to new CPR Part 7 claims issued after that date in the Business and Property Courts of England and Wales.[127] It will remain in force for two years.[128]

The provisions of the pilot are detailed. In summary, it is suggested that the following points are likely to be particularly relevant in rectification claims.

1. The pilot creates a new concept of 'Initial Disclosure'.[129] This is the requirement that each party provides the other parties at the same time as its statement of case – and thus before any directions for disclosure are given by the court – an 'Initial Disclosure List of Documents' that "*lists and is accompanied by copies of: (1) the key documents on which it has relied (expressly or otherwise) in support of the claims or defences advanced in its statement of case (and including the documents referred to in that statement of case); and (2) the key documents that are necessary to enable the other*

126 In relation to the application of the pilot in CPR Part 8 claims, see "Disclosure – Part 8 Claims" above.

127 Paragraph 1.2 of CPR Practice Direction 51U.

128 Paragraph 1.2 of CPR Practice Direction 51U.

129 Paragraph 5 of CPR Practice Direction 51U.

parties to understand the claim or defence they have to meet."[130] Initial Disclosure does not apply if it would require a party to disclose more than the larger of 1,000 pages or 200 documents.[131] It is suggested that this threshold is unlikely to be met in most rectification claims, and Initial Disclosure is therefore likely to apply. The parties can also agree in writing prior to the commencement of proceedings that Initial Disclosure should not apply; however, they should only do so with good reason, as the court may review the parties' reasons for disapplying Initial Disclosure at the first case management conference and may set aside such an agreement aside if it considers that Initial Disclosure "*is likely to provide significant benefits and the costs of providing Initial Disclosure are unlikely to be disproportionate to such benefits*".[132]

2. Once proceedings have commenced, the parties are under a duty "*to disclose, regardless of any order for disclosure made, known adverse documents, unless they are privileged*"[133] in accordance with the provisions of the pilot. 'Known adverse documents' are "*documents (other than privileged documents) that a party is actually aware (without undertaking any further search for documents than it has already undertaken or caused to be undertaken) both (a) are or were previously within its control and (b) are adverse.*"[134] A document is 'adverse' if "*it or any information it contains contradicts or materially damages the disclosing party's contention or version of events on an issue in dispute, or supports the contention or version of events of an opposing party on an issue in dispute*".[135] The duty to disclose adverse documents applies throughout the proceedings[136] and irrespective of any order for Extended Disclosure: "*if adverse*

130 Paragraph 5.1 of CPR Practice Direction 51U.

131 Paragraph 5.3(3) of CPR Practice Direction 51U.

132 Paragraph 5.8 of CPR Practice Direction 51U.

133 Paragraph 3.1(2) of CPR Practice Direction 51U.

134 Paragraph 2.8 of CPR Practice Direction 51U.

135 Paragraph 2.7 of CPR Practice Direction 51U.

136 Paragraph 3.3 of CPR Practice Direction 51U.

documents in the control of a party come to its knowledge at a later date they must (unless privileged) be disclosed without delay".[137]

3. A party wishing to seek disclosure of documents in addition to, or as an alternative to, Initial Disclosure must request 'Extended Disclosure'.[138] This is done by completing a 'Disclosure Review Document' in advance of the first case management conference in accordance with paragraph 7 of CPR Practice Direction 51U (no application notice is required).[139] An order for Extended Disclosure will only be made where the court "*is persuaded that it is appropriate to do so in order fairly to resolve one or more of the Issues for Disclosure*".[140] The order "*must be reasonable and proportionate having regard to the overriding objective*"[141] and to the seven factors listed in paragraph 6.4 of CPR Practice Direction 51U.[142] The 'Issues for Disclosure' are "*those key issues in dispute, which the parties consider will need to be determined by the court with some reference to contemporaneous documents in order for there to be a fair resolution of the proceedings*";[143] however, this does not extend

---

137 Paragraph 9.3 of CPR Practice Direction 51U.

138 Paragraph 6.1 of CPR Practice Direction 51U.

139 *Ibid.*

140 Paragraph 6.3 of CPR Practice Direction 51U.

141 Paragraph 6.4 of CPR Practice Direction 51U.

142 These are:

(1) the nature and complexity of the issues in the proceedings;

(2) the importance of the case, including any non-monetary relief sought;

(3) the likelihood of documents existing that will have probative value in supporting or undermining a party's claim or defence;

(4) the number of documents involved;

(5) the ease and expense of searching for and retrieval of any particular document (taking into account any limitations on the information available and on the likely accuracy of any costs estimates);

(6) the financial position of each party; and

(7) the need to ensure the case is dealt with expeditiously, fairly and at a proportionate cost.

143 Paragraph 7.3 of CPR Practice Direction 51U.

"*to every issue which is disputed in the statements of case by denial or non-admission.*"[144] The parties are required to identify and to try to agree the List of Issues for Disclosure in section 1A of the Disclosure Review Document.[145] In relation to each Issue for Disclosure, the parties must also consider which of the five 'Disclosure Models' identified in paragraph 8 of CPR Practice Direction 51U should apply.[146] Although the parties may agree that a particular Model should apply to a particular Issue for Disclosure, no Model will in fact apply without the approval of the court,[147] who will usually consider whether to make an order for Extended Disclosure and, if so, on what terms at the first case management conference.

4. The pilot also imposes a duty to "*to take reasonable steps to preserve documents […] that may be relevant to any issue in the proceedings*".[148] This duty applies to:

   (a) "*[a] person who knows that it is or may become a party to proceedings that have been commenced or who knows that it may become a party to proceedings that may be commenced*";[149] and

   (b) "*[l]egal representatives who have the conduct of litigation on behalf of a party to proceedings that have been commenced, or who are instructed with a view to the conduct of litigation where their client knows it may become a party to proceedings that have been or may be commenced*".[150]

The duty to preserve documents applies to "*documents which might otherwise be deleted or destroyed in accordance with a doc-*

144 *Ibid.*

145 Paragraph 7 of CPR Practice Direction 51U.

146 See also paragraph 9 of CPR Practice Direction 51U.

147 Paragraph 8.2 of CPR Practice Direction 51U.

148 Paragraph 3.1(1) and 3.2(1) of CPR Practice Direction 51U.

149 Paragraph 3.1 of CPR Practice Direction 51U.

150 Paragraph 3.2 of CPR Practice Direction 51U.

> *ument retention policy or in the ordinary course of business*"[151] and "*[p]reservation includes, in suitable cases, making copies of sources and documents and storing them.*"[152] Legal representatives are also under a duty to notify their client of the duty to preserve documents "*within a reasonable period of being instructed*"[153] and to obtain written confirmation from the client that any document deletion or destruction processes have been suspended for the duration of the proceedings in accordance with paragraphs 4.2 and 4.3 of CPR Practice Direction 51U.

As indicated above, in most rectification claims the key – and possibly the only – documentary evidence is likely to be the file relating to the instrument. In practice, this will usually be disclosed during pre-action correspondence. It also seems likely that in most cases all other relevant documentary evidence will be disclosed either pre-action or during Initial Disclosure, and that it will therefore rarely be necessary to seek an order for Extended Disclosure.

Depending on the circumstances, it may also be worth considering whether disclosure should be sought from a non-party pursuant to CPR rule 31.17.

<u>Witness statements</u>

In CPR Part 8 claims, witness statements will have already been filed and served at the early stages of the proceedings (as discussed above).

In CPR Part 7 claims, directions for the exchange of witness statements are normally given at the CCMC. Who should be asked to give evidence and what that topics that evidence should cover will depend on the particular circumstances of the case. In general terms, the topics which the evidence is likely to have to cover are the same which the particulars of claim should cover, viz.:

---

151 Paragraph 4.1 of CPR Practice Direction 51U; see also paragraph 4.2 and 4.3.

152 Paragraph 3.2 of CPR Practice Direction 51U.

153 Paragraph 4.4 of CPR Practice Direction 51U.

(a) the claimant's role and the capacity in which he brings the claim;

(b) the factual background;

(c) the current drafting of the trust instrument and its construction;

(d) what the settlor's intentions are alleged to have been;

(e) how the current drafting of the trust instrument fails to correctly record the settlor's intentions;

(f) how the court is being asked to rectify the trust instrument;

(g) the position of the other interested parties.

In cases involving a professionally prepared trust instrument, the key witness evidence is generally likely to be that of the individual or individuals who were involved in taking instructions for, drafting and/or arranging the execution of the instrument. Indeed, in some cases the draftsman may be the only witness.[154] Depending on how involved they were, any attesting witnesses may also be able to shed light on the settlor's intentions and on the process by which the trust instrument was prepared.

If the settlor discussed his intentions with family and/or friends (who may or may not be beneficiaries or intended beneficiaries of the trust), these individuals may also be able to give evidence on the issue.

Disposal hearing/trial

At the disposal hearing (in CPR Part 8 claims) or trial (in CPR Part 7 claims), the court will hear the argument in favour and against rectification. In CPR Part 8 claims, directions will have previously been given as to whether there should be oral evidence and cross-examination of any of the witnesses (e.g. the draftsman).

154 See e.g. the will case of *Re Bimson* [2010] EWHC 3679 (Ch) at [6].

Disposal hearings/trials in rectification claims are generally listed in public, i.e. in a court which is open to members of the public.[155] Whilst it may be possible in some cases to persuade a court to list the claim in private pursuant to CPR rule 39.2(3),[156] or to impose some other less extensive reporting restriction,[157] a party seeking such an order is likely to have to show compelling reasons why the court should depart from the principle of open justice.[158]

<u>Judgment</u>

The Master or judge will decide how, when and where to deliver judgment. Judgment may be delivered orally immediately at the conclusion of the hearing (a so-called '*ex tempore*' judgment),[159] or may be reserved. A reserved judgment may be delivered orally at a later date or, more commonly, may be circulated in written draft to the parties and then formally handed down at a subsequent date. Sometimes – particularly in urgent cases – the court may announce its decision and make

---

155 Under the general rule in CPR rule 39.2(1).

156 CPR rule 39.2 requires the court to sit in private if it is satisfied (i) that "*it is necessary to sit in private to secure the proper administration of justice*" and (ii) that one or more of the 7 sub-rules of CPR rule 39.2(3) is engaged. Of those sub-rules, those which may be engaged in a rectification claim are likely to be (c), (d), (f) and/or (g), which provide:

> *(c) [the hearing] involves confidential information (including information relating to personal financial matters) and publicity would damage that confidentiality;*
>
> *(d) a private hearing is necessary to protect the interests of any child or protected party;*
>
> *[…]*
>
> *(f) [the hearing] involves uncontentious matters arising in the administration of trusts or in the administration of a deceased person's estate; or*
>
> *(g) the court for any other reason considers [a hearing in private] to be necessary to secure the proper administration of justice.*"

157 See e.g. *A v D* [2017] EWHC 2222 (Ch) and *ABC v JKL* [2019] EWHC 2416 (Ch).

158 See in this regard the Court of Appeal's guidance in *MN v OP* [2019] EWCA Civ 679 regarding privacy and reporting restrictions in the context of applications pursuant to the Variation of Trusts Act 1958.

159 See e.g. *Slattery v Jagger* [2015] EWHC 3976 (Ch).

any necessary order at the conclusion of the hearing and provide its reasoned judgment at a later date.[160]

<u>Costs</u>

As indicated at 5.2.3 above, if the trust instrument was professionally prepared and the circumstances indicate that a professional negligence claim against the draftsman is likely, his insurers may have agreed in advance to fund the costs of the rectification claim. Where the claim is unopposed, the court will often be asked to make no order as to costs, on the basis that the parties will recover their costs from the draftsman's insurer as agreed.[161]

On the other hand, if the rectification claim is contested, the general rule (which applies in all civil litigation) is that the unsuccessful party will be ordered to pay the costs of the successful party.[162] However, costs are ultimately in the discretion of the court,[163] and the court may therefore decide to depart from that starting point and make a different costs order. In general terms, in deciding costs the court will try to ensure that the costs are in fact borne by the negligent draftsman and/or (in contested case) by the party who has lost, and not by the successful party. In deciding precisely how this should be achieved in the circumstances of the case, the court will have to take into account the parties' respective interests under the will, and in particular who would in fact bear the costs if the costs are ordered to be paid out of the trust.[164]

160 See e.g. *Sovereign Trustees Ltd v Lewis* [2016] EWHC 2593 (Ch) at [13] and [43], and *ABC v JKL* [2019] EWHC 2416 (Ch) at [4].

161 See e.g. *Re Bimson* [2010] EWHC 3679 (Ch) at [23] and *Gerling v Gerling* [2010] EWHC 3661 (Ch) at [50].

162 CPR rule 44.2.(2)(a).

163 Section 51(1) of the Senior Courts Act 1981.

164 See e.g. *Marley v Rawlings (costs)* [2014] UKSC 51 and *Slattery v Jagger* [2015] EWHC 3976 (Ch) at [103]-[112].

Order

If the rectification claim succeeds, the order will need to make it clear precisely how the will is being rectified. It will usually be sensible for one of the recitals to record that the court was satisfied that the trust instrument fails to record the settlor's intentions.

How the rectification is best recorded in the order is will depend on precisely what the rectification consists of. In general terms, it is suggested that:

(a) if the rectification is straightforward and can be clearly described in few words, this can be done in the body of the order (e.g. "clause 5 is rectified by the insertion of "Brünnhilde," between "daughters" and "Gerhilde"");[165]

(b) however, if the rectification is less straightforward, it is likely to be sensible for the body of the order to refer to a schedule (e.g. by providing: "the Deed is rectified in the manner set out in the Schedule hereto"), and for the schedule to then set out the rectified version of the relevant provisions of the trust instrument.

Chapter 22 of the Chancery Guide contains guidance in relation to the drafting, filing and sealing of orders.

Appeals

A party who is dissatisfied with the court's decision must obtain the court's permission in order to appeal it.[166] The court will only grant permission to appeal if it considers that the appeal would have a real prospect of success, or that there is some other compelling reason for the appeal to be heard.[167]

---

165 See Example 10.

166 CPR rule 52.3(1).

167 CPR rule 52.6(1).

Although this is not strictly required, it is generally sensible for a party who wishes to appeal to first seek permission from the lower court.[168] This is usually done when judgment is delivered or handed down and consequential issues, such as the terms of the order giving effect to the judgment and costs, are decided.

If the lower court refuses permission, or if permission was not sought from it, permission must be sought from the appeal court by filing an Appellant's Notice.[169] Unless the court orders otherwise, the time limit for doing so is "*21 days after the date of the decision of the lower court*".[170] That is a relatively short time limit, which cannot be extended by agreement between the parties,[171] and it must be borne in mind that the period starts to run from the date of the decision of the lower court and not, if later, the date on which consequential matters are decided or the date on which the order giving effect to the decision is approved and sealed.[172] If – as is quite common – the lower court's judgment is circulated to the parties in draft and then formally handed down in the absence of the parties, and a hearing to decide consequential matter is arranged at a later date, the lower court should be asked to direct[173] that the 21-day period will only start to run from the date of the later hearing, rather than from the date on which judgment was handed down.[174]

---

168 Pursuant to CPR rule 52.3(2)(a); see e.g. *In re T (A Child)* [2002] EWCA Civ 1736 at [12]-[13].

169 CPR rules 52.3(2)(b) and 52.12(1).

170 CPR rule 52.12(2)(b).

171 CPR rule 52.15(2).

172 See e.g. *Sayers v Clarke Walker (A Firm)* [2002] EWCA Civ 645 at [8]-[9] and *Owusu v Jackson* [2002] EWCA Civ 877 at [24]-[27].

173 Pursuant to CPR 52.12(2)(a).

174 See e.g. *Jackson v Marina Homes Ltd* [2007] EWCA Civ 1404 at [8].

Compromise

In some cases it may be possible to compromise a rectification claim after proceedings have been issued.[175] The mechanism by which the compromise should be implemented will inevitably depend on its terms and on the particular circumstances of the case. In most cases, the following will have to be considered:

(a) Whether the compromise has any tax implications and, if so, how these should be addressed.

(b) Whether a court order rectifying the trust instrument is required, and if so whether the court can be asked to make the order by consent without hearing full argument. In *Burford (Fareham) Ltd v Christian Vision*[176] (which involved the rectification of a deed of assignment of warranties) the court held that there is no "*blanket rule that rectification should not be ordered by consent*"[177] and that the question is one of the court's discretion. However, it should be borne in mind that this jurisdiction is exercised sparingly. In this regard, paragraph 29.69 of the Chancery Guide provides: "*It is not the practice of the court to make an order for rectification by default or by consent. The court is sometimes asked to make an order for rectification to which all relevant parties consent, but the court will not, even in such a case, make an order without being satisfied that it is justified by the evidence. The court will therefore wish to scrutinise carefully the changes that are proposed, the reasons for them and the evidence in support*".

(c) Whether the court's approval of the compromise is required, which will be the case where one or more of the parties is a minor,[178] an adult who lacks capacity to conduct litigation[179]

175 The circumstances in which it may be possible to resolve a rectification issue without the need for court proceedings are considered at 5.2.2 above.

176 [2005] EWHC 2533 (Ch).

177 [2005] EWHC 2533 (Ch) at [7].

178 CPR rule 21.10.

and/or a party who has been appointed to represent others pursuant to CPR rule 19.7.[180]

Paragraphs 22.9 to 22.13 of the Chancery Guide contain guidance in relation to consent orders.

---

179 *Ibid.*

180 CPR rule 19.7(5).

CHAPTER SIX
MISTAKE AND HASTINGS-BASS

When dealing with a voluntary lifetime transaction[1] in which something has gone wrong, it is usually worth considering whether the doctrine of mistake and/or the so-called 'rule in *Re Hastings-Bass*' can assist.[2] These doctrines are different from construction and rectification, both in their nature and as regards the remedy they can lead to. This chapter provides a summary overview of the two doctrines and of their interplay with construction and rectification.

6.1 Mistake

<u>The law</u>

The doctrine of equitable mistake has regained popularity following *Pitt v Holt*.[3] In that case the Supreme Court adopted the approach of the Court of Appeal and the House of Lords in *Ogilvie v Littleboy*,[4] a case which was described as having "*emerged from the shadows [...] after a century of obscurity*".[5]

The applicable principles which emerge from *Pitt v Holt*[6] have been summarised as follows:[7]

1 The doctrine of mistake and *Hastings-Bass* discussed in chapter cannot be invoked to address a drafting problem in a will.

2 Other possible vitiating factors which might also need to be considered include lack of capacity, fraud, misrepresentation, duress and/or undue influence. These are outside the scope of this book.

3 [2013] UKSC 26.

4 (1897) 13 TLR 399 and (1899) 15 TLR 294.

5 *Pitt v Holt* [2013] UKSC 26 at [12].

6 [2013] UKSC 26.

7 In *Van der Merwe v Goldman* [2016] EWHC 790 (Ch) at [26]. The references in square brackets are to paragraph numbers of the decision in *Pitt v Holt*. This summary was adopted in *Smith v Stanley* [2019] EWHC 2168 (Ch) at [62]-[63]

(1) a donor can rescind a gift by showing that he acted under some mistake of so serious a character as to render it unjust on the part of the donee to retain the gift: [101], quoting Ogilvie v Littleboy (1897) 13 TLR 399 at 400;

(2) a mistake is to be distinguished from mere inadvertence or misprediction: [104];

(3) forgetfulness, inadvertence or ignorance are not, as such, a mistake but can lead to a false belief or assumption which the law will recognise as a mistake: [105];

(4) it does not matter that the mistake was due to carelessness on the part of the person making the voluntary disposition unless the circumstances are such as to show that he deliberately ran the risk, or must be taken to have run the risk, of being wrong: [114];

(5) equity requires the gravity of the mistake to be assessed in terms of injustice or unconscionability: [124];

(6) the evaluation of unconscionability is objective: [125];

(7) the gravity of the mistake must be assessed by a close examination of the facts which include the circumstances of the mistake and its consequences for the party making the mistaken disposition: [126];

(8) the court needs to focus intensely on the facts of the particular case: [126];

(9) a mistake about the tax consequences of a transaction can be a relevant mistake: [129]-[132];

---

and *Re Clarke* [2019] EWHC 1193 and 1194 (Ch) at [103]. See also the similar 4-point summary in *Kennedy v Kennedy* [2014] EWHC 4129 (Ch) at [36], which was adopted in *Freedman v Freedman* [2015] EWHC 1457 (Ch) at [16], *South Downs Trustees Ltd v GH* [2018] EWHC 1064 (Ch) at [33], *Hartogs v Sequent (Schweiz) AG* [2019] EWHC 1915 (Ch) at [19] and *Rogge v Rogge* [2019] EWHC 1949 (Ch) at [43].

(10) where the relevant mistake is a mistake about the tax consequences of a transaction, then:

> *"[i]n some cases of artificial tax avoidance, the court might think it right to refuse relief, either on the ground that such claimants, acting on supposedly expert advice, must be taken to have accepted the risk that the scheme would prove ineffective, or on the ground that discretionary relief should be refused on grounds of public policy." [135];*

(11) it is not pointless, nor is it acting in vain, to set aside a transaction and to remove a liability to pay tax, even where that is the principal, or the only, effect of the setting aside: [136]-[141]."

The remedy

If the court is satisfied that a relevant type of mistake has occurred, this renders the transaction voidable in equity (not void at law).[8] The remedy is usually rescission, i.e. the setting aside or undoing of the transaction.[9] The remedy is discretionary and the court has to consider whether it should in fact be granted. In doing so it will take into account factors such as any delay in bringing the claim and any rights any third party may have acquired.[10]

If the court rescinds the transaction, it is treated as never having taken place.[11] In the case of voluntary dispositions, the court may rescind a transaction in part and notwithstanding that restitution is impossible.[12]

---

8 *Kennedy v Kennedy* [2014] EWHC 4129 (Ch) at [41].

9 See e.g. *Pitt v Holt* [2013] UKSC 26 at [130] and *Payne v Tyler* [2019] EWHC 2347 (Ch) at [33].

10 See e.g. *Bainbridge v Bainbridge* [2016] EWHC 898 (Ch) at [20].

11 See e.g. *Pitt v Holt* [2013] UKSC 26 at [130] ("*if a transaction is set aside the Court is in effect deciding that a transaction of the specified description is not to be treated as having occurred*") and *Bainbridge v Bainbridge* [2016] EWHC 898 (Ch) at [37] ("*the effect of an equitable rescission for mistake is to undo the transaction from the beginning. It is thereafter treated for the purposes of the general law as if it never took place*").

The interplay with construction and rectification

As the above outline shows, mistake is fundamentally different from construction and rectification. Construction involves asking the court to clarify the terms of the transaction. Rectification involves asking the court to correct a mistake in the way in which the transaction has been recorded (as opposed to a mistake in the transaction itself).[13] Both can affect the consequences of the transaction, including its tax consequences, but in both the hoped-for outcome is one in which the transaction continues to stand, but its terms (and thus potentially its consequences) are clarified and/or corrected.

On the other hand, mistake involves asking the court to set aside the transaction altogether because it was entered into as a result of the mistake. The hoped-for outcome is one in which the transaction is rescinded, i.e. treated as if it had never happened.

In most situations it is likely that the factual circumstances will mean that it is only desirable to seek either construction/rectification or mistake, but not both. For instance, in general terms where the intention was to carry out a transaction at a particular time, rescinding it is unlikely to be desirable. This is the case for example with transactions which are intended to be potentially exempt transfers ("PET") for inheritance tax purposes, which must be made a sufficient number of years[14] prior to the donor's death to achieve a tax advantage, and with deeds varying the devolution of an estate, which must be made within 2 years of the deceased's death in order to be 'read back' for inheritance tax and capital gains tax purposes.[15] With these sorts of transactions, if a mistake comes to light some time – perhaps several years – after the transaction, then rescinding the transaction altogether is unlikely to be

---

12 See e.g. *Kennedy v Kennedy* [2014] EWHC 4129 (Ch) at [46], *Bainbridge v Bainbridge* [2016] EWHC 898 (Ch) at [21]-[22] and *Rogge v Rogge* [2019] EWHC 1949 (Ch) at [167]-[168].

13 See e.g. *Racal Group Services Ltd v Ashmore* [1995] STC 1151 at 1154h.

14 At least 3 and preferably more than 7.

15 See section 142 of the Inheritance Tax Act 1984 and section 62 of the Taxation of Chargeable Gains Act 1992.

desirable. In the case of the former, the donor's death will now inevitably be some years closer or may even have already happened, so it will be undesirable or impossible to rescind the original transaction and make a new PET.[16] In the case of the latter, the 2-year period may have expired by the time the mistake comes to light, and it will therefore be impossible to rescind the original deed of variation and make a new one.[17] In these sorts of cases, the hope will be to remedy the error through construction and/or rectification.

On the other hand, following *Pitt v Holt* the doctrine of mistake is often invoked where the transaction has led to unexpected tax consequences.[18] In such cases, the construction of the relevant instrument will often be clear (so a construction claim will not be necessary or appropriate) and it will not be possible to argue that there is a mistake in the way in which the transaction has been recorded – particularly where the donor/settlor has acted on professional advice and the documentation giving effect to the transaction is clear and accords with the advice (but the problem is the advice is wrong). Instead, in these sorts of cases, the hope will be to remedy the error by setting aside the transaction altogether on the basis of mistake.

In certain particular factual circumstances, it may be desirable to argue construction and/or rectification and mistake in the alternative. This

16 See e.g. *Allnutt v Wilding* [2007] EWCA Civ 412, in which the Court of Appeal expressly acknowledged this point at [8]: "*The trustees here do not ask this court to set aside the settlement on the grounds that a mistake was made by the settlor in executing a discretionary settlement instead of an interest in possession settlement. This is not surprising. The effect of setting aside this settlement would be that the funds would then form part of the settlor's estate and would be liable to inheritance tax. It is, of course, impossible for any new settlement to be executed, which would have the tax advantages that the settlor and his advisers hoped to achieve*".

17 See e.g. *Ashcroft v Barnsdale* [2010] EWHC 1948 (Ch), *Vallings v Gibbon* [2013] EWHC 2862 (Ch), *Giles v Royal National Institute for the Blind* [2014] EWHC 1373 (Ch) and *Vaughan-Jones v Vaughan-Jones* [2015] EWHC 1086 (Ch).

18 See e.g. *Pitt v Holt* [2013] UKSC 26 itself, *Freedman v Freedman* [2015] EWHC 1457 (Ch), *Van der Merwe v Goldman* [2016] EWHC 790 (Ch), *Smith v Stanley* [2019] EWHC 2168 (Ch), *Hartogs v Sequent (Schweiz) AG* [2019] EWHC 1915 (Ch) and *Payne v Tyler* [2019] EWHC 2347 (Ch).

might be, for example, where the argument would run along the following lines: the transaction should be construed in way X; alternatively, the documents recording it should be rectified so as to record X. However, if that is not possible as a matter of construction or rectification, and the court concludes that instead of being X the transaction is in fact Y, then the transaction was entered into as a result of a mistake and should be rescinded.

6.2 Hastings-Bass

<u>The law</u>

Until *Pitt v Holt*[19] it seemed that the so-called 'rule in *Re Hastings-Bass*'[20] had developed into a powerful weapon which allowed trustees and other fiduciaries[21] to unravel a transaction which had unexpected consequences (often fiscal). One of its best-known formulations came from *Sieff v Fox*:[22]

Where trustees act under a discretion given to them by the terms of the trust, in circumstances in which they are free to decide whether or not to exercise that discretion, but the effect of the exercise is different from that which they intended, the court will interfere with their action if it is clear that they would not have acted as they did had they not failed to take into account considerations which they ought to have taken into account, or taken into account consideration which they ought not to have taken into account.

However, in *Pitt v Holt* the Court of Appeal and then the Supreme Court made it clear that the 'rule' had been misunderstood and misapplied, and reformulated it in a much narrower way by requiring that the failure by the trustee to take into account a relevant consideration, or

19 [2013] UKSC 26.

20 The 'rule' derives its name from the Court of Appeal decision in *Re Hastings-Bass* [1975] Ch 25.

21 The 'rule' only applies to trustees or other fiduciaries: see e.g. *Pitt v Holt* [2013] UKSC 26 at [6]. The doctrine of mistake is not restricted in this way.

22 [2005] EWHC 1312 (Ch) at [119].

his taking into account an irrelevant consideration, must amount to a breach of fiduciary duty before the rule is engaged.

As a result, all decisions pre-dating *Pitt v Holt* in which the rule in *Re Hastings-Bass* was applied must now be treated with considerable caution. It also seems that in most factual situations in which before *Pitt v Holt* trustees would have invoked the rule in *Re Hastings-Bass*, the doctrine of mistake is now likely to be invoked instead.[23] The main reason for this is that to rely on mistake it is not necessary to establish that there has been a breach of trust, which is often likely to be difficult where the transaction was entered into following receipt of (incorrect) professional advice.

The remedy

The remedy is similar (if not identical) to that available in relation to mistake. If the court is satisfied that the rule applies, the effect of this is to render the transaction voidable in equity (not void at law).[24] The remedy is usually rescission, i.e. the setting aside or undoing of the transaction.[25] The remedy is discretionary and the court has to consider whether it should in fact be granted. In doing so it will take into account factors such as any delay in bringing the claim and any rights any third party may have acquired.[26]

---

23 This is the position in England and Wales. However, several offshore jurisdictions have passed legislation to reverse *Pitt v Holt* and enact what is in effect a statutory rule in *Re Hastings-Bass*, so the jurisprudence is likely to develop differently there.

24 *Pitt v Holt* [2013] UKSC 26 at [93].

25 See e.g. *Pitt v Holt* [2013] UKSC 26 at [130].

26 See e.g. the mistake case of *Bainbridge v Bainbridge* [2016] EWHC 898 (Ch) at [20].

If the court rescinds the transaction, it is treated as never having taken place.[27] In the case of voluntary dispositions, the court may rescind a transaction in part and notwithstanding that restitution is impossible.[28]

The interplay with construction and rectification

The interplay between construction and rectification on the one hand and the rule in *Re Hastings-Bass* on the other is very similar (if not identical) to the interplay between construction and rectification and mistake, which is considered at greater length above.

In summary, once again the main point is that the result of a successful construction and/or rectification claim is that the transaction will stand but its terms will be clarified and/or corrected, whereas the result of a successful *Hastings-Bass* claim is that the transaction will be set aside altogether and treated as having never occurred. This is something to be carefully considered when deciding whether to pursue a claim for construction/rectification, or a *Hastings-Bass* claim, or perhaps both.[29]

27 See e.g. *Pitt v Holt* [2013] UKSC 26 at [130] ("*if a transaction is set aside the Court is in effect deciding that a transaction of the specified description is not to be treated as having occurred*").

28 See e.g. the mistake cases of *Kennedy v Kennedy* [2014] EWHC 4129 (Ch) at [46], *Bainbridge v Bainbridge* [2016] EWHC 898 (Ch) at [21]-[22] and *Rogge v Rogge* [2019] EWHC 1949 (Ch) at [167]-[168]. The statements made in those cases appear to be of general application (and not restricted to mistake claims).

29 See e.g. the pre-*Pitt v Holt* case of *Jiggens v Low* [2010] EWHC 1566 (Ch), in which the court set aside a deed of appointment which had had unintended capital gains tax consequences on the basis of *Hastings-Bass*, and therefore considered it unnecessary to decide the alternative claims for construction and/or rectification of the deed (at [19]).

MORE BOOKS BY LAW BRIEF PUBLISHING

A selection of our other titles available now:-

'Ellis on Credit Hire – Sixth Edition' by Aidan Ellis & Tim Kevan
'Tackling Disclosure in the Criminal Courts – A Practitioner's Guide' by Narita Bahra QC & Don Ramble
'A Practical Guide to TOLATA Claims' by Greg Williams
'Artificial Intelligence – The Practical Legal Issues' by John Buyers
'A Practical Guide to Prison Injury Claims' by Malcolm Johnson
'A Practical Guide to Hackney Carriage Licensing in London' by Stuart Jessop
'A Practical Guide to Advising Clients at the Police Station' by Colin Stephen McKeown-Beaumont
'A Practical Guide to Antisocial Behaviour Injunctions' by Iain Wightwick
'Practical Mediation: A Guide for Mediators, Advocates, Advisers, Lawyers, and Students in Civil, Commercial, Business, Property, Workplace, and Employment Cases' by Jonathan Dingle with John Sephton
'Planning Obligations Demystified: A Practical Guide to Planning Obligations and Section 106 Agreements' by Bob Mc Geady & Meyric Lewis
'A Practical Guide to Crofting Law' by Brian Inkster
'A Practical Guide to Spousal Maintenance' by Liz Cowell
'A Practical Guide to the Law of Domain Names and Cybersquatting' by Andrew Clemson
'A Practical Guide to the Law of Gender Pay Gap Reporting' by Harini Iyengar
'A Practical Guide to the Rights of Grandparents in Children Proceedings' by Stuart Barlow
'NHS Whistleblowing and the Law' by Joseph England
'Employment Law and the Gig Economy' by Nigel Mackay & Annie Powell
'A Practical Guide to the General Data Protection Regulation (GDPR)' by Keith Markham

'A Practical Guide to Noise Induced Hearing Loss (NIHL) Claims' by Andrew Mckie, Ian Skeate, Gareth McAloon
'An Introduction to Beauty Negligence Claims – A Practical Guide for the Personal Injury Practitioner' by Greg Almond
'Intercompany Agreements for Transfer Pricing Compliance' by Paul Sutton
'Zen and the Art of Mediation' by Martin Plowman
'A Practical Guide to the SRA Principles, Individual and Law Firm Codes of Conduct 2019 – What Every Law Firm Needs to Know' by Paul Bennett
'A Practical Guide to Licensing Law for Commercial Property Lawyers' by Niall McCann & Richard Williams
'A Practical Guide to Adoption for Family Lawyers' by Graham Pegg
'Essential Motor Finance Law for the Busy Practitioner' by Richard Humphreys
'A Practical Guide to Industrial Disease Claims' by Andrew Mckie & Ian Skeate
'A Practical Guide to the Law of Armed Conflict' by Jo Morris & Libby Anderson
'A Practical Guide to Redundancy' by Philip Hyland
'A Practical Guide to Vicarious Liability' by Mariel Irvine
'A Practical Guide to Claims Arising from Delays in Diagnosing Cancer' by Bella Webb
'A Practical Guide to Applications for Landlord's Consent and Variation of Leases' by Mark Shelton
'A Practical Guide to Relief from Sanctions Post-Mitchell and Denton' by Peter Causton
'Butler's Equine Tax Planning: 2nd Edition' by Julie Butler
'A Practical Guide to Equity Release for Advisors' by Paul Sams
'A Practical Guide to Unlawful Eviction and Harassment' by Stephanie Lovegrove
'A Practical Guide to the Law Relating to Food' by Ian Thomas
'A Practical Guide to the Ending of Assured Shorthold Tenancies' by Elizabeth Dwomoh
'A Practical Guide to Financial Services Claims' by Chris Hegarty
'The Law of Houses in Multiple Occupation: A Practical Guide to HMO Proceedings' by Julian Hunt
'A Practical Guide to Unlawful Eviction and Harassment' by Stephanie Lovegrove

'A Practical Guide to Solicitor and Client Costs' by Robin Dunne
'A Practical Guide to Wrongful Conception, Wrongful Birth and Wrongful Life Claims' by Rebecca Greenstreet
'Occupiers, Highways and Defective Premises Claims: A Practical Guide Post-Jackson – 2nd Edition' by Andrew Mckie
'A Practical Guide to Financial Ombudsman Service Claims' by Adam Temple & Robert Scrivenor
'A Practical Guide to the Law of Enfranchisement and Lease Extension' by Paul Sams
'A Practical Guide to Marketing for Lawyers – 2nd Edition' by Catherine Bailey & Jennet Ingram
'A Practical Guide to Advising Schools on Employment Law' by Jonathan Holden
'Certificates of Lawful Use and Development: A Guide to Making and Determining Applications' by Bob Mc Geady & Meyric Lewis
'A Practical Guide to the Law of Dilapidations' by Mark Shelton
'A Guide to Consent in Clinical Negligence Post-Montgomery' by Lauren Sutherland QC
'A Practical Guide to Running Housing Disrepair and Cavity Wall Claims: 2nd Edition' by Andrew Mckie & Ian Skeate
'A Practical Guide to Digital and Social Media Law for Lawyers' by Sherree Westell
'A Practical Guide to Holiday Sickness Claims – 2nd Edition' by Andrew Mckie & Ian Skeate
'A Practical Guide to Elderly Law' by Justin Patten
'Arguments and Tactics for Personal Injury and Clinical Negligence Claims' by Dorian Williams
'A Practical Guide to QOCS and Fundamental Dishonesty' by James Bentley
'A Practical Guide to Drone Law' by Rufus Ballaster, Andrew Firman, Eleanor Clot
'A Practical Guide to Compliance for Personal Injury Firms Working With Claims Management Companies' by Paul Bennett
'A Practical Guide to the Landlord and Tenant Act 1954: Commercial Tenancies' by Richard Hayes & David Sawtell
'A Practical Guide to Psychiatric Claims in Personal Injury' by Liam Ryan
'A Practical Guide to Dog Law for Owners and Others' by Andrea Pitt

'RTA Allegations of Fraud in a Post-Jackson Era: The Handbook – 2nd Edition' by Andrew Mckie
'RTA Personal Injury Claims: A Practical Guide Post-Jackson' by Andrew Mckie
'On Experts: CPR35 for Lawyers and Experts' by David Boyle
'An Introduction to Personal Injury Law' by David Boyle
'A Practical Guide to Claims Arising From Accidents Abroad and Travel Claims' by Andrew Mckie & Ian Skeate
'A Practical Guide to Chronic Pain Claims' by Pankaj Madan
'A Practical Guide to Claims Arising from Fatal Accidents' by James Patience
'A Practical Approach to Clinical Negligence Post-Jackson' by Geoffrey Simpson-Scott
'Employers' Liability Claims: A Practical Guide Post-Jackson' by Andrew Mckie
'A Practical Guide to Subtle Brain Injury Claims' by Pankaj Madan
'A Practical Guide to Costs in Personal Injury Cases' by Matthew Hoe
'The No Nonsense Solicitors' Practice: A Guide To Running Your Firm' by Bettina Brueggemann
'The Queen's Counsel Lawyer's Omnibus: 20 Years of Cartoons from The Times 1993-2013' by Alex Steuart Williams

These books and more are available to order online direct from the publisher at www.lawbriefpublishing.com, where you can also read free sample chapters. For any queries, contact us on 0844 587 2383 or mail@lawbriefpublishing.com.

Our books are also usually in stock at www.amazon.co.uk with free next day delivery for Prime members, and at good legal bookshops such as Wildy & Sons.

We are regularly launching new books in our series of practical day-to-day practitioners' guides. Visit our website and join our free newsletter to be kept informed and to receive special offers, free chapters, etc.

You can also follow us on Twitter at www.twitter.com/lawbriefpub.

www.ingramcontent.com/pod-product-compliance
Lightning Source LLC
LaVergne TN
LVHW052311200926
848481LV00002B/524

* 9 7 8 1 9 1 2 6 8 7 2 0 6 *